D0412942

# Social Media Marketing

BATH SPA UNIVERSITY
NEWTON PARK
LIBRARY

REFERENCE ONLY

B.S.U.C. - LIBRARY

00348123

Sara Miller McCune founded SAGE Publishing in 1965 to support the dissemination of usable knowledge and educate a global community. SAGE publishes more than 1000 journals and over 800 new books each year, spanning a wide range of subject areas. Our growing selection of library products includes archives, data, case studies and video. SAGE remains majority owned by our founder and after her lifetime will become owned by a charitable trust that secures the company's continued independence.

Los Angeles | London | New Delhi | Singapore | Washington DC | Melbourne

Stephan Dahl

# Social Media Marketing

## Theories & Applications

## 2E

Los Angeles | London | New Delhi
Singapore | Washington DC | Melbourne

Los Angeles | London | New Delhi
Singapore | Washington DC | Melbourne

SAGE Publications Ltd
1 Oliver's Yard
55 City Road
London EC1Y 1SP

SAGE Publications Inc.
2455 Teller Road
Thousand Oaks, California 91320

SAGE Publications India Pvt Ltd
B 1/I 1 Mohan Cooperative Industrial Area
Mathura Road
New Delhi 110 044

SAGE Publications Asia-Pacific Pte Ltd
3 Church Street
#10-04 Samsung Hub
Singapore 049483

© Stephan Dahl 2018

First published 2015

This second edition published 2018

Apart from any fair dealing for the purposes of research or private study, or criticism or review, as permitted under the Copyright, Designs and Patents Act, 1988, this publication may be reproduced, stored or transmitted in any form, or by any means, only with the prior permission in writing of the publishers, or in the case of reprographic reproduction, in accordance with the terms of licences issued by the Copyright Licensing Agency. Enquiries concerning reproduction outside those terms should be sent to the publishers.

Editor: Matthew Waters
Editorial assistant: Jasleen Kaur
Production editor: Sarah Cooke
Copyeditor: Gemma Marren
Proofreader: Christine Bitten
Indexer: Judith Lavender
Marketing manager: Alison Borg
Cover design: Francis Kenney
Typeset by: C&M Digitals (P) Ltd, Chennai, India
Printed in the UK

**Library of Congress Control Number: 2017955496**

**British Library Cataloguing in Publication data**

A catalogue record for this book is available from the British Library

ISBN 978-1-4739-8233-8
ISBN 978-1-4739-8234-5 (pbk)

At SAGE we take sustainability seriously. Most of our products are printed in the UK using responsibly sourced papers and boards. When we print overseas we ensure sustainable papers are used as measured by the PREPS grading system. We undertake an annual audit to monitor our sustainability.

# Contents

Visit https://study.sagepub.com/businessandmanagement for **PowerPoint slides** prepared by the author to support your teaching.

3.  Sites which can be used as both social networking sites and social media sites, integrating functionality for both elements dependent on the user. For example, a photographer can use Flickr to showcase user-generated pictures and share this with relative strangers, in the same way as the site can be used to circulate pictures from a family event to other members of a family.

Knowing the types of interactions that are likely to occur on different types of sites is important when considering how communication takes place on these sites, and the likely motivators for interactions. For instance, as interactions on primary social networking websites are amongst usually personally known users, considerations such as established interpersonal trust or social conformity are likely to be important. Conversely, on primary sites where the target audience remains largely unknown, such as TripAdvisor or similar review sites, trust in the message needs to be established first, and social conformity pressures are likely to be relatively insignificant, as users do not focus on interacting with each other. Thus, understanding the type of communication, social relevance and intended audience of user-generated content posted on these sites is important for successful interactions with users. For instance, social media disasters like the #AskBG campaign may have been avoidable if the social media managers had considered the primary audience of people on Twitter. As the majority of Twitter users seek to connect with like-minded individuals, and therefore will pander to their perceived audience, trying to get users to engage with an unpopular brand is likely to backfire – who would be a user that asks a serious question instead of entertaining their followers by posting a witty and cynical comment?

Accordingly, having an in-depth understanding of the culture and type of site (or application as per the definition) and understanding the nature of the communication is important for social media managers. And while having a wide variety of different communication tools and types may seem revolutionary, the question is, is it really such a paradigm shift from previous communication methods – especially the early Internet?

## EVOLUTION OR REVOLUTION?

It is not uncommon to find expressions such as 'social media explosion', as one advertising agency called the phenomenon (Euro RSCG, 2009). Similarly, characterisations of social media as 'the democratization of information, transforming people from content readers into publisher … the shift from a broadcast mechanism, one-to-many, to a many-to-one model, rooted in conversations between authors, people, and peers' (Solis, 2010: 37) are commonplace when describing social media. Yet, these characterisations are remarkably similar to predictions about the future of business made much earlier in the history of the Internet, for example, in 2000 prior to any notion of social media, the Cluetrain Manifesto proclaimed that the effect of the Internet is that 'your organization is becoming hyperlinked. Whether you like it or not. It's bottom-up; it's unstoppable' (Levine, 2000: 199).

The reason for the similarity is that many of the qualities ascribed to social media are neither novel nor did consumption co-creation and user generation start with Facebook,

Twitter, LinkedIn and other social media apps. Consumer and interest groups did not arise following the 'introduction' of social media. Groups such as the **Boston Computer Group (BCG)**, founded in 1977, were active long before social media or even the widespread adoption of the Internet was conceivable. BCG would later on become a Macintosh User Group. These groups, popular in the 1980s, co-created computer consumption experiences of the emerging Apple computer technology. Consequently, web technology probably enhanced and increased visibility of such behaviour, but it has not created a new form of 'social media behaviour'. Before the first World Wide Web browser, Mosaic, was released in 1993, the Internet had already been characterised as presenting a 'growing diversity of user communities' (Hart et al., 1992: 683), and two years after the 1995 development of the first Internet Explorer, scholars remarked that 'the Internet is as much a collection of communities as a collection of technologies' (Leiner et al., 1997: 106).

What can be said with some certainty is that the widespread adoption of communication technology has increased the speed of and lessened the effect of geographical boundaries on information exchange. This book aims to contribute to a more informed debate about the real impact of social media by looking beyond the hype and examining how current theories can be used to explain social media, and particularly, how such theories can help to develop effective and successful social media marketing campaigns.

To examine the questions, the book is divided into three parts: Actors, Platforms, Content and Contexts as shown in Figure I.2.

Part 1 looks at the actors and their immediate activities, and how these shape, or are shaped by, social media. The first chapter examines consumers and their motivation to form tribes and engage with other, similar individuals in various media forms. This is followed by a look at the process of co-creation in Chapter 2, looking at the processes that emerge when organisations and customers work together. Chapter 3 then focuses specifically on organisational actors, specifically from a branding perspective, and investigates the increasingly anthropomorphic nature that brands adopt as co-creators and content-providers in a user-generated environment.

Part 2 examines closely the media platform in which these actors are operating. Reflecting on the increasing convergence of different media types, the three chapters of this part chart the development of computer-based social networking, game-driven social networking and finally mobile and location-based social networking.

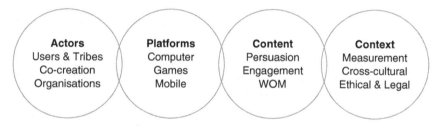

**Figure I.2**   Structure of the parts in the book

In Part 3 the chapters examine different aspects of communication taking place amongst the actors in the various channels. Persuasion is the focus of Chapter 7, while Chapter 8 focuses on engagement. Chapter 9 then combines much of the discussion from the previous chapters and applies it to the most important aspect of user-generated media: the exchange of word of mouth.

Finally, Part 4 examines the contextual elements of social media marketing. Chapter 10 critically reviews measuring social media effectiveness, while Chapter 11 discusses cross-cultural aspects of social media. Chapter 12 focuses on important ethical and legal aspects of social media marketing.

The book concludes by taking a look towards the future, and how new technological developments will shape future communication between users and organisations – and how theories discussed during the course of the preceding chapters can help to guide marketers, by making sense of the changes and by being active participants.

## REFERENCES

Berners-Lee, T. (n.d.) developerWorks Interviews [Online]. Available at: www.ibm.com/developerworks/podcast/dwi/cm-int082206txt.html (accessed 15 January 2014).

boyd, D.M. and Ellison, N.B. (2007) 'Social network sites: Definition, history, and scholarship', *Journal of Computer-Mediated Communication*, 13: 210–30.

Corstjens, M. and Umblijs, A. (2012) 'The power of evil: The damage of negative social media strongly outweigh positive contributions', *Journal of Advertising Research*, 52(4): 433–49.

Euro RSCG (2009) Social media explosion: Americans are redefining their lives online and offline with social media tools [Online]. Available at: www.prnewswire.com/news-releases/social-media-explosion-americans-are-redefining-their-lives-online-and-offline-with-social-media-tools-70471552.html (accessed 21 December 2013).

Hart, J.A., Reed, R.R. and Bar, F. (1992) 'The building of the Internet: Implications for the future of broadband networks', *Telecommunications Policy*, 16: 666–89.

Kaplan, A.M. and Haenlein, M. (2010) 'Users of the world, unite! The challenges and opportunities of social media', *Business Horizons*, 53: 59–68.

Khang, H., Ki, E.-J. and Ye, L. (2012) 'Social media research in advertising, communication, marketing, and public relations, 1997–2010', *Journalism & Mass Communication Quarterly*, 89: 279–98.

Kopecki, D. (2013) JPMorgan's #AskJPM Twitter hashtag backfires against bank [Online]. Available at: www.bloomberg.com/news/2013-11-14/jpmorgan-twitter-hashtag-trends-against-bank.html (accessed 12 March 2014).

Leiner, B.M., Cerf, V.G., Clark, D.D., Kahn, R.E., Kleinrock, L., Lynch, D.C., Postel, J., Roberts, L.G. and Wolff, S.S. (1997) 'The past and future history of the Internet', *Communications of the ACM*, 40: 102–8.

Levine, R. (2000) *The Cluetrain Manifesto: The End of Business as Usual*. Cambridge, MA: Perseus Books.

Solis, B. (2010) *Engage: The Complete Guide for Brands and Businesses to Build, Cultivate, and Measure Success in the New Web*. New York: Wiley.

Twitter (2013a) Twitter/Tesco: 'It's sleepy time so we're off …'. Available at : https://twitter.com/Tesco/status/292043677897994240 (accessed 12 March 2014).

Twitter (2013b) Twitter/jpmorgan: 'Tomorrow's Q&A is cancelled …'. Available at: https://twitter.com/jpmorgan/status/400782415641059328 (accessed 12 March 2014).

Twitter (2013c) Twitter/LeeJamesVincent: 'Hi Bert, which items of furniture …'. Available at: https://twitter.com/LeeJamesVincent/statuses/390812693026054144 (accessed 12 March 2014).

Twitter (2013d) Twitter/jamesrbuk: 'Will you pass on the cost savings …'. Available at: https://twitter.com/jamesrbuk/statuses/390811931785064448 (accessed 12 March 2014).

# PART 1

## Understanding Actors in Social Media Marketing

In the following three chapters, the book looks at the actors who engage in social media in different ways: who is acting, and why are they participating in and acting out a given scenario? What are the participants creating, and why? Which roles do other objects, tools and accessories play in enabling the participants to act and create? Consequently, these chapters focus on these three topics and which role they play as a means to help marketers understand consumer behaviour in social media environments, and to successfully engage with consumers.

The first chapter examines the social environment in which first digital and later social media emerged as a viable marketing tool. In the first section, the chapter examines the perquisite of 'usefulness' to explain the rise of ubiquitous new communication tools for consumers. It conceptualises the rise of social media both in terms of the technological acceptance as well as uses and gratifications derived from the 'new' media. Clearly, a pervasive presence of new media cannot arise without a strong perception of usefulness. A wider discussion follows to show how improved communications has influenced consumer behaviour. This latter section examines how the emergence of consumer tribes has synergistically facilitated and been enabled by new communication methods, expedited by the flexibility and adaptability of Internet-based tools and widespread Internet adoption.

Chapter 2 examines the interface between organisations and consumers by focusing on the value consumers perceive when engaging in collaborative activities using social media, and what value they are creating by collaboratively working. Based on the notion that value is 'the consumer's overall assessment of the utility of a product based on perceptions of what is received and what is given' (Zeithaml, 1988: 14), the chapter shows that consumers as co-creators are taking over active control in creating their consumption experiences, especially if consumption experiences enable consumers to associate themselves to tribes as discussed in Chapter 1. As co-creation is integral to the brand experience, understanding the roles and processes in co-creation is essential for marketers curating brands. Much has been written about the rising consumer power in the context of social media, and many marketers have come to fear, loathe and love social media tools. This chapter will enable future marketers to understand and engage with co-creating consumers and engage positively with the 'working consumer'.

Finally, Chapter 3 scrutinises the changing role of brands, messages and social media tools themselves as the essential constituents of social media marketing. The chapter is based on the observation that consumers treat computers and technology as independent social actors (c.f. Wang et al., 2007), and consequently that in order to be successful, brands have to assume a role of independent social actors, alongside human actors (such as other tribe members). Aided by the ubiquitous virtual communication environment, the chapter examines how communication messages need to adapt, by focusing more on relationship and brand personality creation and less on overtly selling products. Using the notion of anthropomorphic marketing, the chapter shows, given the characteristics of the social media environments, that brands have to assume an increasingly humanoid appearance in their communication – effectively anthropomorphising commercial communication.

## REFERENCES

Wang, L.C., Baker, J., Wagner, J.A. and Wakefield, K. (2007) 'Can a retail web site be social?', *Journal of Marketing*, 71: 143–57.

Zeithaml, V.A. (1988) 'Consumer perceptions of price, quality, and value: A means-end model and synthesis of evidence', *Journal of Marketing*, 52: 2–22.

# 1

# Consumer Tribes and Communities

## CHAPTER OVERVIEW

This chapter puts the rise of the Internet and social media in particular into the wider societal context, which occurred concurrently with the advancement in and popular adoption of information technology. The chapter shows that emerging tribal and symbolic consumption patterns and subcultures of consumption were substantial driving forces of technological adoption, with subcultures adopting online technology as a means to network, before a more widespread adoption and adaptation in mainstream culture.

## LEARNING OUTCOMES

On completing this chapter, you should be able to:

*   understand how marketing and consumer behaviour have moved from an exchange-based emphasis to emphasising the experience
*   appreciate the importance of subcultures and subcultures of consumption on consumer behaviour
*   be able to distinguish between tribes and brand communities, and critically evaluate the influence of symbolic consumption on everyday purchase decisions
*   understand the basics of researching brand communities online, through the use of netnography.

## TOWARDS TRIBAL CONSUMPTION

To understand the rise of the Internet and the emergence and influence of social media as a particular evolution of the widespread adaptation of information technology, it is essential that we put these two phenomena into a broader context of culture shifts occurring at the end of the twentieth and the beginning of the twenty-first century. Although it is tempting to think of the emergence of social media as the game-changing event that swept away any of the previous models and theories, when the phenomenon is looked at from a more holistic, cultural perspective, the development and subsequent popularity of social media is more a lucky combination of technological advancement combined with post-modern consumption behaviour.

Social media 'gurus' love to amaze by showing impressive numbers about the explosive growth of websites like Facebook, Twitter and other social networking sites. A favourite comparison is comparing the time it took for radio and television to reach a similar audience, for example, it is claimed that it took 13 years for television to reach 50 million viewers, yet only 3.5 years for Facebook to accumulate the same amount of users (Annan, 2012). However, these comparisons are problematic, as fundamentally such comparisons imply that it is the appearance of Facebook, or similar social media platforms, that has sparked a revolution in consumer behaviour, which could not have happened without the appearance of the particular platform being talked about. An alternative view is that social media emerged to fulfil a need online that was already evident offline. In other words, social media did not actually change existing consumer behaviour, but rather it brought it online and made it more visible.

To clarify these issues, the remainder of this chapter examines whether social media was the spark that lit the fire, or if it simply added fuel to an existing fire. In other words, was social media accelerating a change in society and with it a change in consumption behaviour, or was it the initiator?

### The 'Usefulness' of Social Media

If regarded from a purely theoretical and practical perspective, any technology, including social media, the Internet, the video recorder, the telephone or any other innovation, needs to achieve widespread adoption to become 'significant'. The **Technology Acceptance Model (TAM),** amongst other models described in more detail in Chapter 4, highlights the importance of **usefulness** as a key component.

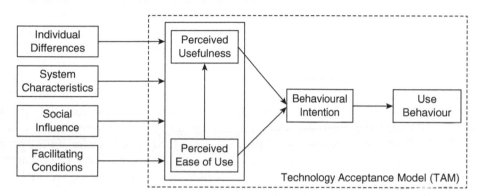

**Figure 1.1**　Technology Acceptance Model

## Technology Acceptance Model

To achieve adoption on a large scale, technology needs to be perceived as 'useful' by the adoptees, a variable well recognised in technology adoption, for example, 'perceived usefulness', alongside perceived ease of use, is the starting variable influencing directly the intention to use new technology in the well-established **Technology Acceptance Model** (Davis, 1989).

Thus, new technology must be considered useful by many, if not a majority of, consumers to be successful. It does not become successful because it is simply easy to use, as social media tools in comparison to traditional online media doubtlessly are, nor does it become successful because it is a new technology *per se*. The important questions to ask are therefore: Why was social media considered so useful that it did spread rapidly? Which underlying needs did social media fulfil? And which social trends and consumer behaviours were affected by the widespread adoption of social media?

To investigate these questions, we briefly look at the conceptualisation of consumption behaviour by the individual, before we look at the wider, social context of consumption.

## Consumption in Context: From Exchange to Experience

Traditionally, marketers focused rather narrowly on the concept of exchange, for example the exchange of money for goods or services (Bagozzi, 1975). In a very traditional view, therefore, consumption is seen as a matter of pre-purchase activities, such as identification of need, search for information, evaluation of alternatives, followed by an exchange (purchase) succeeded by a series of post-purchase activities, such as assessing if the product met the desired objectives. In essence, consumption is seen as an essentially utilitarian concept, which enables both parties in the process (consumer and producer) to achieve their means through exchange, i.e. the producer earns money from the consumer, and the consumer gains satisfaction through the use of a product or service.

However, since the 1960s and 1970s, this utilitarian view of consumption, based on a strictly rational view of the consumer, has been replaced by more interpretative methodologies seeking to go beyond one-dimensional approaches to market exchange and consumption. Consumer behaviour research and marketing have broadened their research focus to include non-utilitarian attributes, such as experiences and meanings in the consumption process as well as going beyond a simple purchase-focused approach. This extension enabled a much broader view of consumption. Consumption is no longer seen as restricted towards the sequential processes involved in purchasing a new product, for example a new computer. With a broader perspective, using the purchased computer, and even disposing of the computer once it has outlived its usefulness, are included in the concept of consumption, studied and explained.

Of particular note within this broader theoretical framework are two lines of enquiry – **Consumer Culture Theory (CCT)** and experiential consumption – both of which merit a brief review here, as they will help to frame the discussion of marketplace and consumer behaviour, especially in a social context, including when using social media.

### Consumer Culture Theory

CCT as a research tradition emerged around the middle of the 1980s. CCT refers to a 'family of theoretical perspectives that address the dynamic relationships between consumer actions, the marketplace, and cultural meanings' (Arnould and Thompson, 2005: 868). In other words, CCT focuses on the contextual aspects of consumption, such as the symbolic nature of consumed products and services, and experiential aspects of consumption activity.

By taking a holistic view of marketplace behaviour, CCT challenges the traditional focus on studying marketplace behaviour merely at the purchasing stage. Arnould (2004) contends further that the experiential aspects of consumption, i.e. consumer experiences during the wider stages of consumption preceding and proceeding the purchase, have become an important, if not the most important, aspect for contemporary consumers. Fundamentally, Arnould and CCT theorists in general describe consumption as experiences encountered during four stages of consumption:

1. *Pre-consumption stage*: Searching for, planning and imagining the actual consumption experience, for example, looking at fashion magazines, imagining what it would feel like to wear a certain coat, etc.
2. *Purchasing stage*: The definite purchase experience involving choosing, paying and service experience linked to the actual purchase, such as the experiences encountered when choosing the coat, trying it on, paying and leaving the shop.

3. *Core consumption stage*: The actual sensation and experiences during and immediately after the consumption of the product, including satisfaction or dissatisfaction. For example, occasions where the coat is worn, such as a special occasion or the occasion where the coat was worn for the first time.

4. *Remembered consumption stage*: The nostalgic stage following the consumption experiences, in which the experience is relived, for example through looking at photos of one wearing the coat, and remembering certain events and sensations or feelings related to this occasion.

Extending the focus allowed researchers to explore how for contemporary consumers, the consumption-associated experiences, for example feelings and sensations, rather than the product's utilitarian function, are the main aspect of consumption. These experiences, encountered during the extended consumption process, can be more important (or valuable) for the consumer than the product itself.

Many of these stages require an active involvement on behalf of the consumer. This challenges the traditional view of the passive consumer, considering instead the 'productive aspect of consumption'. Rather, consumers are seen as active participants in the consumption process, in fact, the consumers co-produce, together with vendors or producers, their experiences and the meanings attributed to the consumption process during each of the stages of consumption. For example, in the context of social media, this wider focus can elucidate the practice of 'unboxing', where consumers share videos or pictures of themselves opening a package of a new, often coveted item (Jenkins, 2011), such as a mobile phone. They are extending the core consumption experience, and sharing the emotions with their wider social network, a practice that can be observed in some 370,000 videos on YouTube showing individuals ritually 'unboxing' goods.

An extensive body of research, much of which is in the CCT tradition and beyond, has looked further at how consumers rework and reinterpret meanings they encounter throughout the consumption process, for example, when exposed to advertisements, the brands themselves, or through the consuming of goods. The overwhelming consensus is that consumers consume as a way to express their individual personal and social circumstances – or to assert their identity or advance personal lifestyle goals. While we will revisit the notion of the active, i.e. co-producing, consumer in depth in the next chapter, it is important to recognise that the focus of consumption for contemporary consumers has shifted significantly from a utilitarian consumption motive to become a largely symbolic act through which consumers aim to express themselves.

Early works highlighting the symbolic nature of consumption can be found in the 1960s and 1970s (Holbrook and Hirschman, 1980), and it is therefore reasonable to assume that current technology has played little role in instigating this type of consumption. Modern technology has, nevertheless, been useful for symbolic consumption, for example, social media enables people to rapidly share consumption with friends, such as in the example of unboxing above, therefore extending the experience beyond people present during the consumption process.

## THINKBOX SYMBOLIC CONSUMPTION

Clothes are probably the most symbolic item many people are consuming (or wearing), because they signal a lot about the wearer. Thinking about the clothes that you are wearing now, try to answer the following questions: Why are you wearing these? What do they say about you? Are there brands that you particularly like to wear? Why? Are there certain brands that you would never wear? Why?

## The Social Context: Subcultures and Tribes

Wider society has been in a state of flux and change well before the widespread adoption of social media in the mid-2000s – or in fact even the widespread adoption of the Internet in the 1990s. In the late twentieth century, individuals around the world progressively sought to liberate themselves from social restrictions and established social norms. This liberation resulted in a fragmentation of society, a severe social dissolution and, what some researchers have called, 'extreme individualism' (Cova and Cova, 2002). Following significant cultural shifts, often attributed to the aftermaths of two world wars, individuals were no longer adhering to the constraints of previous generations, and following collective ideals. Rather, people increasingly sought to personalise their existence (and with it their personal consumption), based on relatively few constraints and on individual choice maximisation.

Paradoxically though, as Goulding and colleagues (2001) point out, mounting **individualism** did not result in everyone pursuing their life alone. Rather, individualism impelled individuals to seek alternative social arrangements, new 'communities' in which they could find a sense of belonging. Such communities were often away from what the individuals regarded as the mainstream, and free from traditional and established social structures. An analogy that is often used to describe this phenomenon is the idea of the mainstream breaking up into a 'plethora of subcultures'. These 'subcultures' offered a community, or spiritual home, to post-modern consumers seeking a replacement for vanished conventional, social bonds. Many early researchers into consumer behaviour focused particularly on consumption behaviour in subcultures as representative examples of consumers breaking away from the societal mainstream. We therefore briefly explore the research into subcultures – and related to this the emergence of the 'plethora of subcultures' in the next section.

## The Emerging Importance of Subcultures

Long before the widespread adoption of the Internet, at the beginning of the 1970s, researchers became interested in the consumption practices of subcultures. Examples include the work done at the Birmingham **Centre for Contemporary Cultural**

**Studies (CCCS)**. Much of their work focused on the relationship between various sub-cultures and the perceived dominant (or mainstream) culture. What emerged, against the background of social upheaval in the 1970s, was an overabundance of 'subcultures', frequently young consumers rebellious against the alleged mainstream, usually adult, culture. Yet, the rebellious nature of these subcultures did not result in an unswervingly antagonistic relationship with mainstream culture. Rather, with time, mainstream culture incorporated aspects of many subcultural meanings or behaviours back into the mainstream and adopted these (Hebdige, 1979). An example is the originally 1960s London-based subculture of 'mods', with various revivals in different places in later years. While the original mod culture started to fade away in the second half of the 1960s, many of the brands and even places became adopted for mainstream consumption – brands such as Fred Perry, motor scooters such as Lambretta or Vespa, insignias such as the original Royal Air Force roundel all of which were originally associated with the mods – re-emerged in the mainstream. Carnaby Street, the original shopping street of many mods, became the focal point of 'Swinging London' in the late 1960s. It continues to draw on this legacy today as an upmarket, youth-oriented shopping area, although there are no connections with the original mod subculture anymore.

Over time, researchers studied an increasing number of subcultures, which originally were largely based on readily identifiable groups, existing 'away' from the mainstream. For example, ethnic minorities, gays or 'alternative lifestyle' groups – ranging from punks to skinheads, from hippies to rockers – were researched, and behaviour first identified in subcultures increasingly became a prototype for subsequent, mainstream consumer behaviour (such as the mods example above).

Historically, subcultures existed away from the mainstream, drawing together individuals who felt neglected or outcast by the majority culture, creating their own social norms, behaviours and knowledge. Researchers realised that subculture members appropriated commercially available material taken from the mainstream culture, and interpreted these items according to a different set of values shared amongst subculture members. An example of this is Dr Martens shoes. The shoes were originally popular with people who walked a lot as part of their profession, for example police officers and postal workers. Within the skinhead subculture, the Dr Martens shoes were reinterpreted away from the functional aspect of being a product that provided the wearer with comfort to walk, to a sign of belonging to the subculture. Therefore, the shoes, within the context of the skinhead subculture, identified the wearer as a fellow skinhead, and the consumption of these shoes (i.e. wearing them) carried symbolic and potentially political meaning.

Increasingly though, researchers uncovered that the behaviour they observed in the subcultures was by no means restricted to subcultures: individuals of all walks of life used commercially available goods, reinterpreted these and used them as a symbol of their individual beliefs or persuasions. Referring to these groupings as **subcultures of consumption**, these subculture-like groups, largely comprising self-selected members, defined themselves based on a communal commitment to a particular brand, product or other consumption activity (Schouten and McAlexander, 1995). Similar to traditional subcultures, members of these subcultures of consumption often came from different socio-economic backgrounds, crossed diverse age ranges, had different ethnic backgrounds or bridged the gender divide. Instead of specific demographic similarities, members of these 'subcultures' shared certain experiences, arising from a particular consumption activity. For example, the ownership of a motor cycle brand, such as the Harley Davidson community (Schouten and McAlexander, 1995), or watching specific television shows, such as *Star Trek* (Kozinets, 2001).

However, while membership of subcultures of consumption was largely self-selected, rather than ascribed, it was not entirely free of the influences of established factors such as social class, gender or ethnicity. Holt (1997) cautioned that basic demographic principles were still influential factors for consumption behaviour. However, Holt conceded that existing social patterns became subtler and started to be increasingly complemented by consumption activities. Nevertheless, members needed to have the financial means to purchase certain goods that were required to participate in these subcultures, for example purchasing and owning an Apple computer, despite members not sharing other, traditional socio-demographic similarities.

Concurrent with the research into subcultures and consumption taking place in Britain, the French sociologist Michel Maffesoli (1988) studied a similar phenomenon though his work was based on work with French 'conventional' consumers, rather than based on rebellious youth subcultures in Britain. He focused particularly on the rise of the perceived individualism in mainstream culture. However, paradoxically, in his book *Le Temps des Tribus* (*The Time of the Tribes*, published in 1996) he concluded that, rather than rising dramatically as many people feared, individualism is outdated in contemporary society. Instead, he found that post-modern society is best understood as an assortment of intermittent social groupings, which are characterised as fluid, occasional and in constant formation and dispersal. Alluding to indigenous structures, Maffesoli called these communities 'tribes'. In his view, contemporary 'tribes' replaced traditional tribes, which were life-long, static and based on membership by ascription or birth, such as social class. Tribes, as described by Maffesoli, had strong similarities with the subcultures of consumption described by Cova and Cova, both being 'inherently unstable, small scale, affectual and not fixed by any of the established parameters of modern society; instead they can be held together through shared emotions, styles of life, new moral beliefs and consumption practices' (Cova and Cova, 2001: 67), and many researchers started to use both terms, often interchangeably.

Some scholars, for example Bennett (1999), suggested distinguishing between historical tribes, such as Indian tribes in America, and contemporary, fluid **tribes,** by using the term 'neo-tribes' to describe these contemporary communities of belonging, where members enact particular, shared lifestyles. However, works by, for example, Cova and Cova, Maffesoli and Godin (2008) popularised the simpler notion of 'tribes'.

Fundamentally, both subcultures of consumption and tribes describe similar concepts characterising contemporary consumer behaviour, based on a post-modern, fluid society, where consumers self-ascribe to communities of meaning and belonging. In other words, consumers choose to be part of several, occasionally even seemingly contradictory, communities or tribes. Consumers can navigate between the selected communities, while choosing to join and relinquish their membership from communities as they wish. For example, people can opt freely to join a Mac User Group, or to no longer take part in meetings of a local Mac User Group. Or they can buy a different computer. It is important to note that much of the research into consumer tribes significantly predates the emergence and widespread adoption of social media.

These tribes have primarily three functions:

1. They enable sharing of functional knowledge, for example, how to use emerging technology in the case of computers, or share new software and experiences with new hardware in the local Mac User Group.
2. They offer a place of social bonding, support and belonging, allowing individuals to create an identity that helps distinguish them from 'others'. For example, Mac users vs. PC users, also famously used in Apple's 'I'm a PC, I'm a Mac' advertising campaigns.
3. These tribes create and share a set of collective rules and behaviours, which allows tribe users to distinguish each other from non-tribe members, for example, camping out in front of Apple stores before their opening.

While social barriers, in principle, were coming down as early as the 1970s and 1980s, geographical distance often made it difficult for consumers to join tribes they wanted to be a part of, but which were not local to their community. Think of being a solitary punk in a small community, or the only gay in the village in the 1970s or 1980s – or simply the only Mac user based in a small township where another Mac User Group was far away. If a specific tribe was not established in the local community, consumers had no access to any of the support functions of the tribe. For example, there was no access to shared social support, such as personal support *vis-à-vis* non-tribe members who may question the rationale for tribe membership. Similarly, a geographically remote tribe member had no easy access to knowledge about tribe practices and behaviours, for example, for *Star Trek* fans, practising speaking or writing Klingon, reading about events organised for other 'Trekkies' or knowing where to purchase Trek memorabilia. The evolution of technology brought the possibility of tribal support beyond confined geographical borders, offering access to global support and access to knowledge independent of locality. Maybe it is therefore unsurprising that many 'traditional', ascribed subcultures, for example homosexual men, ethnic minorities as well as other self-selected, alternative lifestyle tribes, were amongst the earliest adopters of the Internet (boyd and Ellison, 2007).

The Internet, almost from the beginning, offered subcultures 'social networking' features by enabling individuals to connect to fellow subculture members globally. More details of these features are discussed in Chapter 4, but especially the introduction of the World Wide Web made connecting to fellow tribe members via the Internet easy and convenient. Gay.com, arguably the first social networking site in the world, launched in 1994 (Campbell, 2005). It offered 'perceived usefulness' and enhanced ease of use, by enabling access to social and emotional support from other gay men. It therefore encouraged the early adoption of new technology in this particular subculture around a decade before the emergence of 'mainstream' social networks.

Similarly, as boyd and Ellison (2007) point out, other minority groups quickly followed in the 'social networking' footsteps with their own sites: Asian-American social networking site AsianAvenue and African-American social networking site BlackPlanet both launched

2009), are equally influenced by tribal connections. This is somewhat counterintuitive when considering traditional models of involvement, which conventionally suggested that consumers tend to create emotional bonds nearly always with high-involvement products (Martin, 1998).

## THINKBOX TRIBAL CONSUMERS

List some of the 'tribes' you are familiar with.
   Can you identify three consumption behaviours that identify tribe members for each tribe?
   Describe how each of these behaviours signals membership to the tribe.

## Tribal Consumers and Traditional Marketing Concepts

As can be seen from the preceding discussion, modern consumers are best characterised by tribes rather than socio-demographic variables. This has significant impact on the way marketing should approach such consumers, as much of traditional marketing theory suggests a static approach to marketplace behaviour.

Bearing this in mind, it seems tempting to think of tribes as comparable to, if not synonymous with, traditional 'market segments'. However, there are some stark differences. Segments are usually seen as subgroups of a market, made up of clearly defined, homogenous consumers who share similar characteristics. Customers are seen as passive in selecting which segment they belong to and segments are furthermore mutually exclusive.

However, tribes, while indeed subgroups of a market, don't share any of the other characteristics of traditional segments:

- Tribes are commonly not clearly defined, particularly on social networks, where people may follow a brand religiously – or indeed visit a brand community sporadically. Therefore, membership of a tribe is by definition hard to establish.
- Tribes are often a community of heterogeneous consumers, bound by consumption behaviour and shared experiences, but few other demographics. While some common demographics may be evident in some cases, for example, in the case of tribes related to highly priced goods members are likely to have a relatively high income, this is not true in other cases. For example, income, age, gender or many other segmentation variables cannot be used to characterise *Star Trek* fans effectively. Therefore, traditional tools have only limited validity in a tribal marketplace.
- Tribes are often interconnected and tribe 'members' can be a member of seemingly contradicting tribes. For example, owning a VW Beatle does not preclude the owner from owning another car, maybe even a similar 'cult-like' car such as a Mini.

- Tribe members are seen as active, although to varying degrees. Often tribe members don't simply consume – they are advocates and active promoters of consumption in their own right. This view is different from segments, which see members as passive consumers, incapable of collective action (Cova and Cova, 2002).

For example, a netnographic study of 'wine lovers' on Instagram showed that this tribe is best segmented considering their knowledge and awareness of different wines. Traditional, more rigid market segmentation ideas are less useful (Cuomo et al., 2016). The more fluid view of tribes is therefore contradictory to some established marketing assumptions, challenging the static and positivistic conventions underlying many traditional marketing approaches.

Moreover, tribal consumers challenge some other assumptions made in traditional marketing, for example, marketing practices such as relationship marketing, which place great emphasis on enhancing customer–brand relationships. Customers in a traditional marketing view are enticed and loyalty gained through frequent contact and consistent, personalised customer service at the point of contact between customer and brand. In the tribal view, the contact between brand and customer is subordinate to the contact between customers: the brand supports the relationship between different consumers and acts as a link between individuals.

Importantly for tribes, brands are not consumed for their utilitarian value and contemporary consumers, especially when engaging in tribal marketplace behaviour, are not focusing on rational, utilitarian, logical or largely cognitive brand choices. Rather, consumers choose brands because of their experiential or indeed affectionate value. One could argue consumers are developing an affective loyalty (Cova and Cova, 2002) to the products they consume because of the consumption experiences at different stages, rather than the product attributes.

Consequently, brands depend upon their consumers to forge relationships. Thus, the traditional view of the exchange between organisation and consumer has lost importance. This view is replaced by a more fluid view, where brand and a community of consumers are in a perpetual state of 'mutual indebtedness' (Cova and Cova, 2002: 614), whereby the brand enables the consumer to recognise fellow tribe members while simultaneously individual tribes rely on brands to provide products in accordance to the values of the tribes, and to provide the tribes with means to recognise fellow tribe members. Many social media sites rely on rapid identification of fellow tribe members, for example, when reading reviews on a user-generated website like TripAdvisor, small clues in the reviews can identify reviewers as tribe members and make their reviews more relevant to the reader, for instance, when a child is mentioned (tribe = parents), or a preference for healthy food at breakfast (tribe = green), etc. Similarly, when posting pictures on Twitter, Instagram or Facebook, brands that appear and the type of picture are all part of self-expression by the individual users, enabling browsers to quickly identify the poster as a fellow tribe member, or not. Brands in particular have then become paradoxical in a social media context. On the one side, they are uninvited, commercialising a space originally made for people to connect. On the other side, they are essential tools for recognising tribal allegiances and enabling social networking beyond the point of close friends. But to do so, brands need to be prominently displayed or alluded to, so that casual friends or browsing bypassers can recognise the individual characteristics of the poster through the embedded meaning, or linking value, of the brands.

## SUMMARY

This chapter discussed how consumption and consumer behaviour have changed in the last part of the twentieth century. Consumption has moved from a largely utilitarian function, to a symbolic and experiential one. Concurrently, modern society became increasingly individualistic, abandoning established socio-cultural structures and rejecting established social norms and networks. Tribal structures, often centred around shared consumption activity, have taken the place of established social structures. Technical advancement, such as the Internet and social media, have further accelerated these changes by allowing tribe members to communicate and share consumption experiences almost irrespective of geographical location.

Tribal consumption challenges established marketing thinking, because tribe members are by their very nature fluid, frequently contradictory and exist in a mutual indebtedness with brands, that are used for tribal membership recognition and providing social links.

## RESEARCH DIRECTIONS

Much research has already focused on explaining tribal behaviour, especially within online communities, as these are often more accessible and easier to research than offline consumption communities. However, there are still some interesting areas that can be explored as most of the current research has been based on active participants of these communities, i.e. people that post rather than merely lurk. Similarly, there is only limited research on events prior to, or indeed post, participation in brand community groups.

A further interesting potential area to explore is the interaction between online and offline consumer behaviour. As many brand communities are not purely virtual, the difference between the virtual consumption experience and, for example, gatherings, shows and meet-ups in real life could be an interesting avenue for future research.

Finally, intertribal behaviour and tribal rivalry could yield interesting results. A prominent example might be the 'Rich Kids of Instagram' (http://richkidsofin stagram.tumblr.com/) phenomenon, where members of one tribe try to ridicule members of the other tribe and their consumption practices relying on social media tools.

# RESEARCH HIGHLIGHT
# NETNOGRAPHY

Netnography is a type of ethnographic research used to study behaviour of individuals online. The word is a contraction of eth*nography* and Inter*net*. While netnography shares many aspects with ethnographic research, such as being immersive, adaptable and naturalistic, it offers some advantages over traditional ethnographic research, namely, data collection is frequently faster and less expensive as researchers can rely largely on existing, textual data available rather than having to conduct, for example, interviews or observe participants over an extended period of time.

Kozinets (2002) divides the netnographic research process into five stages:

1 Selecting an appropriate online community.
2 Gathering and analysing data.
3 Analysing the data.
4 Ensuring ethical research standards.
5 Triangulating the findings.

## 1 Selecting an appropriate online community

After formulating specific research questions, researchers have to spend some time getting to know the online community they are researching, which includes identifying where community participants congregate, that is, they need to identify specific websites, newsgroups, forums or chat rooms for investigation – and evaluate which of these, or which combination of these, will be included in the research project.

Because each online group may be made up of different participants, use group-specific language and have other interests and behaviours distinguishing the group, the researcher should take care to know as much about each of the groups as possible prior to selecting appropriate groups and starting the data collection.

Kozinets (2002) suggests that when deciding between different groups, preference should be given to communities which have five research-relevant advantages:

1 communities that are focused as much as possible on the research question
2 communities that have a high enough traffic, i.e. number of postings
3 communities that have a large number of posters (or participants) to yield potentially fruitful results
4 communities that yield rich and detailed postings or data
5 communities that offer appropriate between-member interactions related to the research question.

*(Continued)*

## 2 Gathering and analysing data

Once the researcher has chosen the online communities to be investigated, the data selection process can begin, focusing on two types of data – firstly the copied data from the online groups, or originating from group members and secondly data in relation to researchers' observations, feelings and ascription of meanings.

In order to deal with the likely large amounts of data the researcher encounters upon data gathering, Kozinets recommends a number of ways to categorise the data to help the researcher make sense of the online interactions.

Firstly, messages can be categorised into primarily social and primarily informational messages – or on-topic messages and off-topic messages – depending on which is more suitable for the research context. For example, an online forum about handbags may contain messages in which members talk to each other in a social way, such as playing word games with each other. These messages are likely to be off-topic. Messages relating to identifying handbags in television shows and messages discussing newly released handbags would be classified on-topic messages.

Secondly, the contributors (or posters) of the messages may be categorised based on their involvement with the community. Kozinets, in previous research (1999), identified four levels of involvement with the community, which may be used to classify the contributors:

1   *Tourists* are contributors that have loose ties to the community and are not highly involved in the community. This type of contributor can often be identified by trivial questions being posted.
2   *Minglers* have well-established social ties in the community – but do not, or only to a minimal extent, engage in the consumption behaviour of the group.
3   *Devotees* are the opposite of minglers, in that they engage significantly in the consumption behaviour that is the subject of the group, but have relatively few ties.
4   Finally, *insiders* combine both strong social ties to the group and engage in extensive consumption behaviour.

A particular focus point for researchers is also not just the information related to the consumption activity, but also the interaction between different groups of contributors, specifically, researchers should focus on how consumption is socially reinforced and minglers and tourists are converted to become more engaged in either or both consumption activity or online community.

During the research it can useful to write reflective notes on the messages reviewed, including notes on how many messages were evaluated and from how many participants. However, as most online data can be stored relatively easily, an alternative way to collect data is to download the data without writing notes. Data collection online should continue until no new insights are produced.

## 3 Analysing the data

Data analysis in netnography relies on analysing the textual data derived from the data collection. Relying only on the analysis of textual data makes netnography different from ethnography, which aims to balance both observational (behavioural) and discursive (spoken) data. Therefore the focus of netnography shifts towards recontextualising the data collected rather than contextualising behaviour in ethnographic research (c.f. Kozinets, 2002 for a discussion of this shift).

Some of the data analysis can be assisted by software traditionally used in qualitative research, such as NVivo, as well as widely available web-based tools in order to enhance the analysis. See Kozinets (2010a) for a discussion of several tools that researchers may find helpful for locating online groups and analysing the data.

## 4 Ethical considerations

Contrary to traditional ethnographic methods, where participants agree to take part in an interview or focus group, posts and messages used by netnographic researchers are unlikely to have been created with the intention or consideration of being studied. Therefore, it is important that netnographers follow strict ethical guidelines to ensure that netnographic research does not become perceived as disrespectful or intrusive, potentially damaging the reputation and possibility of future research efforts.

To avoid ethical problems, Kozinets recommends that netnographic researchers should follow four steps:

1   They must disclose their identity, affiliations and presence when conducting the research openly and fully.
2   Researchers should reassure participants that any data collected will be kept confidential and anonymous.
3   Researchers should seek to triangulate their results (see also step 5), i.e. they should incorporate feedback from participants when reporting about the online communities they have studied.
4   Kozinets further recommends in the case of quoting participants verbatim, for example, by inserting postings directly from a bulletin board or Twitter updates, participants should be contacted directly and permission sought, even if the material is available in a public forum.

## 5 Triangulation of results

As a final step, the researcher should make the findings available to the communities studied, for example, by posting the report or report highlights on a web page and

*(Continued)*

invite comments and feedback, or by sending the report to community members. This final step is useful as it can enable the generation of additional insights, can prevent ethical issues from arising, and importantly, can establish an on-going interaction between researcher and online community.

For a more extensive discussion of using netnography as a research approach, see Kozinets, 2010b.

# CASE STUDY VANCOUVER OPERA

Operas around the world desperately need to attract new audiences, but it is often not easy with a product that is largely assumed to be irrelevant especially to younger audiences. Although operas often try to connect to younger audiences and are extensively using social media, simply posting material is often not enough. In fact, the material often doesn't reach younger people, as they are unlikely to follow opera on social media.

Vancouver Opera (VO) is one of the most innovative opera companies in North America, yet, similar to other opera houses, suffered from declining ticket sales and low perceived relevance for people under 40 years of age. Trying to reach out to a younger audience, they commissioned a new opera that focuses on bullying, a theme very likely to be relevant to a younger audience. However, simply staging a topical opera and relying on posting about the new work using their traditional social media channels wasn't going to be enough to engage the audience they were trying to target – not least because much of the audience was unlikely to follow them in the first place! Thus, VO needed to find a way to challenge preconceived ideas about operas and talk to the audience they were trying to reach. VO was particularly interested in reaching 20–40 year olds, who, while considering themselves interested in arts and culture, wouldn't normally visit the opera. Often, people in this target group assumed that opera was too traditional and associated it with elitism and conservatism – rather than being a progressive art form.

One of the key messages the opera company wanted to convey was the idea that opera has traditionally been a voice of the voiceless, and many revolutionary, underground ideas were often conveyed through operas in the past. The newly commissioned opera obviously picked up this message, and gave a voice to a victim of bullying – who in turn turned perpetrator. To bring this message to 'the streets', VO focused its promotion on street art, combining real life murals on street corners with online 'murals' on Tumblr, which allowed audiences to share their experiences of bullying. The real life murals in Vancouver were created specifically by known street artists. In addition to being seen by passers-by, the artists also shared their work using social media.

The results of the campaign were astonishing: ticket sales to new patrons doubled, and the new opera generated almost three times as many conversations on social media as other operas produced by VO. A large proportion of the audience watching the opera was also much younger than other VO operas.

## Questions to Consider

1 How would you describe VO's chosen tribe?
2 How do you rate the relative importance of social media and real life murals in this case?
3 VO relied heavily on Tumblr to create a background story to the opera. Would you make the same media choice?
4 Discuss what makes you follow organisations (such as VO or others) on social media networks. How do you think an organisation can reach out to people beyond their traditional followers?

# FURTHER READING

Kadirov, D. and Varey, R.J. (2010) 'Symbolism in marketing systems', *Journal of Macromarketing*, 31(2): 160–71.

Kozinets, R.V. (2010) *Netnography: Ethnographic Research in the Age of the Internet*. London: Sage Publications.

Levy, S.J. and Luedicke, M.K. (2012) 'From marketing ideology to branding ideology', *Journal of Macromarketing*, 33(1): 58–66.

O'Reilly, D. (2012) 'Maffesoli and consumer tribes: Developing the theoretical links', *Marketing Theory*, 12(3): 341–7.

## REFERENCES

Annan, K.G. (2012) Radio took 38 yrs to get 50 million users, Angry Birds Space took 35 days [Infographic] – Trickle-Up [Online]. Available at: http://innovation.gkofiannan.com/radio-took-38-yrs-to-reach-50-million-users-o#!/ (accessed 16 March 2013).

Arnould, E.J. (2004) *Consumers*, 2nd edn. Boston, MA: McGraw-Hill/Irwin.

Arnould, E.J. and Thompson, C.J. (2005) 'Consumer Culture Theory (CCT): Twenty years of research', *Journal of Consumer Research*, 31: 868–82.

Bagozzi, R.P. (1975) 'Marketing as exchange', *Journal of Marketing*, 39(4): 32–9.

Belk, R.W. and Tumbat, G. (2005) 'The cult of Macintosh', *Consumption Markets & Culture*, 8: 205–17.

Bennett, A. (1999) 'Subcultures or neo-tribes? Rethinking the relationship between youth, style and musical taste', *Sociology*, 33: 599–617.

boyd, D.M. and Ellison, N.B. (2007) 'Social network sites: Definition, history, and scholarship', *Journal of Computer-Mediated Communication*, 13: 210–30.

Bromberger, C. (1998) *Passions Ordinaires: Du Match de Football au Concours de Dictée*. Paris: Bayard.

Campbell, J.E. (2005) 'Outing PlanetOut: Surveillance, gay marketing and Internet affinity portals', *New Media & Society*, 7: 663–83.

Cova, B. (1997) 'Community and consumption: Towards a definition of the "linking value" of product or services', *European Journal of Marketing*, 31: 297–316.

Cova, B. and Cova, V. (2001) 'Tribal aspects of postmodern consumption research: The case of French in-line roller skaters', *Journal of Consumer Behaviour*, 1: 67–76.

Cova, B. and Cova, V. (2002) 'Tribal marketing: The tribalisation of society and its impact on the conduct of marketing', *European Journal of Marketing*, 36: 595–620.

Cova, B. and Pace, S. (2006) 'Brand community of convenience products: New forms of customer empowerment – the case "my Nutella the community"', *European Journal of Marketing*, 40: 1087–105.

Cuomo, M.T., Tortora, D., Festa, G., Giordano, A. and Metallo, G. (2016) 'Exploring consumer insights in wine marketing: An ethnographic research on #Winelovers', *Psychology & Marketing*, 33(12): 1082–90.

Davis, F.D. (1989) 'Perceived usefulness, perceived ease of use, and user acceptance of information technology', *MIS Quarterly*, 13(3): 319–40.

Fournier, S. and Avery, J. (2011) 'The uninvited brand', *Business Horizons*, 54: 193–207.

Godin, S. (2008) *Tribes: We Need You To Lead Us*. London: Piatkus.

Goulding, C., Shankar, A. and Elliott, R. (2001) 'Dance clubs, "rave" and the consumer experience: An exploratory study of a cultural phenomenon', in A. Groeppel-Klien and F.-R. Esch (eds), *European Advances in Consumer Research*, Vol. 5. Provo, UT : Association for Consumer Research. pp. 203–8.

Hebdige, D. (1979) *Subculture: The Meaning of Style, New Accents*. London and New York: Routledge.

Holbrook, M.B. and Hirschman, E.C. (1980) 'Symbolic consumer behavior: An introduction', in E.C. Hirschman and M.B. Holbrook (eds), *Symbolic Consumer Behavior*. New York: Association for Consumer Research. pp. 1–2.

Holt, D.B. (1997) 'Poststructuralist lifestyle analysis: Conceptualizing the social patterning of consumption in postmodernity', *Journal of Consumer Research*, 23: 326–50.

Jenkins, R. (2011) 'Consumption in the everyday imagination: How consumer culture gives shape to everyday thinking', PhD thesis, Bournemouth University.

Khamis, S., Ang, L. and Welling, R. (2016). 'Self-branding, "micro-celebrity" and the rise of Social Media Influencers', *Celebrity Studies*, 2397(September): 1–18.

Kozinets, R.V. (1999) 'E-tribalized marketing?: The strategic implications of virtual communities of consumption', *European Management Journal*, 17: 252–64.

Kozinets, R.V. (2001) 'Utopian enterprise: Articulating the meanings of *Star Trek*'s culture of consumption', *Journal of Consumer Research*, 28: 67–88.

Kozinets, R.V. (2002) 'The field behind the screen: Using netnography for marketing research in online communities', *Journal of Marketing Research*, 39(1): 61–72.

Kozinets, R.V. (2010a) *Netnography: The Marketer's Secret Weapon*. White Paper, Netbase Solutions, Inc.

Kozinets, R.V. (2010b) *Netnography: Ethnographic Research in the Age of the Internet*. London: Sage Publications.

Maffesoli, M. (1988) *Le Temps des Tribus: le Déclin de l'Individualisme dans les Sociétés Postmodernes*. Paris: La Table Ronde.

Maffesoli, M. (1996) *The Time of the Tribes: The Decline of Individualism in Mass Society*. London: Sage Publications.

Martin, C.L. (1998) 'Relationship marketing: A high-involvement product attribute approach', *Journal of Product & Brand Management*, 7: 6–26.

Marzocchi, G., Morandin, G. and Bergami, M. (2013) 'Brand communities: Loyal to the community or the brand?', *European Journal of Marketing*, 47: 93–114.

Muniz Jr, A.M. and O'Guinn, T.C. (2001) 'Brand community', *Journal of Consumer Research*, 27: 412–32.

Scarpi, D. (2010) 'Does size matter? An examination of small and large web-based brand communities', *Journal of Interactive Marketing*, 24: 14–21.

Schouten, J.W. and McAlexander, J.H. (1995) 'Subcultures of consumption: An ethnography of the new bikers', *Journal of Consumer Research*, 22(3): 43–61.

Steenson, M. (n.d.) Burning Man: What Is Burning Man? The Experience [Online]. Available at: www.burningman.com/whatisburningman/about_burningman/experience.html (accessed 3 March 2013).

Veloutsou, C. and Moutinho, L. (2009) 'Brand relationships through brand reputation and brand tribalism', *Journal of Business Research*, 62: 314–22.

Zaglia, M.E. (2013) 'Brand communities embedded in social networks', *Journal of Business Research*, 66: 216–23.

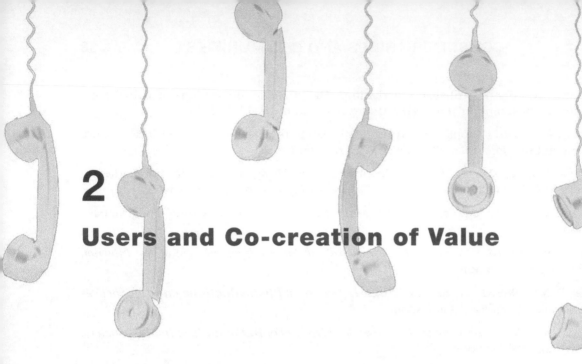

# 2

# Users and Co-creation of Value

## CHAPTER OVERVIEW

Ensuing from the discussion in Chapter 1, this chapter focuses on how the extended consumption process influences consumer behaviour; particularly how social media has created an instantaneous social space in which post-modern consumption-linked practices can readily occur. The chapter asks how do consumers co-create the social consumption experience? How do consumers become active participants in the creation of value using online tools? And which roles do consumers play in the co-creation of experiences and value?

# LEARNING OUTCOMES

On completing this chapter, you should be able to:

- understand the process of co-creation as an integral part of consumption
- be able to critically reflect on the notion of value
- identify consumer roles in the context of co-creation
- understand different consumption communities enabled through social media, including anti-consumption communities
- critically discuss the concept of co-creation and how it relates to traditional marketing.

## CONTROL AND CO-CREATION OF VALUE

## Control

Post-modern, tribal consumption practices pose unique challenges for marketing professionals. Early research into the Newton Community, an online-based brand community which maintained the brand of the Newton, a discontinued personal digital assistant originally manufactured but later abandoned by Apple, shows how hard it is for modern tribes and brand communities to be controlled (Muñiz and Schau, 2007). Whereas previously, consumers were largely unable to influence, or even revive and maintain brands long after brand managers had abandoned them, these communities are now making 'claims on core competencies formerly reserved for the marketer' (O'Guinn and Muñiz Jr, 2005: 269). Tribes and brand communities are laying claims to owning and controlling a brand, thereby taking away brand ownership from the company and claiming the brand as their own (Cova and White, 2010). While Newton is one example, other examples include Cadbury's Wispa chocolate bar, which was relaunched in 2007 following an Internet campaign from consumers. However, it is important to note that although social media tools have made it significantly easier for consumers to voice their dissatisfaction about abandoned or altered brands, or even to keep them alive, that prior to widespread adoption of the Internet, the now legendary relaunch of the 'New Coke', a newly formulated version of the traditional Coca-Cola drink, also resulted in significant protests by consumers resulting in the reintroduction of the 'Classic Coke'.

Moran and Gossieaux describe this phenomenon as **social messiness**, which replaces conventional hierarchy and control in contemporary consumer society (Moran and Gossieaux, 2010). Marketing practitioners are forced to adapt to this social messiness, something that traditional marketing strategies, deeply rooted in a positivist, modernist vision of controllability, equate to a total change of paradigm. Some researchers have asserted that this is a democratisation of the marketplace, where marketers used to have almost total power, but are now finding themselves *primus inter pares*. As Christodoulides describes the change: 'The brand manager [...] has now become a host whose main role is not to control (this is impossible) but to facilitate' (2009: 143).

Consumers now have three basic levels of interaction with brands (Asmussen et al., 2012):

1.  Consumers can choose a passive way of interacting. Thus consumers create meaning out of brand manifestations that they get to experience, but which are not created or co-created by themselves, for instance, when shopping or watching adverts, or when being exposed to brand-originated messages on social media networks, for example retweets by friends, sponsored posts – or indeed online advertising in the conventional form.
2.  Consumers can choose to become active through co-creating brand meaning, aiming to create brand manifestations themselves in a limited way. They can create, with the facilitation of brand stakeholders, their own messages, spreading them across their individual networks. Examples of such practice would include retweeting, sharing or adapting content created by marketers, for instance viral videos or other sharable content posted on Facebook or other social media pages.
3.  Consumers can create brand manifestations autonomously. This means that there is no control of the brand owner, and may include the establishment of rival brands. Typical examples can be found in the **open source (OS)** software community, where amateur developers develop software with similar functionality as commercial software for free. Similarly, users creating or restaging fake adverts and posting them on YouTube, some of which may involve real brands, are examples of this. Other examples are some of the pictures frequently found on some Facebook pages, where brand owners entice fans to submit pictures of them using the product or displaying the brands, which are then posted to all the fans.

Following this shared creation and control over the brand and brand narrative, and taking the consumer perspective as a central point, the remainder of this chapter looks at the idea of the co-creation process, discussing the notion of value and value creation in the process.

The chapter then moves on to explore how the co-creation manifests itself – from positive organisation and consumer collaboration to antagonistic forms of consumer empowerment in the form of value destructive co-creation – and in the form of reactive co-creation. The chapter concludes by looking at critiques of co-creation and implications of co-creating for traditional marketing theories.

## Co-creation

Traditional economic theory, and by extension most traditional marketing models, conceptualises the roles of consumers and producers as distinct and separate – companies were producing goods for consumers. On the other side, most consumers are passive recipients of these goods, not directly involved in the production process (at least beyond market research activities).

However, McLuhan and Nevitt envisaged a more active consumer, directly involved in production, in the early 1970s. They suggested that, aided by technological advancement, the roles of consumer and producer would begin to merge (McLuhan and Nevitt, 1972). They did not foresee social media, or indeed communication technology, as a production tool.

Rather, they assumed a more technical co-production. Nonetheless, through the synergistic rise to popularity of communication technology and a move towards experiential consumption beyond the purchasing process, social media in many ways substitutes the original tools envisaged by McLuhan and Nevitt. However, as Ritzer (2004) argues, even without communication technology advancement, and rather as a result of pressure to rationalise, companies already started to 'put consumers to work': McDonald's restaurants have relied on consumers to perform the role of waiters since the 1940s, and even ATMs rely on 'everyone to work, at least for a few moments, as unpaid bank teller' (Ritzer, 2004: 63). The term **prosumer**, a producing consumer, was coined in the 1980s to describe consumers actively involved in production (Toffler, 1980). Prosumers originally described consumers who customise generally standardised goods by adding limited production to their consumption experience, for example in the case of DIY products, but are also frequently found today, for example, individuals who decorate relatively standard products (e.g. by decorating the cover of a standard Apple laptop) to create an individual computer and consumption experience when using the computer.

Around the turn of the millennium, the concept of co-creation, moving beyond the idea of customisation of products by prosumers, emerged as a way to describe the active involvement of consumers in the creation of goods, services, brands – indeed everything related to a particular organisation. The concept of co-creation can be seen as emergent from the earlier ideas related to prosumers and the Experience Economy and co-creation plays a central role in Service Dominant Logic, being frequently described in marketing terms as a way to empower consumers as active participants in the production process (Prahalad and Ramaswamy, 2004).

## Experience Economy

The management concept of the **Experience Economy** is mostly linked to the work of Pine and Gilmore (1999), who argue that a product is an object around which customers have experiences, and that the value of the object is therefore not the value of the object or product itself, but rather the value of the consumer's experiences surrounding it.

However, the link between experiences and product value has been discussed in the marketing literature well before Pine and Gilmore coined the term. For example, 17 years before Pine and Gilmore, Holbrook and Hirschman (1982) argued for an 'experiential view that focuses on the symbolic, hedonic and aesthetic nature of consumption' (1982: 132). Similar to the view in Experience Economy, Holbrook and Hirschman suggest that consumers do not make consumption choices, or indeed derive value from objects, based merely on rational information processing. Rather, consumers pursue emotions, such as feelings of fun or fulfilment of fantasies, when consuming. Although neither Holbrook and Hirschman nor Pine and Gilmore talk explicitly about social experiences, such as the experiences in tribes, tribal consumption, or indeed online consumption through social media, as covered in the previous chapter, it is easy to see how the pursuit of experiences as a goal in consumption is companionable with a sharing of such experiences, as the literature around brand communities and tribes suggests. Social media aids in this shared experience building: consumption can be shared amongst friends, and life can be constructed as a narrative for fellow tribe members through sharing and interactions. For instance, through sharing of pictures using social media and social networking sites, a consumption experience such as eating food (in the form of food porn) can be extended to the wider social circle. Similarly, various periods of consumption experiences related to a new iPhone can be socialised amongst friends, followers and unknown people, by communal sharing of each step, for instance, through Twitter updates of waiting in line for the launch of the product and posting pictures of the unboxing etc.

## Co-creation Concept

Co-creation, as introduced by Prahalad and Ramaswamy (2000), is going beyond the ideas put forward in the Experience Economy. Co-creation advocates a more interactive stance between company and customer, beyond shared experiences or customisation. Prahalad and Ramaswamy argue that the role of the company has moved beyond focusing on providing experiences for largely passive customers to customers becoming active prosumers, producers and consumers at the same time, stretching way beyond the traditional notion of prosumers' limited involvement. Central to this process is the co-production of value, which goes beyond the price of a product or service. In their words: 'the consumer and the firm [are] intimately involved in jointly creating value that is unique to the individual consumer' (Prahalad and Ramaswamy, 2004: 16). Although Prahalad and Ramaswamy do not explicitly reference online co-creation opportunities in their original work, Ramaswamy and Gouillart (2010) later on acknowledge the pivotal role of social media in the co-creation process, and the influence of social networks, where consumers 'now expect to be able to communicate directly with one another and share and shape their own experiences' (2010: 2). As can be seen from studies into the selfie-culture, consumers now challenge brand assemblages with their own versions of pictures of the brand (Rokka and Canniford, 2016). It could be argued that, through sharing of experiences and stories in the form of selfies and other social media posts, consumers are actually creating competing brand communication.

Co-creation is therefore an interactive and reciprocal action between consumer and producer. And although the power balance in this interaction may be asymmetric, co-creation is frequently described as mutually beneficial – or at least framed as a process which empowers consumers to have an active input into the creation process (Füller et al., 2006), i.e. moving from passive consumer to active co-producer alongside the organisation. Consequently, for managers, providing possibilities for co-creation of the consumption experience becomes a key objective: whether it is through simple facilitation of sharing activities, such as providing free Internet enabling social sharing of consumption, for example in Apple stores, or where co-creation becomes more elaborate, facilitating tribal goals through brand objectives.

### Service Dominant Logic

The concept of co-creation has been further integrated into the **Service Dominant Logic** (sometimes abbreviated to S-D Logic). Proponents of S-D Logic argue that modern consumption is no longer focused on tangible resources and goods. Rather, even around tangible products, the focus has been replaced by an emphasis on the co-creation of value through service, based on the interactions and relationship between producer and consumer (Vargo and Lusch, 2004). S-D Logic therefore evolves the concept of consumers as active agents, who create the value of their consumption experiences through dialogue and actively co-producing 'services'.

Vargo and Lusch argue that these new perspectives are converging to form a new 'dominant logic' where service provision is fundamental to economic exchange.

S-D Logic recognises social media and real life social networks as indispensable tools for facilitating the co-creation of value (Edvardsson et al., 2010), although it aims to be a holistic marketing theory reaching beyond the scope of social media exclusively.

The view of brand creation in S-D Logic also complements the observations made in Chapter 1, as Merz and colleagues (2009) suggest, marketing has evolved from what they call an 'Individual Goods-Focus Brand Era' to a 'Stakeholder-Focus Brand Era'. In this new area of marketing, brands are a dynamic, social process, involving engagement and co-creation of multiple stakeholders. In these aspects, S-D Logic elaborates on the tribal perspective, in that it adds other stakeholders to the creation process, i.e. it is not just friends, or other tribe members, who create a particular brand, but the creation process may also involve the company, brand managers – and even individuals completely unrelated to the consumption process.

While S-D Logic generally tends to see co-creation as a positive process, the potential for a negative outcome has been highlighted (Echeverri and Skålén, 2011; Plé and Cáceres, 2010). See also later in this chapter where destruction of created value is discussed.

## THINKBOX SERVICE OR PRODUCT?

Think of a product you bought recently, for example a coffee or a sandwich. What influence did the service element of the purchasing experience have on you? Have you ever shared such an experience using social media, by for example checking into a place or commenting on the experience? How did the price of the product relate to the experienced value?

## Value

The concept of 'value' is both widely discussed as well as controversial in different disciplines, including in the marketing literature (Sánchez-Fernández and Iniesta-Bonillo, 2007).

From a managerial perspective value is often discussed, simplistically, as a concept of profit maximisation: where a market price exceeds production cost, value is created for a company (Jensen, 2001). Similarly, in the context of marketing, value has been conceptualised in easy terms as the price paid for a product, that is, the value is something that can be measured objectively in terms of monetary value, which again is fundamental to the concept of exchange, conventionally considered at the heart of traditional marketing theory.

On the other side, for the consumer, the concept of value representing the understanding of the 'worth' of an object is significantly more complex. Value can include such diverse factors as the value of the product itself, augmented or linked attributes such as the product's brand, added services, etc. Therefore, value for the consumer is different from just the functional 'worth' or even the 'price' of a given product or service: it has a symbolic meaning at the same time. This symbolic meaning can be different from the purely functional meaning expressed as the price of a product. For example, Curasi and colleagues (2004) discuss how items of small or even no economic value become highly treasured items if they are connected to family history. Consequently, the value attached by consumers to individual items is not reflective of the monetary value of the item.

**Table 2.1**  Consumer value types (Holbrook, 1999)

|                    |           | **Extrinsic**                              | **Intrinsic**                          |
| ------------------ | --------- | ------------------------------------------ | -------------------------------------- |
| *Self-oriented*    | Active    | *Efficiency*<br>Output/input, convenience  | *Play*<br>Fun                          |
|                    | Re-active | *Excellence*<br>Quality                    | *Aesthetics*<br>Beauty                 |
| *Other-oriented*   | Active    | *Status*<br>Success, impression management | *Ethics*<br>Justice, virtue, morality  |
|                    | Re-active | *Esteem*<br>Reputation, materialism, possessions | *Spirituality*<br>Faith, ecstasy, sacredness |

*Source*: Republished with permission of Routledge, from 'Consumer Value: A Framework for Analysis and Research', Holbrook, M.B., 1999.

Consumer value perceptions are, consequently, individual to consumers: consumers perceive value differently depending on how, for example, an item helps them achieve their personal life or career goals. As Firat and colleagues (1995) show, the same product may have a different value – and type of value – attached to it depending on the consumer, for example, one consumer buys a specific brand of sports shoes because they are comfortable to wear, while another consumer may be buying the same shoes in order to look fashionable. Holbrook, expanding on Firat's concept, describes eight different types of consumer values (see Table 2.1).

To add to the complexity of value for the consumer, the perceived value of a product can change over time, that is, the value is fluid and flexible, rather than static as the simple managerial view would suggest (Holbrook, 2006).

Holbrook acknowledges explicitly the role of a specific 'other-oriented' dimension of value, i.e. products being valued explicitly by consumers in relation to others, such as attempting to impress other people through the use of highly priced products, or as a way of entering a tribe.

### Linking Value

Cova and Cova (Cova, 1997; Cova and Cova, 2002), by studying neo-tribal consumption practices, added a further level to the discussion of value creation. Rather than focusing on the value as seen by the consumer or the producer, they argued that products, and especially certain brands, also possess a value arising from the collectives of consumers using them. Thus, their focus on the value is going beyond the individual value perception that underlies Holbrook's work, or the managerial definitions of value.

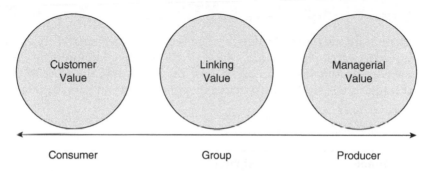

**Figure 2.1** Value types

*Linking value* is derived from the social links a product or brand provides. As such, it is neither the producer who instils linking value into their products, nor is it the consumer individually who can create this value. Rather, linking value arises through the 'social links' a product creates between individual tribe members at a communal level.

In summary, three different sources of value can be identified (see Figure 2.1), all of which can be explicitly modified through social media influence.

Consumers can express different types of customer value in a form of self-expression, for example by posting pictures of products they consume. If they are doing this mainly as a way to increase their own self-perception, or even expecting rewards (for example likes) from friends, then the value arises from within the consumer, rather than the producer. On the opposite extreme, such self-expressions can increase managerial value through (positive) word of mouth, allowing a higher price to be charged. However, ultimately, managerial value arises out of the price paid by consumers. Finally, linking value – arising from the wider group rather than the individual or the producer, in the form of the symbolic value of brands or consumption practices amongst tribes or brand communities – underlies much of social media consumer behaviour as it enables tribe members to identify other tribe members, for example, through identifying other individuals checking in at similar locations using location-based social networks.

## THINKBOX VALUE

Think of different ways in which you can measure the value of an item you are currently wearing. Decide which of Holbrook's value types describes the value you attach to the item.

Check recent social media posts of people you follow. Can you identify brands or objects and attribute different types of value to them?

## Creating Value

Rather than examining the types of value that can be created, Schau and colleagues (2009) focus on the practices that create value, especially in online communities. They identify 12 practices, covering four broad areas, of how brand communities create 'value' (see Table 2.2). Although their study was specifically aimed at brand communities, given the

**Table 2.2**   Value creation in brand communities

| Area | Practice | Description |
|---|---|---|
| *Social networking* | Welcoming | Welcoming new members to the community |
| | Emphasising | Lending emotion or physical support for brand-related issues |
| | Governing | Articulating behavioural expectations within the community |
| *Community engagement* | Staking | Recognising variance in group membership and emphasising intra-group similarity |
| | Documenting | Detailing brand relationships in narratives |
| | Badging | Creating symbols (badges) for individual milestones |
| | Milestoning | Noting seminal events in brand ownership |
| *Impression management* | Evangelising | Sharing good news about the brand to non-community members |
| | Justifying | Deploying rationales for devoting time to the brand community |
| *Brand use* | Customising | Modifying the brand to suit individual or group-level needs |
| | Grooming | Caring or systemising optimal use patterns for brand products |
| | Commoditising | Distancing/approaching and responding to the general marketplace |

*Source*: Schau et al., 2009

discussion in Chapter 1, it is likely that these practices also occur in non-brand-oriented tribes (i.e. tribes where brands or products are not the primary focus).

In line with the previous discussion on the creation of value, the majority of value-creation practices are not directly related to the actual product or brand-related communication, as 11 of the 12 practices can be classified as serving mostly the establishment and existence of the community, i.e. their primary function is building relationships amongst tribe members. They may be linked to the brand, but are not directly connected to brand-related communication under direct control of the marketing managers.

Only one practice of value creation can be indirectly compared to traditional marketing communication activity: evangelising serves both as a way to increase brand usage as well as a way to entice new brand users by positive word of mouth with non-brand users.

Based on Schau et al.'s work, it is evident that much of the emphasis of value creation within brand communities is not on creation of value for the brand *per se*, nor is it intended to create value for the brand owners. Rather, the main focus of value creation is on building ties between members, where the brand is the main link between members, emphasising the importance of social, tribal aspects surrounding post-modern consumption practices.

## Consumer Roles

Cova and Cova (2002) characterised participants in online groups into four groups: from those with low levels of participation (i.e. sympathisers), via active members and practitioners, to the most dedicated group, which they called devotees, who are shown to have extremely high levels of involvement and emotional attachment to both the tribal community and the brand – or indeed brands – representing the tribe.

Lopez (2013) supports the importance of the emotional attachment with the group in her study of antecedents of brand communities. She argues that both a personal and group brand connection lead to engagement in brand communities and subsequent brand loyalty. However, Lopez also cautions that individual need for uniqueness has a negative effect on brand loyalty. This finding further supports the notion that virtual brand communities may be fluid as people may join communities while a brand is relatively unknown, satisfying their need for uniqueness. However, they are then likely to seek alternatives at the point where the brand community is perceived to be becoming more popular.

While Cova and Cova's groups were concerned with activity levels of group members, and Lopez studied antecedents for brand community participation, Pongsakornrungsilp and Schroeder (2011) suggested types of activity as an alternative way of classifying consumer roles. Based on an online football community (see research highlight), they suggested four roles members of online brand communities could perform. At the meta-level, they distinguish between two roles: providers, who are active in the discussion, and beneficiaries. Beneficiaries tend to be less experienced members, who are therefore lurking without much interaction (similar to sympathisers). Providers can act as 'creative posters', 'brand warriors' or 'moderators'.

Creative posters are providers who contribute significant information to the community by sharing opinions and knowledge with co-participants. Brand warriors' contributions focus predominantly on disseminating cultural knowledge about brand values, traditions and history. Moderators focus largely on intergroup cohesion, for example enforcement of rules and creating a welcoming environment for community members.

Other studies have highlighted unique aspects of co-creation in different communities: for instance, using netnography to study university students' activities on Facebook pages, Fujita et al. (2017) found that they created visual narratives, co-authored student/staff brand stories, engaged in co-delivering student services and twisted and played with the narratives and images related to school subcultures. Drawing on both CCT and S-D Logic, Healy and McDonagh extended the number of potential roles taken by consumers to seven, by examining the functions that consumers can play when co-creating value with the brand owners (Healy and McDonagh, 2012). Their study, also based on interactions in an online football supporters forum, highlights the complex social relationships between tribe (or forum) members and traditional brand stakeholders, such as, in their case, the football club itself, the club owners, suppliers of officially branded football clothing, etc. The list of seven roles is given in Table 2.3, together with their management implication.

**Table 2.3** Seven roles

| Type | Description | Management implications |
| --- | --- | --- |
| Voice | Consumer-member response to organisational performance (both positive and negative) | Measurement of 'positive voice' and decrease 'negative voice' by listening to what management could improve |
| Loyalty | Loyal to the brand/organisation but not necessarily loyal to peripheral products | Understand why consumers are loyal, encourage co-creation |
| Exits | Exiting the brand relationship as customers – but not the community | Understand main concerns that lead to exit and look to alter its behaviour and product/service offering to prevent exit |
| Twist | Using consumption symbols in a way not originally intended – or creating unintended items, such as unofficial flags, symbols, etc. | Encourage positive twisting and co-creation of culture and use it as a source of innovation. Negative twisting can be used to understand what drives it and change management behaviour or the product/service offering |
| Entry | New consumers, becoming part of fan tribe | Identify what existing fans believe is necessary to increase new fan entry |
| Non-entry | Don't consume the brand but enter the community because of emotional bond to the main brand | Identify barriers to consumption |
| Re-entry | Boycotting the brand but not the community (but will re-enter if reason for boycott is removed) | Understand why the boycott occurs and use this for change in management behaviour and/or the product/service offering, to encourage re-entry |

*Source*: Reprinted from *Journal of Business Research*, 66/9, Healy, J.C. and McDonagh, P., 'Consumer roles in brand culture and value co-creation in virtual communities', 1-13, 2012, with permission from Elsevier.

The main marketing manager activity is therefore notably based on enabling the various roles that are supportive of the brand's desired position. Failure to acknowledge the potential of co-creation of value can be especially problematic in cases such as football clubs, where fans play a substantial role in creating the value of the brand. Recent rebranding examples of both Cardiff City FC, which changed colours, and Hull City FC, which was supposed to be rebranded as the 'Hull Tigers', are examples of fans with high stakes in value creation using their powers to counteract management decisions. However, while examples such as football clubs are especially noticeable, the roles and potential dangers of ignoring the emotional involvement of customers or creators of value is by no means restricted to football, but can be observed in a wide variety of brand-related communities.

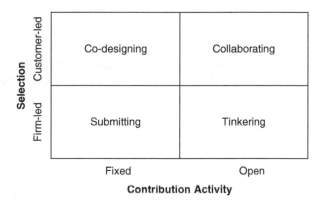

**Figure 2.2**   Typology of customer co-creation

*Source*: Republished with permission of Emerald Group Publishing, from 'Customer co-creation: A typology and research agenda', O'Hern, M. and Rindfleisch, A., *Review of Marketing Research*, N.K. Malhotra (ed.), Vol. 6, 2010; permission conveyed through Copyright Clearance Center, Inc.

## Commercial Co-creation

There are numerous examples of co-creation being used by organisations, both positive and negative, where organisations have used social media in particular to stimulate consumer input all the way to involving their customers in complete product redesigns.

Because co-creation can occur in such a variety of ways, O'Hern and Rindfleisch (2010) proposed a typology of customer co-creation based on different levels of organisation/ customer involvement. The typology distinguishes two activities: firstly, selection of concepts, led by the organisation or by the customer, and secondly, a fixed or open contribution activity. The resultant typology matrix is given in Figure 2.2.

Collaboration is the most customer-led and open, and therefore probably the most extreme, form of co-creation, representing nearly full marketplace democracy, where customers regulate the production of value. Open source software, such as Firefox or Linux, which are managed by non-profit companies, are typical examples of products where contributors have the power to make fundamental changes to the basic structure of the product (e.g. the source code of the software).

Tinkering, on the other hand, allows consumers to use products (i.e. contribute) in a fairly open way and customise the core product, but the organisation still remains in close control of the core product. For example, Google Maps allows the use of its maps in numerous other applications, ranging from running tracking software such as Nike+ to visualisation of crime rates and types of incidences at street level of existing police data in the UK (see www.police.uk/).

Co-designing allows a group of customers to contribute to products, with the final contribution being selected again in an open fashion by all customers. Examples of such co-designing strategies include dig.com, which allows customers to vote for top news stories rather than asserting editorial control over the site's offering.

Finally, the most closely controlled type of co-production both in terms of what is being produced (contribution) and final selection is submitting. Typical examples include design contests where the organisation decides on the final winner. Submitting though is distinguished from traditional market research (e.g. focus groups) by the requirement of a substantial contribution from contestants. For example, O'Hern and Rindfleisch (2010) recount the example of the Electrolux 'Designlab' where participants are asked to design new household appliances, submit these for selection by the company before participating in a six-day retreat to compete for prizes.

Both the on-going popularity as well as academic studies have suggested that many customers perceive co-creation as enjoyable, even if it involves substantial work for no immediate material return, such as in the case of open source software (Shah, 2006). Co-creation leads to increased brand loyalty and more fulfilling consumer–brand relationships (Hajli et al., 2017). O'Hern and Rindfleisch (2010) explain this by arguing that customers achieve psychological satisfaction through being creatively engaged in the creation process. This is, they contend, because creative pursuits fulfil more intrinsic psychological needs than consumption alone. However, Gebauer and colleagues (2012) challenge such a direct link between mere involvement and participant satisfaction. Rather, they argue, perceived fairness when the final selection is made is the key to a positive co-creation experience. Using the example of a bag design contest by an Austrian supermarket chain, where the winners were chosen by a jury, they show that a perceived unfair selection can result in substantial negative word of mouth. They suggest that organisations engaging in co-creation have to ensure an open dialogue to alleviate potential perceptions of unfairness. Pointing towards evidence that co-creation itself can instil a sense of community amongst participants, they further suggest that negative reactions may be mediated by a strong sense of community.

## THINKBOX CO-CREATION

Imagine that you are a brand manager for a new product. Which type of co-creation would you feel most comfortable with?

Think about how you would leverage social media to co-create. What advantages and disadvantages does large-scale co-creation have?

## Anti-consumption

While positive co-creation can be a powerful means to create value, it can also be a powerful way to destroy value, particularly when consumers turn against brands. While anti-consumption is, of course, not immediately linked to social media, the ability to gather tribes and organise for collective action is greatly simplified with the help of social media tools. For example, Buycott.com enables users to set up or join 'campaigns', such as boycotting companies that are linked to political parties or encouraging consumption of products produced by companies with specific ethical standards, on their website. Users then download a phone app that can be used to scan products in order to find out if these products are linked to any of the campaigns – and share these with their social network using Facebook and Twitter.

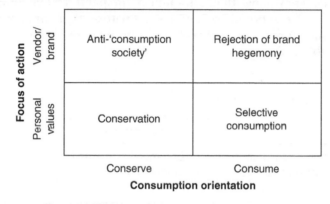

**Figure 2.3**  Anti-consumption typology

Reprinted from *Journal of Business Research*, 62/2,Cromie, J.G. and Ewing, M.T., 'The rejection of brand hegemony', 218-30, 2009, with permission from Elsevier.

Much of the focus of anti-consumption research has traditionally been directed to the groups that try to remove themselves from a society largely focused on consumption activity, through an active reduction of consumption to only essential consumption. However, Cromie and Ewing (2009) contend that anti-consumption can also be expressed through active consumption of competing brands. Therefore, they suggest a wider typology of anti-consumption based on focus of action (i.e. arising from personal values or vendor–brand relationships) and orientation of members towards consumption (i.e. to reject consumption and 'conserve' or to avidly consume). The resultant typology is given in Figure 2.3.

Examples of anti-'consumption society' are numerous, from Adbusters to No Logo movements or in the case of monastic lifestyles.

A narrower focus of consumption reduction can be found in the 'conservation' cluster, where members reduce consumption often of specific products based on personal values. For example, members of www.cooltheearth.org/ try to promote low carbon living through energy reduction and low carbon diets in schools.

Other consumer tribes may encourage consumption as a way to achieve personal or more general goals. For example, members of 'selective consumption' tribes may choose to actively consume certain products linked with causes they support and not consume products they feel are opposing their personal values. For example, Kates (2004) shows how many gay consumers encourage purchase of Levi Jeans because of perceived same-sex-friendly workplace practices.

A distinct group, which actively encourages consumption while rejecting current commercial producers, are tribes located in the 'rejection of brand hegemony' cluster. These groups set up a counter brand community resulting from their frustration or from feeling exploited by major brands in the market. Cromie and Ewing (2009) use the example of OS communities (communities of lay experts who create and maintain software) to show how consumer tribes in this group can move beyond co-creation activities and establish their own products. They show that, although participants in OS communities can be understood to be similar to brand communities in nature, there are some important differences between the more traditional notion of a brand community and an open source community (see Table 2.4).

**Table 2.4** Open source vs. brand community

| Brand community | OS community |
| --- | --- |
| Communities of consumption (other than in the sense of value co-production), not production | Communities are self-consciously communities of production |
| Comprised primarily of consumers engaged with the brand | Comprised primarily of producers engaged with projects |
| Brand/product pre-exist the community and the community is a response to them | The community pre-exists the product and initially the brand; the brand is a result of community effort |
| Brand/product under the control of one or more vendors and/or marketers who decide what degree of influence they will allow the community to exert | Brand and product are substantially under the control of the community – vendors and marketers need to behave in ways approved by the community |

*Source*: Reprinted from *Journal of Business Research*, 62/2,Cromie, J.G. and Ewing, M.T., 'The rejection of brand hegemony', 218-30, 2009, with permission from Elsevier.

Cova and White (2010) extend Cromie and Ewing's 'rejection of brand hegemony' group further by differentiating two alternative types of, what they call, brand community: alter-brand communities and the counter-brand communities.

Alter-brand communities are characterised as a community that creates the brand, i.e. the community is the brand – and go beyond the mere co-creation of value. In alter-brand communities, producers and consumers are the same group, but their motives are largely positive, that is, they are not driven by frustration or dissatisfaction with existing brands, but rather members are likely to be led by altruistic motives.

Counter-brand communities on the other side emerge because of dissatisfaction with existing actors, for example, where consumers felt taken advantage of in the co-creation process. Counter-brand communities are therefore mainly reactive in nature and a consequence of perceived marketplace unfairness.

In summary, anti-consumption activity can be both positive and negative in focus, i.e. customers can focus on rejecting consumption *per se*, or divert or increase consumption of alternative brands. Social media offers networking tools to activate and support (anti-) consumption, for example, through the social learning aspects discussed in the previous chapter, tribe members can exchange knowledge about brand owners and mobilise accordingly. The increased communication flow through social media can greatly increase both the speed of positive and negative (anti-) consumption-related information.

## Critiques of Co-creation

Commercial co-creation has been criticised by some researchers suggesting that the practice when used commercially, to co-create products, is effectively a double exploitation of consumers: consumers are asked to provide free labour in the first instance to create the products, which are then being sold back to them by the organisation who asked the consumers in the first place. However, users or consumers as producers are evidently the main business model of social media and user-generated content, for example, Bonsu (2013) gives the example of the Flickr social networking site. He argues that, as the basic account is too limited to be useful, and must be upgraded to accommodate modern camera usage, the site effectively charges users a subscription fee to post pictures that they have produced, and without which Flickr would not exist. Similarly, Facebook, Twitter or TripAdvisor would all be largely useless if it wasn't for the user-generated content, even if in these cases the business model is not based on direct payment by the consumer, but rather in the consumer being exposed to advertising or sponsored messages in return for 'free' access and usage. Based on this argument, Zwick and colleagues (2008) argue that co-creation, especially using Web 2.0 technology, entangles users in a 'web of control' where consumers work, under the impression of performing a leisure activity.

Ritzer and Jurgenson (2010) go as far as describing online communities, especially social media, as a new form of capitalism, which they call the 'prosumer capitalism'. They describe this form of capitalism as a system where products are free in return for free labour. However, although many prosumers enjoy creating content, this does not, in their view, distract from the fact that prosumers are rendering their labour for free. While the concept of prosumption has often been used interchangeably with co-creation and co-production, some authors maintain that the term 'prosumption' describes a more engaged (from the consumer perspective) form of co-creation. Taking a social media example, on Flickr, individual prosumers are solely responsible for their pictures, with the firm taking little or no responsibility for the individual creations uploaded to the website. Flickr does not provide training in the production of its main content, nor does it collaborate directly with individual site users. This is different from traditional co-production, where firms and consumers are engaged in more frequent interactions, the firms often train the consumer to co-produce or co-create products or value and there is a shared responsibility between firm and consumer for the final product (Alhashem et al., 2013).

**THINKBOX CRITICISMS**

How do you feel about being simultaneously the producer and consumer of social media content? Do you think the idea of double exploitation is justified? Why? Why not?

## Co-creation and Traditional Marketing

The evolvement of co-creation poses some challenges to some traditional marketing assumptions. From a theoretical basis, the blurring of the distinction between consumer and producer creates some challenges in relation to traditional marketing theory. Many of the changes we see today have, however, been incorporated into marketing theory before the rise of social media – for example the role of co-creation in S-D Logic. While therefore similar to the emergence of tribes and the post-modern consumer discussed in Chapter 1, it is difficult to conclude that widespread adoption of social media has caused these effects, although it is probably safe to assume that social media has substantially accelerated changes in the marketplace. For example, the rise of open source as a business and marketing model is difficult, though not impossible to imagine without technological tools. Similarly, alter- and counter-brand communities have probably existed significantly before the Internet or social media was popular. Again, social media does significantly enhance the potential to reach out to many more potential participants, even in organised ways. For instance, by using social media sites such as Thunderclap (see also Chapter 8), activists can harness social media voices to create trending topics.

## SUMMARY

This chapter discussed how consumers co-create value and consumption experiences, including how this co-creation can be mediated and enhanced through social media. Through understanding the roles consumers play, and consumer expectations for co-creation possibilities, marketers can use tools such as social media to complement core products with additional services as per Service Dominant Logic.

**RESEARCH DIRECTIONS**

Much of the research related to co-creation is based on virtual communities, however, the majority of these are distinct communities away from the social media mainstream, that is, the research has focused on dedicated websites and forums rather than on, for example, Facebook groups and pages or how social media tools like Twitter can be used to engage consumers in social co-creation. Exploring how other forms away from dedicated online communities are co-creating value and shared experiences is a necessary future avenue for research.

# RESEARCH HIGHLIGHT VALUE CO-CREATION IN AN ONLINE BRAND COMMUNITY

In the study 'Understanding value co-creation in a co-consuming brand community', Pongsakornrungsilp and Schroeder (2011) examine the roles of consumers in the brand community 'This is Anfield', an online community of fans of Liverpool Football Club, one of the oldest football clubs in the UK. The community is a traditional forum-based community, operated independently from the club, where website members can interact and discuss their team. Pongsakornrungsilp and Schroeder combine netnography (see research highlight in the previous chapter), together with a 'humanist inquiry method' based on Hirschman (1986) in three stages. The three stages are, firstly, an 'a priori' conceptualisation, followed by an exploratory investigation, where initial data is collected and compared to the 'a priori' conceptualisation from the first step. The last step is a 'personal immersion', where the researcher becomes part of the online community, acting both as an observer and participant.

A potential limitation of researcher immersion as both observer and participant is that, as the researcher becomes an active participant in the community, this may result in bias occurring. However, as direct participation is beneficial to form direct relationships and trust with existing group members, the authors argue that the positives outweigh the limitation. The authors also counterbalance the limitation by ensuring that the collected data is analysed by two researchers, one of whom is an active football player and community member, while the other researcher is not. Emerging themes from the research were further analysed relying on an interpretive, three stage, hermeneutical framework originally developed for ethnographic research by Thompson (1997). The framework is useful for evaluating consumer narratives, assuming a game-like description of a phenomenon with different actors 'making moves' according to their agenda, which together form a consumption experience. Such narratives are then interpreted, firstly, by identifying key patterns of meanings for individual participants in their narrative, before secondly detecting common patterns of meanings across several consumption episodes by different participants. In the final step, the researchers

*(Continued)*

derive broad conceptual and managerial implications based on the previous step, which allows researchers to create meaningful insights from a consumer perspective. In the case of Pongsakornrungsilp and Schroeder, the implications are then contextualised with previous research into online communities and roles of co-creating consumers. By comparing the previous insights to the context of the specific online community, Pongsakornrungsilp and Schroeder can critically appraise the validity of previously published role descriptions in the co-creation process and, where appropriate, indicate where the roles are different in the specific community under investigation. Resultantly, they can suggest an improved, richer picture of the co-creation process, specifically demonstrating the dynamic nature of co-creation roles (i.e. in the context of 'This is Anfield', consumers take both beneficiary and provider roles).

To access the full study, please go to the companion website of this book.

# CASE STUDY VISITBRITAIN GREAT NAMES

Chinese visitors have always been an important segment for tourism in Britain. However, Britain as a destination has often been seen as cold and unwelcoming by many tourists from China. Moreover, travelling to places with hard to pronounce names was identified as a challenge to marketing these in China. To challenge the negative perceptions of Britain and to show a more welcoming face, VisitBritain, the British National Tourist Board, hooked into a distinctively Chinese tradition of giving Chinese names to popular foreign places and people.

To find suitable names, VisitBritain launched an online campaign on the web and social media asking Chinese people to come up with alternative names in Chinese for iconic British places and events. The goal was to make these more accessible, get people talking about the attractions – and ultimately encourage Chinese tourists to visit the renamed places and events and to post pictures online.

As part of the campaign, VisitBritain first asked for name suggestions for 101 top tourist attractions – ranging from the Shard building in London to the Highland Games in Scotland. Almost 13,000 names were suggested for the various places. To find the most appropriate name amongst the submissions for each attraction, VisitBritain again asked Chinese Internet users to vote for their favourite names. Appropriately, the Shard is now referred to as Zhai Xing Ta (or the tower that allows us to pluck stars from the sky), while the Highland Games have been renamed Qun Ying Hui (the strong-man skirt party).

The new names will now be used to refer to these attractions on websites, maps and when promoting them.

## Questions to Consider

1 What mechanics did VisitBritain use to achieve co-creation?
2 Why would you submit your idea for a name?
3 Which positive elements can you see for the marketing of the brand 'Britain' in this campaign? What disadvantages can such a contest have?
4 Discuss how VisitBriatin safeguarded the campaign against potential highjacking or jokes?

## FURTHER READING

Grönroos, C. (2011) 'Value co-creation in service logic: A critical analysis', *Marketing Theory,* 11(3): 419–28.

Pongsakornrungsilp, S. and Schroeder, J.E. (2011) 'Understanding value co-creation in a co-consuming brand community', *Marketing Theory,* 11(3): 303–24.

Zwick, D., Bonsu, S.K. and Darmody, A. (2008) 'Putting consumers to work: Co-creation and new marketing governmentality', *Journal of Consumer Culture,* 8(2): 163–96.

## REFERENCES

Alhashem, M., Szmigin, I. and Moraes, C. (2013) 'Collaboration in the marketplace: Identifying the critical differences between prosumption and consumer co-creation', in S. Sezgin, E. Karaosmanoglu and A. Elmadag Bas (eds), *Proceedings of the 42 Annual EMAC Conference, Lost in Translation: Marketing in an Interconnected World*. Istanbul: Istanbul Technical University, 4–7 June.

Asmussen, B., Harridge-March, S., Occhiocupo, N. and Farquhar, J. (2012) 'The multi-layered nature of the Internet-based democratization of brand management', *Journal of Business Research*, 66(9): 1473–83.

Bonsu, S. (2013) 'Value co-creation in virtual environments', in R.W. Belk and R. Llamas (eds), *The Routledge Companion to Digital Consumption*. Abingdon: Routledge. pp. 251–61.

Christodoulides, G. (2009) 'Branding in the post-Internet era', *Marketing Theory*, 9(1): 141–4.

Cova, B. (1997) 'Community and consumption: Towards a definition of the "linking value" of product or services', *European Journal of Marketing*, 31(3/4): 297–316.

Cova, B. and Cova, V. (2002) 'Tribal marketing: The tribalisation of society and its impact on the conduct of marketing', *European Journal of Marketing*, 36(5/6): 595–620.

Cova, B. and White, T. (2010) 'Counter-brand and alter-brand communities: The impact of Web 2.0 on tribal marketing approaches', *Journal of Marketing Management*, 26(3–4): 256–70.

Cromie, J.G. and Ewing, M.T. (2009) 'The rejection of brand hegemony', *Journal of Business Research*, 62(2): 218–30.

Curasi, C.F., Price, L.L. and Arnould, E.J. (2004) 'How individuals' cherished possessions become families' inalienable wealth', *Journal of Consumer Research*, 31(3): 609–22.

Echeverri, P. and Skålén, P. (2011) 'Co-creation and co-destruction: A practice-theory based study of interactive value formation', *Marketing Theory*, 11(3): 351–73.

Edvardsson, B., Tronvoll, B. and Gruber, T. (2010) 'Expanding understanding of service exchange and value co-creation: A social construction approach', *Journal of the Academy of Marketing Science*, 39(2): 327–39.

Firat, A.F., Dholakia, N. and Venkatesh, A. (1995) 'Marketing in a postmodern world', *European Journal of Marketing*, 29(1): 40–56.

Fujita, M., Harrigan, P. and Soutar, G. (2017) 'A netnography of a university's social media brand community: Exploring collaborative co-creation tactics', *Journal of Global Scholars of Marketing Science*, 27(2): 148–64.

Füller, J., Bartl, M., Ernst, H. and Mühlbacher, H. (2006) 'Community based innovation: How to integrate members of virtual communities into new product development', *Electronic Commerce Research*, 6(1): 57–73.

Gebauer, J., Füller, J. and Pezzei, R. (2012) 'The dark and the bright side of co-creation: Triggers of member behavior in online innovation communities', *Journal of Business Research*, 66(9): 1516–27.

Hajli, N., Shanmugam, M., Papagiannidis, S., Zahay, D. and Richard, M.O. (2017) 'Branding co-creation with members of online brand communities', *Journal of Business Research*, 70: 136–44.

Healy, J.C. and McDonagh, P. (2012) 'Consumer roles in brand culture and value co-creation in virtual communities', *Journal of Business Research*, 66(9): 1–13.

Hirschman, E.C. (1986) 'Humanistic inquiry in marketing research: Philosophy, method, and criteria', *Journal of Marketing Research*, 22(3): 237–49.

Holbrook, M.B. (1999) *Consumer Value: A Framework for Analysis and Research*. London and New York: Routledge.

Holbrook, M.B. (2006) 'Consumption experience, customer value, and subjective personal introspection: An illustrative photographic essay', *Journal of Business Research,* 59(6): 714–25.

Holbrook, M.B. and Hirschman, E.C. (1982) 'The experiential aspects of consumption: Consumer fantasies, feelings, and fun', *Journal of Consumer Research*, 9(2): 132–40.

Jensen, M.C. (2001) 'Value maximization, stakeholder theory, and the corporate objective function', *Journal of Applied Corporate Finance*, 14(3): 8–21.

Kates, S.M. (2004) 'The dynamics of brand legitimacy: An interpretive study in the gay men's community', *Journal of Consumer Research*, 31(2): 455–64.

Lopez, M. (2013) 'Identify you! Creating brand loyalty in online social networks', in S. Sezgin, E. Karaosmanoglu and A. Elmadag Bas (eds), *Proceedings of the 42nd Annual EMAC Conference, Lost in Translation: Marketing in an Interconnected World*. Istanbul: Istanbul Technical University, 4–7 June.

McLuhan, M. and Nevitt, B. (1972) *Take Today: The Executive as Dropout*. New York: Harcourt Brace Jovanovich.

Merz, M.A., He, Y. and Vargo, S.L. (2009) 'The evolving brand logic: A service-dominant logic perspective', *Journal of the Academy of Marketing Science*, 37(3): 328–44.

Moran, E. and Gossieaux, F. (2010) 'Marketing in a hyper-social world: The tribaliza-tion of business study and characteristics of successful online communities', *Journal of Advertising Research*, 50(3): 232.

Muñiz, Jr., A.M. and Schau, H.J. (2007) 'Vigilante marketing and consumer-created com-munications', *Journal of Advertising*, 36(3): 35–50.

O'Guinn, T.C. and Muñiz, Jr., A.M. (2005) 'Communal consumption and the brand', in S. Ratneshwar and D.G. Mick (eds), *Inside Consumption: Consumer Motives, Goals, and Desires*. New York: Routledge. pp. 252–72.

O'Hern, M. and Rindfleisch, A. (2010) 'Customer co-creation: A typology and research agenda', in N.K. Malhotra (ed.), *Review of Marketing Research*, Vol. 6. Bingley, UK: Emerald Group Publishing. pp. 84–106.

Pine, B.J. and Gilmore, J.H. (1999) *The Experience Economy: Work is Theatre & Every Business a Stage*. Boston, MA: Harvard Business Press.

Plé, L. and Cáceres, R.C. (2010) 'Not always co-creation: Introducing interactional co-destruction of value in service-dominant logic', *Journal of Services Marketing*, 24(6): 430–37.

Pongsakornrungsilp, S. and Schroeder, J.E. (2011) 'Understanding value co-creation in a co-consuming brand community', *Marketing Theory*, 11(3): 303–24.

Prahalad, C.K. and Ramaswamy, V. (2000) 'Co-opting customer competence', *Harvard Business Review*, 78(1): 79–87.

Prahalad, C.K. and Ramaswamy, V. (2004) 'Co-creating unique value with customers', *Strategy & Leadership*, 32(3): 4–9.

Ramaswamy, V. and Gouillart, F. (2010) 'Building the co-creative enterprise', *Harvard Business Review*, 88(10): 100–9.

Ritzer, G. (2004) *The McDonaldization of Society*. Thousand Oaks, CA: Pine Forge Press.

Ritzer, G. and Jurgenson, N. (2010) 'Production, consumption, prosumption: The nature of capitalism in the age of the digital "prosumer"', *Journal of Consumer Culture*, 10(1): 13–36.

Rokka, J. and Canniford, R. (2016) 'Heterotopian selfies: How social media destabilizes brand assemblages', *European Journal of Marketing*, 50(9/10): 1789–813.

Sánchez-Fernández, R. and Iniesta-Bonillo, M.A. (2007) 'The concept of perceived value: A systematic review of the research', *Marketing Theory*, 7(4): 427.

Schau, H.J., Muñiz, A.M. and Arnould, E.J. (2009) 'How brand community practices create value', *Journal of Marketing*, 73(5): 30–51.

Shah, S.K. (2006) 'Motivation, governance, and the viability of hybrid forms in open source software development', *Management Science*, 52(7): 1000–14.

Thompson, C.J. (1997) 'Interpreting consumers: A hermeneutical framework for deriving marketing insights from the texts of consumers' consumption stories', *Journal of Marketing Research*, 34: 438–55.

Toffler, A. (1980) *The Third Wave*. Boulder, CO: William Morrow.

Vargo, S.L. and Lusch, R.F. (2004) 'Evolving to a new dominant logic for marketing', *Journal of Marketing*, 68(1): 1–17.

Zwick, D., Bonsu, S.K. and Darmody, A. (2008) 'Putting consumers to work: "Co-creation" and new marketing govern-mentality', *Journal of Consumer Culture*, 8(2): 163–96.

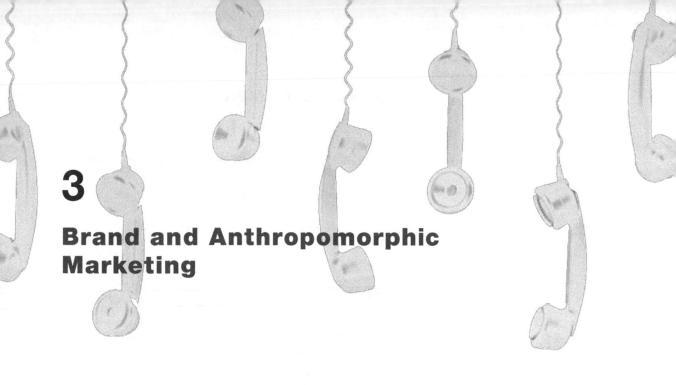

# 3

# Brand and Anthropomorphic Marketing

## CHAPTER OVERVIEW

This chapter introduces anthropomorphic marketing, and explores how brands, particularly in the online world and using technological tools, can 'morph' from inanimate entities to achieve near human qualities, extending brand anthropomorphisation seen in the offline world. As a highly persuasive tool, anthropomorphism has been found to increase brand liking and reduce **persuasion knowledge**. Using examples of spokes characters and anthropomorphised products appearing to act human-like, the chapter explores how social media, more than any other media form, can effectively capture the advantages of anthropomorphic techniques.

## LEARNING OUTCOMES

On completing this chapter, you should be able to:

- critically evaluate different styles of marketing execution, including hard-sell, soft-sell and anthropomorphic appeals
- understand anthropomorphism in marketing, and how social media can be used as anthropomorphic primers
- appreciate why anthropomorphic techniques are persuasive, and how they can be used in different theoretical contexts.

## ANTHROPOMORPHIC MARKETING

Chapter 1 focused on the wider societal changes and was followed by a look at consumer–brand relationship changes in Chapter 2. This chapter now focuses on how organisations can adapt their communication to this change, particularly when communicating within social media environments.

As the last chapter showed, consumers are increasingly taking on an active role in creating brand experiences; therefore, the power of brands (and organisations by extension) has shifted away from a historically asymmetric mode, where the organisation was in charge of brands and products. The result is a shift towards a more symmetric relationship, a relationship of equals, between consumers and brands.

Likewise, consumption has moved from utilitarian to symbolic to experience-creating acts. In social media contexts, brands appear not dissimilar to other humans. Moving away from product-focused selling, as in traditional media, and displaying human characteristics is likely to enhance communication and relationship-building in a social media context.

From a consumer perspective, brands form an interactive part of the tribal life of post-modern consumers, enabling consumers to enhance their individual and social experiences. They have, as has been argued in the two preceding chapters, become extensions of the self for many consumers. While the idea that brands have personalities and consumers can form relationships with brands is well recognised in the branding literature, in social media environments, brands are beginning to play an increasingly human-like role. Here, relationships between consumers and brands, and consumers with other tribe members, are becoming indistinguishable: users can interact and talk to brands using social networks like Twitter, they can like brand actions and brand communications on Facebook and interact with brand-related objects in the same way they would with their human friends.

But favouring interactions that are more human-like is also part of the social media experience. In a context where there is constant communication between consumers and followed brands, a focus on relationship-building in preference to hard-selling is most likely to yield the best results, and keep consumers engaged and receptive.

To create a space where consumers and brands interact positively, brands have to increasingly adopt an anthropomorphic manner of conducting marketing communications.

This chapter therefore focuses on the rise of anthropomorphic marketing in social and traditional media. It briefly revisits how branding has evolved these concepts in the context of traditional media, by reviewing brand personality and brand relationship theories. The chapter then explains how the concept evolved, and the consequences of 'my friend the brand'.

## From Hard-Sell to Brand Personality and Brand Relationships

The emergence of anthropomorphic marketing can be seen as a continuation of the move of marketing away from 'hard' sell. Although 'atmospheric' advertising was mentioned as early as 1911 (Beard, 2004), and some early copywriters acknowledged that simply telling information about a product 'does not excite the reader or create sensations' (Okazaki et al., 2010).

Yet, early advertising is frequently associated with a focus on explicit factual information and functional descriptions or product claims. However, it is important to note that during the early phases of mass media advertising, commercial communication was clearly separated from other forms of communication or entertainment. Advertisers therefore were required to 'shout loudest' to be heard in an environment where they were placed next to another commercial message, and had only a very short period of time to make their sales pitch, for example during an advertising break.

With the rise of branding concepts, especially surrounding the theories of **brand personality** (Aaker, 1997) and **brand relationships** (Fournier, 1998), marketers started to pay more attention to the perceived 'human' aspects of products and services.

### Brand Personality

Since the 1980s, practitioners have increasingly used human characteristics to describe brands, such as young, vivid, fun. For instance, Ogilvy (1985) uses human-like characteristics in his classic book on advertising to describe brands in a near human-like way. Aaker (1997) introduced the first academic concept of using human-like characteristics as a metaphor to describe brands, and to allow for the categorisation of different brands. The term Aaker uses for this framework is 'brand personality'. The brand personality framework consisted of five core dimensions: sincerity, excitement, competence, sophistication and ruggedness. The MTV music channel, for example, is seen as a typical brand embodying excitement, while the *Wall Street Journal* exemplifies competence.

Apart from the five core dimensions, the brand personality framework breaks down brand personality into facets and traits, each linked to the core dimensions in a hierarchical manner. See Table 3.1 for a list of core dimensions and the related facets (in italics) and associated traits.

Using this hierarchical structure, brands can easily be measured based on the perceptions consumers hold about the traits associated with a particular brand. While similar dimensions exist across different countries and cultures, it is important to note that brand personality, similar to the perceived personality of a real person, is culture dependent. For example, different facets were found to describe Japanese and Spanish core dimensions (Aaker et al., 2001) and similarly, research in Brazil showed slightly different core dimensions and facets

(Muniz and Marchetti, 2012). The core dimension of sophistication, for example, was found to be best described in terms of upper-class, glamorous and good-looking in the USA, while in Japan, the dimension was associated with elegance, romance, chic, sophistication and extravagance.

**Table 3.1**  Brand personalities

| Sincerity | Excitement | Competence | Sophistication | Ruggedness |
|-----------|------------|------------|----------------|------------|
| *Down-to-earth* | *Daring* | *Reliable* | *Upper class* | *Outdoorsy* |
| down-to-earth | daring | reliable | upper class | outdoorsy |
| family-oriented | trendy | hard working | glamorous | masculine |
| small-town | exciting | secure | good looking | Western |
| *Honest* | *Spirited* | *Intelligent* | *Charming* | *Tough* |
| honest | spirited | intelligent | charming | tough |
| sincere | cool | technical | feminine | rugged |
| real | young | corporate | smooth | |
| *Wholesome* | *Imaginative* | *Successful* | | |
| wholesome | imaginative | successful | | |
| original | unique | leader | | |
| *Cheerful* | *Up-to-date* | confident | | |
| cheerful | up-to-date | | | |
| sentimental | independent | | | |
| friendly | contemporary | | | |

*Source*: Adapted from: Aaker, J.L. (1997) 'Dimensions of brand personality', *Journal of Marketing Research*, 34(3): 347–56.

Irrespective of the cultural variation of brand personalities, an important aspect of the personality focus is the establishment of emotional, or some would argue pseudo-emotional, connections between a brand and a consumer. As past research shows, brands which are perceived in terms of their personality, rather than their functional values, have a directly positive association between being perceived as having a strong brand personality and increasing consumer brand loyalty (Kim et al., 2001). In other words, the more consumers perceive a brand to be 'person-like', the more they are likely to remain loyal to the brand or product.

The brand personality is created through brand-originating communication, for example in the form of advertising, but may also be created in the consumers' minds through observing brands in use. Traditional media offers relatively few chances to create a strong brand personality, with the main channel being advertising. However, as advertising is both expensive and time-limited, creating successful brand personalities is difficult, as the success depends on high repetition over an extended period of time. For example, Marlborough cigarettes were probably one of the most successful brands to create a 'rugged' brand personality. However, this required extensive advertising and other marketing communications campaigns over several years.

Within the social media sphere, achieving high repetition of brand personality-creating communication is substantially easier and more cost-effective as friends and followers can receive brand personality supportive communication on a daily, or even more frequent, basis. For instance, followers of Yorkshire Tea, a tea brand in the United Kingdom, receive several Twitter updates each day from the brand. Many of these show the brand in use, for example through retweeting pictures taken by consumers, which can influence the brand personality perception through observation of the 'brand in use'. Other tweets sent out by the company are more personal in nature, for instance, on 1 April, the first tweet of the brand asked their followers 'Anyone fancy a coffee? #Aprilfool' (Twitter, 2014).

### Brand Relationships

Rather than focusing on ways to describe the brand itself, Fournier (1998) studied the way in which people relate to the brands they use. Fournier found that people relate to brands in similar ways as to other humans, i.e. the relationship between consumers and brands can be described as one of several human-to-human relationship types (see Table 3.2).

Frequently linked to the notion of creating a brand personality, and by extension anthropomorphising a brand or product, are the notions of soft-sell or hard-sell. Although the connection between creative execution, such as the use of soft-sell versus hard-sell, and brand anthropomorphism remains under-researched (Okazaki, 2006), a number of important links between types of communication and perceived brand image have been made.

Soft-sell appeals are focused on building positive affect towards the advertised product and brand; therefore they are more likely to create positive attitudes towards the ad, decrease any irritation and generally are associated with higher purchase intention (Okazaki et al., 2010). Therefore, soft-sell appeals are more likely to be beneficial for creating positive brand personality attributes, which may explain why advertising has moved increasingly away from utilitarian messages towards the use of soft appeals (Phillips and McQuarrie, 2005).

From this, it can be seen that soft-sell appeals are equally likely to be more effective in an environment where there is constant communication between consumer and brand (or marketers), as is the desired outcome of social media engagement and interaction. Given the danger of hard-sell approaches to lead to irritation, avoidance and potentially reactance, few customers would voluntarily 'op into' a stream of constantly irritating messages. However, in an environment where the focus is on interpersonal relationships, brands acting as 'virtual persons', or anthropomorphised brands, are more likely to be attractive.

## Anthropomorphism in Marketing

Despite being ubiquitous in marketing (Brown and Ponsonby-McCabe, 2012), and especially so in the social media context, anthropomorphism remains almost absent from the marketing research agenda. Marketers have anthropomorphised brands since the middle of the twentieth century, though much of the original 'anthropomorphic' marketing attempts were in the form of cartoon-like spokes characters, for example the talking M&M candies. Although brand spokes cartoons became less common during the latter twentieth century, anthropomorphic marketing has staged a remarkable comeback (Brown, 2010).

In conventional marketing communication, the appearance of these characters was necessarily reserved to the defined spaces of advertising or packaging, and the mascots mostly acted as likable spokespersons for the brands they represented.

One of the ubiquitous effects of social media has, however, been the move away from distinguishable commercial spaces on the one side, such as adverts, and personal spaces, such as news from friends, on the other. Both have increasingly become a blended ensemble. Consider the case of Facebook newsfeeds, or Twitter updates: updates from liked pages, brands, companies – and friends – appear side-by-side, with no clear differentiation, effectively creating a shared 'newsfeed'.

**Table 3.2** Brand relationship types

| Relationship type | Definition | Example |
|---|---|---|
| Arranged marriages | Non-voluntary union imposed by a third party | When sharing a flat, the type of washing-up liquid is determined by the person who does the shopping |
| Casual friendships | Low levels of intimacy, characterised by infrequent and irregular use and low levels of expected reciprocity | When choosing a snack food, a consumer may choose one brand of crisps one day and a different one the next |
| Marriages of convenience | Long-term committed relationship precipitated by environmental factors | Having moved to a new area, a householder finds that there is only one company that offers a doorstep delivery of milk |
| Committed partnership | Long-term relationship, high levels of love and intimacy, socially supported and committed to stay together despite adverse circumstances | When a consumer particularly enjoys a brand of premium coffee and is prepared to make sacrifices in the family budget to ensure that he or she can continue to drink it when money becomes short |
| Best friendships | Voluntary union based on the principle of reciprocity, characterised by mutual reward, honesty and intimacy | Consumers become loyal to a brand of shampoo because it recognises their shortcomings (e.g. greasy hair, dandruff, etc.) and they feel they can rely on it to make their hair look good |
| Compartmentalised friendships | Relationships are specialised and situationally confined | Consumers who only drink eggnog or mulled wine at Christmas |
| Kinships | Non-voluntary union with lineage lines | Teenagers who, on first leaving home, use the same brand of washing powder or toothpaste as their parents |
| Rebounds | Relationship precipitated by the desire to move away from another partner | People who, on giving up smoking, develop an attachment to a particular brand of sweet |

| Relationship type | Definition | Example |
| --- | --- | --- |
| Childhood friendships | Infrequently engaged relationship based heavily upon nostalgia, yields comfort and security | When people buy a brand of jelly out of nostalgia because it was the sort of food they had as a child |
| Courtships | An interim relationship state on the road to a more committed partnership | When someone tries a new brand and likes it, but are yet to be totally convinced |
| Dependencies | Obsessive, highly emotional, separation leads to anxiety, strong feeling that the other is irreplaceable | Brands that people feel they cannot live without |
| Flings | Time-bounded engagements with high emotional reward but devoid of commitment and reciprocity | When a consumer breaks up with a boyfriend or girlfriend, he or she indulges in comfort eating with a favoured brand of ice-cream |
| Enmities | Negative relationship based upon a desire to avoid or inflict pain on the other | A consumer boycotts a brand because he or she feels that it has behaved badly or unethically |
| Secret affairs | Highly emotive, privately held relationship, considered risky if exposed to others | A member of a diet club who secretly indulges in a love of chocolate |
| Enslavements | Non-voluntary relationship that exists because of circumstances that result in a lack of alternative, involves negative feelings | Where a consumer is limited to a provider of mobile phone service operator because of a limited signal despite the fact that they feel it is inferior |

*Source*: Reprinted from *Journal of Consumer Research*, 24, Fournier, S., 'Consumers and their brands: developing relationship theory in consumer research', 343-53, 1998, with permission from Oxford University Press.

Companies have been quick to adapt to this different form of communication environment. For example, Mr Peanut, brand mascot for Planters, informs his half a million followers that he likes to 'work out' as well as taking 'leisurely lunches in the park' and 'reading nature essays to a beautiful woman' (www.Facebook.com/mrpeanut). When liked, the mascot will also inform his fans daily about what he is up to – in his spare time.

While brand mascots being 'active participants' in social networks is a relatively straightforward transfer of traditional anthropomorphic marketing communication techniques to social media, other brands do not engage with users via their mascots – but some are actually 'acting' as the brand themselves. This changes the relationship between brand and follower distinctly, resulting in what can be characterised as a 'complete humanisation of the brand', going beyond the traditional concept of anthropomorphism observed in conventional media.

When consumers perceive brands as having human-like qualities, i.e. the brand is seen as anthropomorphic, this has a positive effect on brand relationships even in different cultures. In a study comparing data from France, the UK and the US, Hudson et al. (2016)

showed that those consumers who perceived a brand as anthropomorphic were more likely to have a positive relationship with the brand and, crucially, to follow the brand on social media.

## Definition of Anthropomorphic Marketing

There is, as yet, no recognised definition of anthropomorphism or related terms, and different authors have used the term to describe message characteristics as well as feelings induced in the audience. Dahl and Desrochers (2013) propose the framework given in Figure 3.1 to describe the various properties of anthropomorphic marketing.

Personification describes a communication strategy where a brand logo or the product assume human-like characteristics, for example, the characters in *Toy Story* are personifications of toys, similarly the talking M&Ms in the candy advertising represent personifications (of the actual product).

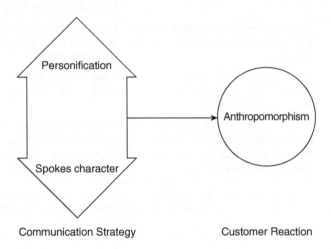

**Figure 3.1**   Anthropomorphic marketing

Spokes character strategies employ inanimate objects, animals or cartoon characters, but not products or brands as the main actor. Aleksandr Orlov, the meerkat from the hugely successful comparethemarket.com campaign in the UK, for example, would fall into this category (Patterson et al., 2013).

Ultimately, the goal of anthropomorphic marketing is to evoke an anthropomorphic reaction in the targeted audience. Delbaere and colleagues describe this process as an attribution 'of human like qualities to things' (2011: 121), or specifically to brands. Therefore, anthropomorphic techniques aim to invoke attributions of 'intelligent, animated beings, like beliefs, desires, intentions, goals, plans, psychological states, powers, and will' (Turner, 1987) to brands and products.

The communication strategy associated with anthropomorphic marketing can be described as a continuum ranging from using inanimate objects as spokes characters to animating products or brand images in advertising. Delbaere and colleagues (2011) define messages used to elicit such anthropomorphic reactions as 'personification', referring, for example, to a product being portrayed as the main 'actor' in a commercial. They give the example of a moisturiser pack drinking water in an advert as a form of personification, which is consequently perceived as human by the audience. Their research shows that such personification of the product generates anthropomorphic reactions in the audience, leading to the desired effect of attributing human-like characteristics to an inanimate object (e.g. the moisturiser is perceived as 'thirsty'). Taking a different view, Brown (2010) uses the term 'anthropomorphic marketing' to describe the use of inanimate spokes characters, such as cartoon characters. Brown uses the popular brand spokes character Aleksandr Orlov, the anthropomorphic meerkat used in comparethemarket.com advertising in the UK, as an example. In this case, the spokes character is neither the product nor the brand logo of the company – it is a stand-in for a human spokesperson. The insurance company using Aleksandr as a spokesperson also engages successfully in anthropomorphising social media communication: Aleksandr also has a Twitter account (https://Twitter.com/Aleksandr_Orlov) where fans can follow which products Aleksandr buys in a supermarket for his new baby boy, or consumers can read Aleksandr's blog on the corporate website (www.comparethemarket.com/meerkat/blog/).

Other researchers have suggested brand characters such as the two M&Ms used in the chocolate's adverts – half product, half cartoon character – are prime examples of anthropomorphism. Again, both characters make extensive use of social media to engage fans. Thus, attempts to induce an anthropomorphic reaction can be said to include both personification of products themselves, as well as using (usually inanimate) objects as spokes characters in advertising. In practical terms, these don't represent distinct categories, but rather endpoints of a continuum.

Therefore, anthropomorphic marketing is a marketing technique that attempts to connect human emotional feelings to products or brands. The desired outcome is that the audience transfers perceived attributes and human qualities to the brand.

## THINKBOX ANTHROPOMORPHIC MARKETING

Can you think of other advertisements that use usually inanimate objects as spokes characters? Can you think of examples of personifications in advertising? Analyse the last 10 updates of a brand you follow on Twitter or Facebook. How many of these try to create anthropomorphic feelings towards the brand? How do they do this?

## Persuasiveness of Anthropomorphic Marketing

Most of the research related to the effectiveness of anthropomorphic marketing is related to animated spokes characters. Practitioners have previously talked about a 'suspension of disbelief': people accept product claims made by animated presenters which would be unacceptable – or at least unbelievable – if conveyed by a normal human being (Baldwin, 1982). Academic research suggests that likable spokes characters have been linked to successfully creating an emotional connection between brand and consumer (Phillips, 1996). In turn, a positive emotional connection enhances both the perception of brand personality and brand trust (Garretson and Niedrich, 2004).

In comparison with spokes characters, there is only relatively scant research related to the personification of products. However, the existing research suggests that the effects are similar to those observed for spokes characters. Research has found that personification of products leads to a stronger and more positive evaluation of brand attributes (Aggarwal and McGill, 2007). For example, when car owners develop anthropomorphic feelings towards their vehicle, they are less likely to change the brand in future purchases and will be more likely to excuse any shortcomings of the car. Moreover, personification can lead to a reduction in risk perception, for example in the case of perceived risk when gambling (Kim and McGill, 2011). Hart and colleagues (2013) show that anthropomorphism is most likely to occur for complex products, such as a car or computer, although limited anthropomorphism has also been observed for simple products.

Delbaere and colleagues (2011) offer the most comprehensive, comparable study of the effect of personification in print advertising versus traditional, non-anthropomorphism-inducing advertising. They show that personification used as an advertising tool elicits more attributions of brand personality and more emotional response than conventional advertising. Additionally, personification increased brand liking, which in turn is a precursor for purchase intention, in line with previous research.

In relation to online anthropomorphic marketing, in their explorative research Dahl and Desrochers (2013) show that, similar to print advertising, personification of brands as agents in social media creates increased brand liking, a stronger emotional response and clearer, more varied attribution of brand personality aspects. This finding is echoed by Thompson et al. (2016), who showed that consumers are more likely to perceive sport events as positive and engaging, if these actively used brand anthropomorphism in their social media marketing. Therefore, personification in social media is likely to lead to increased purchase intention. As there is to date no comparative research between different media, such as traditional media (e.g. print media) and social media, there are no studies to suggest whether social media offers a more persuasive platform for personification apart from circumstantial evidence. One could speculate that social media is socially and emotionally more engaging, and therefore may well prove to be superior in terms of eliciting an emotional response. However, there are no studies to support this conjecture.

Similarly, future research is needed to compare personification with spokes characters – when used both in traditional media and social media. While it seems plausible that both elicit similar reactions and the reactions are based on the same processes, there is, as yet, no conclusive evidence to prove or explain the phenomenon.

Notwithstanding these limitations, many companies are employing anthropomorphic principles in social media marketing with great success. In the next section, we therefore discuss the potential theoretical explanations of this.

## Theoretical Explanations

Two theoretical perspectives have been suggested to explain why anthropomorphism is an effective communication strategy – the Elaboration Likelihood Model, as stated by Delbaere et al. (2011), and Cultivation Theory, as suggested by Dahl and Desrochers (2013).

### The Elaboration Likelihood Model

**The Elaboration Likelihood Model (ELM)** recognises two different routes to 'persuading' individuals: a peripheral and a central one, as can be seen in Figure 3.2. The peripheral route relies on understated cues to subtly shift or associate attitudes towards a product or brand. Conversely, the central route relies on 'elaboration' (or cognitive engagement) on behalf of the consumer to aid consumers in forming or changing attitudes towards a product/service or brand.

Central processing can be preferable in terms of persuasive power, as it involves active engagement of the consumer with the message. In the context of anthropomorphism, this is achieved by presenting the consumer with a visual 'puzzle', i.e. the active realisation that an inanimate object is behaving in a human-like way. For example, Burger King's 'Subservient Chicken' campaign used a supposedly 'live webcam' to support its traditional media advertising online. The website consisted of showcasing a chicken which seemingly responded to typed consumer commands (Mara, 2004). The campaign required a person to engage with the on-screen chicken, which is likely to trigger elaboration, and thus a processing of the message using the central route – and activating a direct transfer of the campaign message ('Get chicken just the way you like it') this way. Similarly, as Delbaere et al. (2011) suggest, seeing a personification in advertising is likely to trigger a similar response. Different from traditional advertising with overt product claims, in the cases of anthropomorphic marketing, the consumer is likely to engage with (and elaborate on) how the portrayal is created, for example, how the chicken can behave in exactly the way the consumer tells it to. If such an elaboration occurs, cognitive resources are occupied with this process, leaving fewer resources to activate defence mechanisms against persuasion. Consequently, such attempts at 'indirect' persuasion, particularly by using visual metaphors, have been found to be more persuasive to consumers (McQuarrie and Phillips, 2005). A further desirable effect of anthropomorphic activation in the consumers' minds for the marketer was previously researched in a different context using rhetorical figures, where the consumer uses resources for information processing of the heavily coded message, which reduces counter-arguing and source derogation (Mothersbaugh et al., 2002). Delbaere and colleagues observe that the same effect explains consumer reactions towards seeing a visual representation of a rhetorical figure – for example, a representation of a chicken 'just the way you like it': consumers engage in less critical reasoning with the core message and instead transfer emotions more readily to the brand.

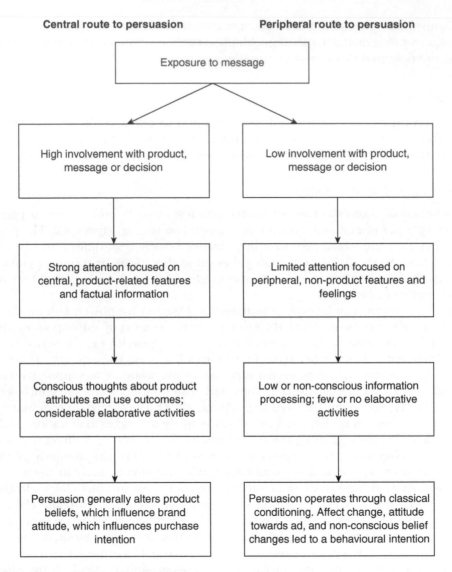

**Figure 3.2** Elaboration Likelihood Model

*Source*: adapted from: Hawkins, D.I. (2004) *Consumer Behavior: Building Marketing Strategy*. Maidenhead: McGraw-Hill Education.

However, not every social media communication is necessarily engaging to consumers or followers. In fact, many messages may be more peripherally processed, i.e. the consumer engages with the messages only fleetingly, rather than elaborating on the message content. In traditional media advertising, peripheral processing has significant disadvantages: it is less persuasive, attitudes formed are less strong and, above all, require more repetitions than elaboration via the central route. Such heavy rotation is, inevitably, costly (e.g. paying for several repeat exposures of an advertisement). Typical examples of peripheral routes to persuasion being used in traditional media are perfume ads as the ads often contain no (obvious) message, and simply rely on the person(s) depicted in the advert and general brand ideas to convey the perfume attributes. Celebrity endorsements are an alternative, typical sign of peripheral strategies, i.e. the positive image of the celebrity is expected to be associated with the brand. Again, such advertising usually relies on repeat exposure through costly, high rotation.

Within the context of social media, once a person becomes a follower or friend, the cost of achieving repeat exposures is dramatically reduced (or almost zero). Through repeated exposure to these messages, for example, frequent party pictures shown to people who like an alcohol company's page on Facebook (Dahl and Desrochers, 2013), a similar effect to repeated advertising exposure can be achieved, at a fraction of the cost.

## THINKBOX PERIPHERAL VS. CENTRAL PROCESSING

Look at some brand pages on Facebook or Twitter. Analyse the updates that you see. Are they designed to be peripherally or centrally processed? Which strategy do you think is more effective for people following the brand versus people not following or unfamiliar with the brand?

### Cultivation Theory

**Cultivation Theory** (Gerbner and Gross, 1976; Gerbner et al., 1986) offers a further theoretical perspective as to why social media influences, including exposure to social media messages, may be effective as a persuasive tool. Cultivation Theory was originally developed to explain why people watching a lot of television commonly have a distorted perception of reality – their view of reality becomes based on what is portrayed in television programmes, rather than what is happening in the 'real world' around them. This effect holds even if television programmes are acknowledged as fictional, for example, high television consumption is related to viewers overestimating the numbers of doctors and lawyers in society, as these professions are repeatedly shown in television programmes (Shrum, 2001), amongst numerous other reality-distorting effects. Although no work to date has directly addressed the relevance of cultivation theory for social media environments, Morgan and Shanahan (2010) argue that Cultivation Theory is more applicable today than it has been in the past, indicating that media consumption as a whole has increased significantly, with social media making it easier than before to consume content. Similarly, cultivation effects have been observed in virtual environments and online games (Williams, 2006), and are therefore likely to apply to other media exposures in a similar way as they would apply to traditional media.

Despite the significant evidence that connects media exposure to behavioural or belief changes, the usefulness is limited in commercial advertising settings due to the high frequency of exposure needed. A meta-analysis of previous studies has shown the effect to be relatively small (correlation coefficient of about 0.09) (Morgan et al., 2008), however, it is important to remember that even a small effect can have some important consequences over time when the effects accumulate. Moreover, if users follow brands or even interact with brands using social networks, it is likely that the messages they receive from the brands are both recurrent and repetitive over a significant amount of time, a key prerequisite for cultivation effects to occur.

Cultivation Theory categorises the effects attributed to high media, especially television, consumption into first-order and second-order effects. First-order effects relate to direct perception changes – for example the amount of murders committed – and are more widely researched and are generally found to be larger. Second-order effects are subtler and relate to values and beliefs a person holds. Second-order effects are, however, less well researched, though research shows that, somewhat surprisingly, first-order and second-order effects are not always related and are different psychological concepts (Hawkins and Pingree, 1982). The reason for the difference is that first-order effects are the result of fairly concrete information recalled from memory, and people's perception of the frequency of crimes or number of doctors in society is influenced by the ease of 'access' to an example, i.e. if they can easily recall an appropriate example. If people can recall an example quickly, then the probability is estimated as high, regardless of whether the example is fictional or real.

Second-order effects are the result of updating currently held values and judgements as a consequence of media exposure, a process that is evolving and gradual. These judgements, and the gradual adoption or updates of judgements, are made more frequently, as they occur spontaneously, for example when watching an advert or reading a status update.

An interesting point is the central role of narrative immersion, similar to the idea of Flow (see Chapter 5) in some aspects. Research suggests that people who are immersed in a story show suspend disbelief, even ignoring facts that may contradict a message (Green et al., 2004), an effect that also influences persuasion knowledge (Escalas, 2007).

Similarly, subtle, emotional persuasion has been shown to avoid activation of persuasion knowledge, at least for children (Nairn and Fine, 2008). Thus, one can argue that immersion into social networks may have a similar effect, even for grownups.

## THINKBOX CULTIVATION THEORY

Compare a social media stream, for example your Facebook profile, with reality. Which aspects of your life are more pronounced for your followers? Which aspects do you rarely mention? Consider the effect this might have on a person evaluating your life. What effect would this distortion effect have when aggregated across all of your friends?

## Anthropomorphism in Social Media

Dahl and Desrochers (2013) show that anthropomorphism is used extensively in social media across different product categories as companies use personification extensively in updates and shared content. Similarly, spokes characters are used frequently, with a majority of spokes characters using social media 'as if they were real humans'.

Hart and colleagues (2013) show that consumers tend to anthropomorphise more complex products more readily than simple products, in fact, consumers tend to anthropomorphise complex products even in the absence of any personification, possibly as a means to simplify these products. However, importantly, Hart et al. show that consumers also anthropomorphise simple products, such as a toothbrush, potentially more so in the presence of anthropomorphic priming, for example by personification of products. It may therefore be especially useful for companies with less complex products to engage in anthropomorphic marketing – especially using the personification tools that social media offers – as a way to create anthropomorphic reactions in consumers.

## Criticism

Despite the growing research into the links between brand personality, brand relationships, anthropomorphic marketing, customer loyalty and emotional involvement, some researchers have voiced concerns about the validity of conceptualising brands in similar ways to humans. Despite research claims that consumers form strong and lasting relationships with brands, and that consumers perceive these brands as 'complete humans' (Puzakova et al., 2009: 413), some researchers advocate that consumers mentally separate strongly between brands and fellow humans. For instance, Avis and colleagues (2012) argue that more evidence is needed to support the view that either consumers see brands as having human-like features, or consumers form relationships with brands which are similar to interhuman relationships. Rather, Avis et al. imply that consumers merely use terminology akin to the terminology used to describe human-to-human relationships or personalities as a way of describing brands and brand relationships. Subsequently, in Avis et al.'s view, brand personality and brand relationships are merely metaphors, used due to a lack of a different set of words describing these phenomena related to inanimate objects. Consequently, they suggest further research is necessary in theorising why the expression through metaphors might have an influence on consumer purchasing behaviour, as implied by the concepts of brand personality, brand relationships and anthropomorphic marketing.

## SUMMARY

Brand relationships and brand personality are important concepts in the marketing literature, and explain why consumers make choices based often on emotional impulse, rather than on logical and rational decisions. In particular brand personality has received widespread attention from scholars. However, in traditional media, establishing a brand personality has been relatively costly and time consuming. With social media, and **opt-in** marketing communication, there are more opportunities to directly and regularly communicate with friends and followers of a brand. Therefore, the cost aspect of establishing and maintaining perceived brand personality has decreased substantially. Moreover, social media allows brands to behave in nearly human-like ways. While anthropomorphism is already ubiquitous in traditional marketing communications, online human–brand interactions are frequently nearly indistinguishable from those between humans and humans: users can interact and talk to brands using social networks like Twitter, they can like brand actions and brand communications on Facebook and interact with brands in the same way they would with their human friends. Similar to print advertising, personification of brands as agents in social media create increased brand liking, a stronger emotional response and clearer, more varied attribution of brand personality aspects.

## RESEARCH DIRECTIONS

Anthropomorphism remains vastly under-researched, with extensive possibilities for future research. For example, little research has been conducted on anthropomorphic priming, and to what extent suspension of disbelief can be achieved. Repeat exposure, as for example in the case of following 'anthropomorphic brands' in social media, is also vastly under-researched and the long-term effects are not well understood. Equally, to what extent does emotional transfer take place even in the presence of disbelief? While there is anecdotal evidence of this occurring, no research has yet formally examined these effects.

Further avenues of research can include cross-cultural aspects, i.e. examining if the effect is comparable or different across culturally different populations.

## RESEARCH HIGHLIGHT
## MY FRIEND BUD

In the study 'My friend Bud', Dahl and Desrochers show how the British alcohol industry uses social and interactive functions offered by social networks to communicate with their customers. The exploratory study relies on **quantitative data** about usage and type of interactions, rather than **qualitative data** or, more specifically, netnographic methods.

Using market research data, the authors identified the top 10 largest advertising spenders in three product categories: beer, spirits/ready-to-drink (pre-mixed) and cider. The researchers then visited the brands' websites, and where available, the Facebook and Twitter pages, recording how the brands interacted with the visitors. As no previous coding instrument for interactivity was available, the authors developed scoring sheets for tools encouraging interactivity (e.g. encouraging consumers to share, like or comment on posts in Facebook, or @-replies to consumers on Twitter).

The study highlights the interactive nature of social media, where users are encouraged to interact more with the brand than in traditional media – and more so than on company websites. The study shows that alcohol advertisers have moved away from promoting products, and are embracing social media tools to encourage consumers to interact with brands in a similar way as they interact with their friends using social media, for example, by tagging the brand in pictures on Facebook or by talking to the brand on Twitter. Because of the constant communication between consumers and brands, the tone of the commercial communication is often significantly more like something a friend would say, rather than promoting the brand or product. Thus, the boundaries between private and commercial communication are increasingly blurred, both in terms of the space in which the communication takes place (social networks) as well as in terms of the language and tools used by advertisers.

A significant limit of the study is that it is quantitative and therefore the data is not suitable to derive the intention of advertisers or the actual effect that such a blurred and anthropomorphic communication has on the consumers.

The full study is available on the companion website of this book.

# CASE STUDY CHARMIN

Making a fast moving consumer good interesting is challenging – even more so if it is something most people don't like to talk about: such as toilet paper. Procter & Gamble faced exactly this conundrum for its Charmin brand: How do you make people follow the brand on social media – and keep it relevant and interesting?

Traditionally, Charmin advertising relied on a fictional store keeper recommending the brand to his customers. But in the times of social media, communication about the brand needed to change. Charmin had already moved over to new spokes characters: the Charmin Bears. Since 2000 Charmin bears appeared in television adverts of the brand, explaining why the toilet paper was better than competitor brands. However, simply transferring these hard sales tactics to a social media context could be problematic, as few customers follow social media accounts that use traditional hard-selling methods, especially for goods that are of relatively low importance to the customers.

While retaining a sales-focused approach in traditional advertising, Charmin decided to take a tongue in cheek approach on social media: blurring the line between brand and spokes character (e.g. the Charmin bears), the brand engaged in more fun banter on social media, ranging from tweeting about awkward toilet moments under the hashtag #tweetsfromtheseat to sending out playful love notes (using the #Charminlovenotes tag), not just to followers – but also to other brands on Twitter. For example, Charmin tweeted the pizza brand DiGiorno Pizza with the tweet 'Hey @DiGiornoPizza OLIVE YOU #CharminLoveNotes').

*(Continued)*

This playful approach is a great example of making a potentially unattractive product brand successful on social media and well liked (with nearly 75,000 followers on Twitter). It was also named the sassiest brand on social media by *Time* magazine in 2014. *Time* especially praised the 'LOL-worthy' social media presence of Charmin, concluding: 'Congratulations, Charmin, you're officially the sassiest' (Grossman, 2014).

## Questions to Consider

1   Why does Charmin use both hard-sell and soft-sell tactics?
2   Visit the Charmin social media accounts. Discuss how Charmin has kept the campaign alive.
3   What role do emotional brand connections have in a competitive marketplace? Can they be convincing?
4   Discuss for which type of products a tongue in cheek approach would be most suitable. For which type of products would you use a hard-sell approach?

## FURTHER READING

Avis, M., Aitken, R. and Ferguson, S. (2012) 'Brand relationship and personality theory metaphor or consumer perceptual reality?', *Marketing Theory*, 12: 311–31.

Bucy, E.P., Kim, S.C. and Park, M.C. (2011) 'Host selling in cyberspace: Product personalities and character advertising on popular children's websites', *New Media & Society*, 13(8): 1245–64.

Lee, E.-J. (2010) 'What triggers social responses to flattering computers? Experimental tests of anthropomorphism and mindlessness explanations', *Communication Research*, 37(2): 191–214.

Phillips, B.J. and Gyoerick, B. (1999) 'The cow, the cook, and the quaker: Fifty years of spokes-character advertising', *Journalism & Mass Communication Quarterly*, 76(4): 713–28.

## REFERENCES

Aaker, J.L. (1997) 'Dimensions of brand personality', *Journal of Marketing Research*, 34(3): 347–56.

Aaker, J.L., Benet-Martinez, V. and Garolera, J. (2001) 'Consumption symbols as carriers of culture: A study of Japanese and Spanish brand personality constructs', *Journal of Personality and Social Psychology*, 81: 492.

Aggarwal, P. and McGill, A.L. (2007) 'Is that car smiling at me? Schema congruity as a basis for evaluating anthropomorphized products', *Journal of Consumer Research*, 34: 468–79.

Avis, M., Aitken, R. and Ferguson, S. (2012) 'Brand relationship and personality theory metaphor or consumer perceptual reality?', *Marketing Theory*, 12: 311–31.

Baldwin, H. (1982) *Creating Effective TV Commercials*. New York: Crain Books.

Beard, F.K. (2004) 'Hard-sell "killers" and soft-sell "poets": Modern advertising's enduring message strategy debate', *Journalism History*, 30: 141–9.

Brown, S. (2010) 'Where the wild brands are: Some thoughts on anthropomorphic marketing', *The Marketing Review*, 10: 209–24.

Brown, S. and Ponsonby-McCabe, S. (2012) 'Editorial: They're gr-r-reat! Introduction to the special issue on Anthropomorphic Marketing', *Journal of Marketing Management*, 29(1/2): 1–4.

Dahl, S. and Desrochers, D.M. (2013) 'My friend Bud: Alcohol promotions using social media', in S. Sezgin, E. Karaosmanoglu and A. Elmadag Bas (eds), *Proceedings of the 42nd Annual EMAC Conference, Lost in Translation: Marketing in an Interconnected World*. Istanbul: Istanbul Technical University, 4–7 June.

Delbaere, M., McQuarrie, E.F. and Phillips, B.J. (2011) 'Personification in advertising', *Journal of Advertising*, 40: 121–30.

Escalas, J.E. (2007) 'Self-referencing and persuasion: Narrative transportation versus analytical elaboration', *Journal of Consumer Research*, 33: 421–9.

Fournier, S. (1998) 'Consumers and their brands: Developing relationship theory in consumer research', *Journal of Consumer Research*, 24: 343–53.

Garretson, J.A. and Niedrich, R.W. (2004) 'Spokes-characters: Creating character trust and positive brand attitudes', *Journal of Advertising*, 33: 25–36.

Gerbner, G. and Gross, L. (1976) 'Living with television: The violence profile', *Journal of Communication*, 26: 172–94.

Gerbner, G., Gross, L., Morgan, M. and Signorielli, N. (1986) 'Living with television: The dynamics of the cultivation process', in J. Bryant and D. Zillman (eds), *Perspectives on Media Effects*. Hillsdale, NJ: Lawrence Erlbaum. pp. 17–40.

Green, M.C., Brock, T.C. and Kaufman, G.F. (2004) 'Understanding media enjoyment: The role of transportation into narrative worlds', *Communication Theory*, 14: 311–27.

Grossman, S. (2014) The 13 sassiest brands on Twitter [Online]. Available at: http://time.com/5151/sassiest-brands-on-twitter-ranked/ (accessed 6 November 2017).

Hart, P.M., Jones, S.R. and Royne, M.B. (2013) 'The human lens: How anthropomorphic reasoning varies by product complexity and enhances personal value', *Journal of Marketing Management*, 29: 105–21.

Hawkins, D.I. (2004) *Consumer Behavior: Building Marketing Strategy*. Maidenhead: McGraw-Hill Education.

Hawkins, R.P. and Pingree, S. (1982) 'Television's influence on social reality', in D. Pearl, L. Bouthilet and J. Lazar (eds), *Television and Behavior. Ten Years of Scientific Progress and Implications for the Eighties*, Vol. 2. Washington, DC: Government Printing Office. pp. 224–47.

Hudson, S., Huang, L., Roth, M.S. and Madden, T.J. (2016) 'The influence of social media interactions on consumer–brand relationships: A three-country study of brand perceptions and marketing behaviors', *International Journal of Research in Marketing*, 33(1): 27–41.

Kim, C.K., Han, D. and Park, S.-B. (2001) 'The effect of brand personality and brand identification on brand loyalty: Applying the theory of social identification', *Japanese Psychological Research*, 43: 195–206.

Kim, S. and McGill, A.L. (2011) 'Gaming with Mr. Slot or gaming the slot machine? Power, anthropomorphism, and risk perception', *Journal of Consumer Research*, 38: 94–107.

Mara, J. (2004) Burger King hen whets chicken yen [Online]. Available at: www.clickz. com/clickz/news/1690908/burger-king-hen-whets-chicken-yen (accessed 2 April 2013).

McQuarrie, E.F. and Phillips, B.J. (2005) 'Indirect persuasion in advertising: How consumers process metaphors presented in pictures and words', *Journal of Advertising*, 34: 7–20.

Morgan, M. and Shanahan, J. (2010) 'The state of cultivation', *Journal of Broadcasting & Electronic Media*, 54: 337–55.

Morgan, M., Shanahan, J. and Signorielli, N. (2008) 'Cultivation processes', *Media Effects: Advances in Theory and Research*, 10: 34.

Mothersbaugh, D.L., Huhmann, B.A. and Franke, G.R. (2002) 'Combinatory and separative effects of rhetorical figures on consumers' effort and focus in ad processing', *Journal of Consumer Research*, 28: 589–602.

Muniz, K.M. and Marchetti, R.Z. (2012) 'Brand personality dimensions in the Brazilian context', *Brazilian Administration Review*, 9: 168–88.

Nairn, A. and Fine, C. (2008) 'Who's messing with my mind? The implications of dual-process models for the ethics of advertising to children', *International Journal of Advertising*, 27: 447–70.

Ogilvy, D. (1985) *Ogilvy on Advertising*, 1st Vintage Books edn. New York: Vintage Books.

Okazaki, S. (2006) 'Excitement or sophistication? A preliminary exploration of online brand personality', *International Marketing Review*, 23: 279–303.

Okazaki, S., Mueller, B. and Taylor, C.R. (2010) 'Measuring soft-sell versus hard-sell advertising appeals', *Journal of Advertising*, 39: 5–20.

Patterson, A., Khogeer, Y. and Hodgson, J. (2013) 'How to create an influential anthropomorphic mascot: Literary musings on marketing, make-believe, and meerkats', *Journal of Marketing Management*, 29(1/2): 69–85.

Phillips, B.J. (1996) 'Defining trade characters and their role in American popular culture', *Journal of Popular Culture*, 29: 143–58.

Phillips, B.J. and McQuarrie, E.F. (2005) 'The development, change, and transformation of rhetorical style in magazine advertisements 1954–1999', *Advertising & Society Review*, 6(4): 1–13.

Puzakova, M., Kwak, H. and Rocereto, J.F. (2009) 'Pushing the envelope of brand and personality: Antecedents and moderators of anthropomorphized brands', *Advances in Consumer Research*, 36: 413–20.

Shrum, L. (2001) 'Processing strategy moderates the cultivation effect', *Human Communication Research*, 27: 94–120.

Thompson, A.J., Martin, A.J., Gee, S. and Geurin, A.N. (2016) 'Fans' perceptions of professional tennis events' social media presence: Interaction, insight, and brand anthropomorphism', *Communication & Sport*. http://doi.org/10.1177/2167479516650442.

Turner, M. (1987) *Death is the Mother of Beauty: Mind, Metaphor, Criticism*. Chicago, IL: University of Chicago Press.

Twitter (2014) Twitter/Yorkshire Tea: 'Anyone fancy a coffee? #Aprilfool' [Online]. Available at: https://twitter.com/YorkshireTea/status/450913077454983168.

Williams, D. (2006) 'Virtual cultivation: Online worlds, offline perceptions', *Journal of Communication*, 56: 69–87.

# PART 2

## Understanding Platforms in Social Media Marketing

Following the first part focusing on the individual and organisational actors and how they interact in the social media sphere, this second part now turns the attention to the media context in which the interactions take place.

The dominant theme in the media context is the convergence of three technologies – traditional computing, gaming and mobiles – merging into a universally accessible platform, enabling access across multiple devices. While merging, each of these technologies brings with it its own version of 'socialisation', and therefore contributes concepts to the emergent cross-platform social media landscape. For instance, traditional, desktop-based computing contributes social functionality in the form of simple sharing of information amongst both known and unknown individuals. Chapter 4, the first chapter of this part, therefore explores how the social functionality of traditional computing has evolved from the early **Bulletin Board Systems** (BBS) to **Usenet** newsgroups and web forums to current social media technology in the form of blogs and websites. The chapter also highlights the important contribution that early technologies have made, including the role early technologies played in world events, decades before the omnipresence of social media, but also noting the changes that have occurred as a result of the technology becoming more widely accessible, but arguably more narrowly focused than it has been historically. In other words, what are the effects of focusing on, as Mike Zuckerberg puts it, 'a squirrel dying in your front yard' more than on people 'dying in Africa' (Pariser, 2011)?

A different contribution is made by originally game-focused devices. Chapter 5 explores the rise to popularity of this technology and these devices, and highlights how games-related principles, such as **gamification**, have grown beyond games and find application in behaviour change, health and social marketing and the wider marketing context. The chapter explores the various theoretical and practical aspects of gaming, and how these can be applied to marketing, highlighting marketing applications such as **in-game advertising** and advergames along the way.

The final chapter in this part focuses on the rise of mobile communication – from an originally exclusively voice-only technology to modern devices which mimic desktop computer functionality. A particular contribution from this technology is the location-independence of accessing information, and the merging of location-relevant and personal data. For instance **location-based social networking** allows users to connect to others nearby, discover new places and receive location-specific information, including marketing communication relevant to the person and current position.

## REFERENCES

Pariser, E. (2011) 'When the Internet thinks it knows you' [Online], *New York Times*, 22 May. Available at: www.nytimes.com/2011/05/23/opinion/23pariser.html?_r=1& (accessed 6 November 2017).

# 4
# Traditional Social Media Platforms

## CHAPTER OVERVIEW

This chapter reviews the rise of social interactivity in the context of the history of the Internet, from early forms of computer-mediated communication in the form of BBSs and Usenet to the declaration and development of Web 2.0, and how this controversial notion has, although thin on substance, focused web development towards a more social experience.

## LEARNING OUTCOMES

On completing this chapter, you should be able to:

- critically discuss the notion of Web 2.0, and how it evolved historically
- explain the adoption of technology using TAM/UTAUT
- consider how users choose amongst different media channels and websites, and offer a suitable theoretical explanation
- critically evaluate the effect of text-based communication on the formation of relationships.

## TRADITIONAL SOCIAL MEDIA

Web 2.0, social media and related buzzwords are frequently portrayed as revolutionary new technologies that have dramatically transformed the communication landscape, both on a personal as well as organisational level. It is certainly indisputable that communication has changed dramatically in recent decades. As digital and social media-based communication has proliferated significantly, it is frequently overlooked that current social media sites are the outcome of a long list of prior computer-mediated communication tools, leading up to the current interest in Web 2.0. To appreciate how social media evolved, and how individuals and organisations adopted their communication to fit the changing environment, it is useful to review briefly the history of computer-mediated communication prior to the establishment of the Web 2.0 concept, before reviewing theoretical foundations which can explain the rise of the Internet and contemporary emphasis on social media.

### Early 'Social Media': BBS, Usenet, Forums

For many current marketing practitioners the history of communities and social networking on the Internet is almost synonymous with current social media websites such as Facebook, Twitter and LinkedIn. However, nothing could be further from the truth as before even the first popular World Wide Web-browser, Mosaic, released in 1993, the Internet had already been characterised as presenting a 'growing diversity of user communities' (Hart et al., 1992). And, just two years after development of the first Internet Explorer, in 1995, scholars remarked that 'the Internet is as much a collection of communities as a collection of technologies' (Leiner et al., 1997).

In fact, some aspects of social media, such as user-generated, universally shared and computer-mediated content within 'virtual' or 'online' communities, predate even the widespread adoption of the Internet as a communication platform in the 1990s, although on a relatively small scale in comparison to the current social media phenomenon. As Kindsmüller and colleagues (2008) indicate, online communities (or virtual communities) in their original form were neither dependent on the World Wide Web, nor did they actually depend on the Internet as a means to connect communities or members. For example, Rheingold (1993a) writes about his experiences in the WELL, an early example of an online, virtual community. The WELL launched in 1985 as a dial-up service with no connection to the already existing, but not widely used, Internet. As Rheingold observed, these virtual communities are:

> cultural aggregations that emerge when enough people bump into each other often enough in cyberspace ... A virtual community [...] is a group of people who may or may not meet one another face to face, and who exchange words and ideas through the mediation of computer bulletin boards and networks. (Rheingold, 1993b: 57)

Communities like the WELL were often run by enthusiasts from their homes using a single computer with a modem running specific software that allowed users to interact, also often called Bulletin Board Systems, or **BBS** for short. Many BBSs emerged during the late 1970s as modems became widely available and relatively cheap. As private computer ownership was not common in those days, this meant BBS users largely consisted of early adopters, such as computer fans – or people with a specific professional or private interest in information technology, for example, the majority of WELL users were writers, journalists and academics.

Taking part in a BBS required the user to dial up into a central computer that acted as the 'host' of the BBS. Once connected, a user could exchange messages with other users, read and partake in public discussions, including, occasionally, chatting directly with other users connected at the same time. Further, many BBSs allowed users to download and upload software or share pictures and other items with fellow users – some BBSs even had online games. At the height of BBS activity, in the US alone, there were an estimated 60,000 systems in operation, each supporting a user-base from a few dozen to several thousand users (Rheingold, 1993b). Most of these BBSs were topic-focused virtual communities centred on hobbies or shared interests, from cooking to religious interests, from political conversation to communication of a sexual nature. As such, they were early representations of the subcultures of consumption discussed in Part 1 in a computer-mediated environment.

As the Internet became more prolific, especially amongst academic users who had access to the technology through educational networks, it was only a question of time until similar environments surfaced. During the 1980s, Usenet emerged as a virtual, global discussion system (and technology) on the Internet. In many ways, Usenet was similar to the original BBSs' public discussion groups. However, as Usenet connected many more users than was possible via dial-up BBSs, groups tended to be much larger and more numerous, with some sources claiming over 100,000 different discussion groups. Usenet required special software to view the available groups, in which individual messages were displayed threaded, like in traditional BBSs and, later, in web forums. This allowed for an on-going discussion on a particular topic. From the beginning, Usenet was designed as a networked platform, capitalising on the interconnectedness created by its Internet technology. Rather than relying on a single host as the original BBSs did, Usenet ran on interconnected servers, each of which stored messages (referred to as news). Local users could retrieve these news items, and the servers distributed these news items to other servers, which in turn made the news items available to users local to them. Usenet was therefore, much like the original Internet, designed to circumvent any attempts to censor it, by spreading the news relatively quickly from the original source server, and copying it across thousands of Usenet servers connected with each other.

As a result of the global nature of Usenet, rapid mass distribution of messages, albeit limited to a small group of Internet users, became possible. And, although Twitter is occasionally credited as a 'revolutionary tool' achieving exactly this global mass distribution, for example in the case of the Arab Spring, a very similar role was played around 20 years earlier by Internet-based technologies such as Usenet, for example, during the USSR military coup in 1992, media in the US relied, amongst other sources, on Usenet reports from the USSR. In particular the talk.soviet.politics group on Usenet became a valuable source of information. The group was an important supplier of news for the outside as state media ceased to broadcast and the group became the first source from inside the USSR to confirm the coup attempt taking place – and making the news available to a global audience (Press, 1992).

In a similar vein, students in China used early Internet services to communicate with students both in Mainland China and abroad to organise protests in the run up to the Tiananmen Square Massacre (Grier, 1998). Even news of the actual massacre and aftermath were distributed via Usenet. These news were sourced by activists in Taiwan via conventional telephones, as Mainland China cut off most forms of communications (Rheingold, 1993b). Although based on a different technology, **Internet Relay Chat**, an early real-time, text-based chat programme, in which users could join or create common chat rooms, served as a way to communicate with Israelis under attack by Saddam Hussein during the first Gulf War (Werman, 1993). Users from abroad relayed information to Israelis who suffered media outages during air raids while Israelis described the situation as it unfolded from their vantage point.

A different innovation stemming from early computer-mediated social activity was collaboratively produced content, as Usenet groups developed topical documents as guides for novices joining them. These Frequently Asked Questions (**FAQ**s) documents became extensive sources of information, produced collaboratively, with individual readers of the newsgroup contributing to questions and answers that were then archived and/or posted regularly for the benefit of new readers. While the format followed a question and answer style, and was therefore different from an encyclopaedia, FAQs could be seen as an early form of wiki. Available on a wide range of topics, these FAQs explained anything from the difference between chocolate and coverture to why motorcycle users need to wear gloves.

Marketing literature has paid little attention to BBSs (c.f. Caywood and Bauer, 1986 as one of the few items discussing the technology), although the history of some of the well-known ones, like the WELL, has been documented in non-academic literature (e.g. Rheingold, 1993b). Researchers have paid more attention to Usenet groups. Usenet groups have in fact been the basis for some seminal virtual communities' literature in the marketing area, for instance, Godes and Mayzlin's (2004) study of electronic word of mouth relied on Usenet discussion groups.

While the initial virtual communities, much like the early Internet, required relatively advanced technical skills to access and operate, the emergence of the simpler to operate and visually more appealing **World Wide Web** in 1991 changed the platforms where social online interactions took place. Because of its increasing popularity, web-based technology became the de facto communication standard (apart from email). This slowly replaced the previously manifold technologies and tools. Some of the original BBSs started to migrate their user-base to web-based services, for example, Delphi or the WELL, two of the oldest original BBS forums, and started to make their discussion groups available in a web-based and web-accessible format in 1992. Moving to a web-based format meant engaging with the growing audience of Internet users, who started to discover the overabundance of new information, tribes and groups often by briefly visiting many different websites during an online session, an activity that became commonly referred to as 'surfing' the Internet.

The contemporary counterparts of the original dial-up BBSs and Usenet groups are Internet forums or message boards. In many ways, these mirror the functionality of the early BBSs as the forum content is centrally stored on a specific web-server, and the forum is always owned by an individual, organisation or group of people who act as administrator and/or moderator of the activity in the forum, and who maintain ultimate control over the forum activities, layout and design.

The original forums were often rudimentary and based on proprietarily developed code, programmed by forum operators. More user-friendly software, which could be installed on web-servers with relatively little knowledge of programming, emerged in the middle of the 1990s. Examples are the **Ultimate Bulletin Board (UBB)** software and WWWThreads, both developed around 1996, making them pioneers of web-based Internet forums. With the help of software like UBB or WWWThreads, website owners could designate parts of, or indeed the whole of, their website as a space where virtually no content was generated by the website owners. Instead, visitors to the website created the content in the form of discussions, i.e. an early form of user-generated and shared content, albeit for a smaller audience and text-only.

No Internet history would be complete without mentioning, at least in passing, the rivals of the early Internet. Walled-garden services, such as **CompuServe** and **AOL**, provided a mix of exclusive, easy-to-navigate forums, chat rooms and, later on, access to the Internet and World Wide Web based on proprietary software. However, as more people started to use the Internet, and particularly web-based services on the Internet, these early online providers struggled, merged and faded into almost insignificance.

As can be seen from the above discussion, the Internet has been, from the beginning, a space where social interaction was central. Thus, many of these original developments which were later incorporated into the notion of Web 2.0 – such as user-generated, collaborative, sharing of information, etc. – already took place more than a decade before. O'Reilly (2005) publically described the concept in 2005, a date which is often portrayed as the official 'birthday' of Web 2.0.

## The Creation of the 'Social Web' and Web 2.0

When the first web-browser, Mosaic, and the related technical protocol for transferring information (Hypertext Transfer Protocol or **HTTP**) was publically released in 1993, it was initially just one of many different applications using the technological infrastructure of the Internet to make available, distribute and retrieve information. **Mosaic** (and later web-browsers, such as Internet Explorer) distinguished itself by the ability to include text, graphics and very basic layout (e.g. bold typeface, horizontal lines, etc. in the early stages) in the information it was displaying. Prior to Mosaic, similar applications and Internet protocols, such as **Gopher**, already allowed the transfer of static, text-only information. However, information retrieval using these applications was cumbersome, the information lacked graphics, there was little content and the user could only interact with the retrieved information in a limited way, for example moving from a 'page' to a different 'page' (e.g. Gopher lacked forms and other inputting capabilities).

The ease of use, technical flexibility and free availability of World Wide Web software, together with the rising interest in the Internet as a communication tool, gave the web an important advantage over the existing myriad of different software and technical protocols for transmitting information across the Internet. With widespread adoption, the web became the de facto standard for communicating over the Internet, with many other services being discontinued in favour of the web – or migrating to a web-based version. The popularity of the web became so overwhelming that in the 1990s the word 'web' became practically synonymous with the Internet itself in popular vernacular.

From the start, the early web experience offered interactive capabilities, and websites allowed for user-generated content, a fact that is regularly overlooked in contemporary discussions about Web 2.0. However, many early websites, especially those of traditional 'brick and mortar' companies, did not capitalise on this. Many early, especially commercial, websites were little more than an online version of previously available print material, or material that was presented in a way that it could have been easily printed, offering little more functionality than a traditional, printed catalogue, where users clicked from one page to another. This lack of imagination in the implementation of online strategies was widely criticised at the time, with only a few companies making use of the interactive features that web-based technology allowed for. Sadly, this cautious approach to new technology has remained today, as Grunig (2009) contends, with many companies continuing to avoid using dialogic and interactive features of social media. From a historical perspective, the lack of a more imaginative application of the emerging technology sealed the fate of numerous companies perishing as a result of ignoring or dismissing the technology. Concurrently, new companies emerged rapidly. Some of them became major players, arguably because they understood the need to adapt to more interactive communication methods. For example, Amazon, now one of the world's largest retailers, was founded in 1994. Amazon embraced user-generated content and interactive communication from the beginning. For example, Amazon allowed user reviews from 1995, even critical reviews of its merchandise, making it effectively one of the first review sites on the web (Alba et al., 1997).

Despite, or maybe because of, the lack of interactivity and the ability to adapt by some of the traditional companies, web-based services, commercial and personal ones, built almost exclusively on user-generated content grew substantially in the late 1990s.

Other examples of the rapid acceleration of user-generated content included personal homepage sites, such as **GeoCities**, launched in 1994. GeoCities offered an early means of online self-publishing in the form of personal web pages. It was organised as a series of tribe-like themed neighbourhoods in which users located their homepages, for example Heartland Neighbourhood for users interested in parenting issues, Yosemite Neighbourhood for outdoor pursuits, Vienna Neighbourhood for classical music related topics, and so forth. However, although GeoCities later introduced tools to make self-publication easier, it was complex to operate, and it ceased to exist in 2009 in all but Japan.

Another milestone quietly occurred in 1998, when '**Open Diary**' was launched, the first community website allowing users to easily publish 'diary entries' in a publicly accessible format on the web. Organised by interest-communities, which made it easy to find people of your tribe, 'Open Diary' became the first blogging website – without originally using the term.

The communality of these services is that they are built on the technological platform of the web, meaning they use the HTTP to transfer information across the Internet infrastructure and display this information using web-browser-based technology. Increasingly, through the evolution of technological standards, such as the **HTML** – or the language that makes up the code and tells a web-browser what and how to display information – and the creative adaptation and application of existing technologies, additional functionality was added to the existing web. Therefore, the definition of **Web 2.0**, as delivered by O'Reilly in 2005, was not a radical new definition of a completely different 'web', as some people have falsely imagined. Rather, O'Reilly described a set of existing technological and philosophical concepts, focusing on making the web more interactive – the vision vocalised the existing tendency for web users to move from passive consumption to active participation (and therefore collective co-creation of content, social sharing, etc.). Because the definition of Web 2.0 did not contain any novel ideas, but was rather a summary of activities on the Internet away from the commercial mainstream, the term has been heavily criticised in some circles, especially by early adopters of the Internet. Amongst the most vocal critics is Tim Berners-Lee, the original inventor of the web. Berners-Lee maintains that the term Web 2.0 is flawed and simply jargon, as the web itself is designed to be 'a collaborative space where people can interact'. Subsequently, he argues, a new terminology is not needed to describe 'moving some of the thinking client-side' (Berners-Lee, n.d.), that is, making it 'user-generated' in Web 2.0 jargon.

Similarly, the term Web 2.0 has been described as unclear and ambiguous. Despite attempts to define the term, the concept of Web 2.0 remains vague. Critics argue that O'Reilly and others using the term only offer examples of extreme cases, for example, Encyclopaedia Britannica as archetypal Web 1.0 and Wikipedia as representative of Web 2.0. Yet, it is not clear where, between these two extremes, the boundary between Web 1.0 and 2.0 falls. This ambiguity is further compounded by a myriad of terms such as the social web, social media and user-generated media or content being used often interchangeably with Web 2.0.

Within the marketing literature, to clarify the different concepts and avoid confusion, Kaplan and Haenlein (2010) proposed a series of definitions. In what has become a seminal definition in the field, they characterised the term Web 2.0 as an ideological set of principles and technologies underlying the user-generated content creation and sharing on social media sites (see the Introduction for the full definition).

However, despite these criticisms, the popularity and rise of the notion of Web 2.0, and related terms, can undoubtedly be credited with focusing online activity on the World

Wide Web on user-generation – or at least user-contribution and social interactions, that is, websites started a 'socialisation' of the web experience as a way to engage with website visitors.

Websites, which prior to Web 2.0 resisted some of the typical notions popularised by Web 2.0, started to adapt. For example, prior to the popularity of sharing information amongst users, several high-profile, commercial websites tried to stop individuals from 'deep linking' website content, i.e. linking from a second party website directly to a specific page of a website, rather than linking only to the front page. This fear of deep linking lead to several major news organisations filing a complaint against the news aggregator site Total News in 1997, trying to stop the site deep linking directly to their news stories (Gomez, 1998). Prior to this, a Scottish court stopped sharing of 'deep links' (Connolly and Cameron, 1998). Today, all of these organisations, including the first organisation to seek a court injunction against bypassing their front page in 1996, the *Shetland Times*, urge their website users to share links directly to relevant news items using social media tools embedded in their pages, to comment on news items and generally to interact with their website in a 'social media' way.

---

## THINKBOX WEB 1.0 THINKING VS. WEB 2.0 THINKING

Discuss the shift in thinking between Web 1.0 and Web 2.0.
　Taking the role of the editor of the *Shetland Times*, make a list of pro- and counter-arguments about people sharing your content directly (e.g. deep linking).

---

## Theoretical Underpinnings

Chapter 1 already briefly discussed the notion of usefulness as a key component for explaining the rise of Internet technology. As *The Social Shaping of Technology* (MacKenzie and Wajcman, 1985) postulates, although technology is often seen as something unstoppable and following its own logic, technology is in reality largely dependent upon underlying social and cultural phenomena. In other words, despite the widespread feelings of individuals that they are passive recipients and therefore directed by technological progress, actually, human beings are active designers, definers and changers of technology through the way they use it – and humans can also ultimately decline to use new technology. Consequently, it is the users and not the inventors who decide how, if and why technology is used, for example, while email was initially intended to serve purely as a communication platform for messages, through individual use and redefinition of the technology it now also serves as a tool to store important information, a reminder tool, etc. It is accordingly important to use different theoretical lenses when trying to explain conceptually how social media became such a prolific communication tool. Importantly, theory can't only be used to retrospectively understand the rise of social media. Theory can further help to inform the debate as to how social media can or should be used, and potentially what the future trajectory of technological developments may be.

The remainder of the chapter therefore focuses on frequently used theoretical frameworks that have been used to explain the rise of social media. Because of differences in approach, each theoretical lens offers a different, though often complementary, explanation.

### Technology Acceptance Model/UTAUT

The **Technology Acceptance Model** (TAM) (Davis, 1989) has been used extensively to describe the popularity of the Internet, social media and other forms of technology. Its basic form remains one of the easiest to grasp theoretical frameworks explaining why people choose to adopt technology – or not. The model itself is a technology-focused adaptation of the Theory of Reasoned Action (Fishbein and Ajzen, 1975), a model for predicting behaviours as a result of attitudes and behavioural intentions, widely used in social sciences, including in marketing. TAM in its early versions relied on two fundamental variables to explain resultant behaviour: these two variables are 'Perceived Usefulness' and 'Perceived Ease of Use' on behalf of the user. Both shape the attitude towards new technology. Where the attitude is positive, a behavioural intention to use the technology is formed, which itself is a precondition for the actual behaviour to occur (i.e. actual technology usage).

Considering the history of the Internet, it is easy to see how the medium has become simultaneously more useful as well as easier to use, providing more perceived usefulness – and therefore became popular. While computer technology was comparatively complicated prior to the 1990s, the introduction of a single and popular communication standard (HTTP/World Wide Web) made using the Internet significantly easier for people. It combined functionality previously performed by separate applications into a single, convenient application.

Likewise, as the theory would predict, the early adopters of the Internet were those who perceived they would derive the greatest usefulness from the new technology, that is, individuals from a subcultural background who expected the most usefulness from a global communication network with other tribe members. This perceived usefulness possibly offset initial perceived inconveniences and limitations of early technology, such as slow loading times and complicated set-ups. As the technology became more user-friendly, adoption spread to individuals outside of these defined subcultures. Concurrently, with increasing information, material and services being available, the perceived usefulness increased and spread beyond subcultural groups, in turn achieving wider adoption.

While the notion of Web 2.0 may be debatable, as a philosophical and technological construct with popular recall it nevertheless emphasised ease of use explicitly. During the early years of the Internet, for example, GeoCities' users needed to code complex HTML pages to create their virtual presence. With advancements in technology, users now can set up a significantly more complex web presence in the form of a blog – without ever thinking about the technological aspects of it. Therefore, the rise in usage of the Internet and 'social media' in particular is readily explained using the original TAM variables.

Similar to the Theory of Reasoned Action, TAM has undergone a number of revisions, making the model more complex than the original version from the late 1980s in an attempt to allow for more predictive power. These changes included changing the name to become the **Unified Theory of Acceptance and Use of Technology (UTAUT)** in 2003 (Venkatesh et al., 2003) – although TAM is still widely used and recognised. UTAUT adds several variables, significantly expanding the original model, although it does not fundamentally change the relevance of usefulness and ease of use. Rather, both variables are more differentially explained in the UTAUT, incorporating additional variables, such as 'effort' and 'performance expectancy', instead of a single 'ease of use' variable.

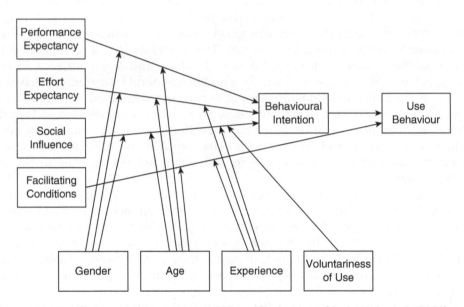

**Figure 4.1**    Unified Theory of Acceptance and Use of Technology (Venkatesh et al., 2003)

This increase of variables has, however, lead to some criticism of the new model. Specifically, that UTAUT is overly complicated to apply and measure, and hard to implement in practice. A further criticism of both TAM and UTAUT is that they assume users to be self-deterministic, i.e. they assume technology adoption is a goal-directed and rational process (Bagozzi, 2007). Social variables, while being one of the variables in the UTAUT, are largely played down, although they may have a significant impact on adoption and maintained usage of technology.

### Social Contagion

While **Social Contagion** is not strictly speaking a theoretical framework, it is a widely recognised social phenomenon, complementing individual-focused, self-deterministic frameworks such as TAM/UTAUT. Specifically, Social Contagion focuses on social influence on decision making. Although it is not technology-specific, Social Contagion can be easily applied to social media, for instance in explaining how certain websites become important and 'spread like an infection' in some groups.

Simply put, Social Contagion posits that if an increasing number of people start using a particular technology, it will be harder for those not using the technology to resist adopting the technology. This effect has long been recognised: French sociologist Gustave Le Bon described the effect in the nineteenth century (Le Bon, 1896). He observed that individuals within a group tended to support the group's attitudes, perform similar behaviours and share knowledge. These Social Contagion 'effects' arise through a combination of heightened awareness, social learning and/or the desire of group members to adhere to perceived shared norms within a group, and as such have been applied in numerous contexts. Within the context of marketing, contagion effects have been studied, for example, in relation to new product development (Du and Kamakura, 2011), focusing on word of mouth as a driver of Social Contagion (Iyengar et al., 2011) and Social Contagion as a tool for wider marketing activity (c.f. Van den Bulte and Wuyts, 2007).

A critical requirement for contagion to occur is communication and exposure to 'group ideas', including through computer-mediated communication networks, with other group members. Increased exposure accelerates contagion.

Two main types of contagion have been identified. Firstly, the classic form of contagion through social contact, for example by having close friendships with other individuals or a group as a whole. This form of contagion is also occasionally referred to as contagion by cohesion, for example, where many people in the immediate surroundings of an individual start using a particular website, and praise the content available, other individuals are likely to follow suit.

Secondly, contagion can be based on vicarious learning, i.e. where there is no direct personal contact between individuals or organisations. Nevertheless, individuals can learn by observation (effectively replacing direct communication). Typical for this 'contagion by structural equivalence' is the self-evaluation of individuals or organisations vis-à-vis others they consider alike. For example, if a competitor uses a new technology, then a competing organisation is likely to consider using the technology as well, even in the absence of any direct contact with the competitor. Consider the case of customer reviews. In the early stages these appeared on Amazon, but not on most other store sites, as many owners feared negative reviews. Today, customer reviews are a ubiquitous feature on virtually all Internet shopping sites – and a major source of customer information.

Contagion theory supplements TAM/UTAUT in that it provides a further explanatory perspective of why technological tools, including for example social media, spread across networks. Specific to social media, Rapp and colleagues (2013) show how social media usage spreads through supply chains – they found that retailers and consumers imitate social media usage of reputable brands. This suggests that a positive, trustworthy brand image outside of the social media realm accelerates contagion in addition to contact, and results in a 'downstream', from manufacturer to retailer and consumer, contagion through a supply chain network.

**THINKBOX** SOCIAL CONTAGION

Write down a list of websites you visit regularly, and a list of your friends. Now compare the website list with the list of your friends.

Which websites do you have in common with your friends?
How did you originally find out about them?
Why are you visiting the websites?

### Uses and Gratifications Theory

While TAM and Social Contagion emphasise the adoption of new technology, for example people starting to use Facebook, complementary theoretical models are needed to examine more closely the 'usefulness' concept, and particularly why people seek out particular websites, continue to frequent them and interact in a social media sphere after they had started using technology. **Uses and Gratifications Theory (UGT)** is an audience-centred theory that focuses on understanding mass communication. While the theoretical framework is derived from traditional media, and predates the Internet and social media significantly, the theoretical assumptions make UGT wholly suitable for Internet and social media research.

The key assumptions of the theoretical framework can be summarised as follows:

- The audience is an active participant in media selection and selects media based on individual goals.
- Media channels compete amongst themselves as well as with other resources for the audiences' attention.
- People are active, self-aware and motive-driven when making media choices. This enables them to articulate the reasons for media choices (e.g. to a researcher).

Given these assumptions, UGT asserts that an audience actively seeks gratification and the type of gratification will drive media choices. Thus media selection is goal-directed and utility-driven. For example, if an individual seeks entertainment gratification, the individual is likely to choose media channels which promise entertainment, such as a movie channel on television or Netflix online. Alternatively, if an individual seeks companionship gratification, he or she is more likely to turn towards a social media website to virtually interact with friends. Individual needs underlie the types of gratifications, and these needs can be classified as either emotional needs (such as companionship) or cognitive needs (for example information seeking).

Since the 1940s, when UGT initially surfaced, the framework has been applied extensively in different media environments, for example, Blumler and McQuail used the framework to study media choices by voters, specifically the types of channels and programmes watched in the 1960s (Blumler and McQuail, 1969). Blumler and McQuail later on categorised the gratifications sought from (traditional) media into four broad categories:

1. diversion, encompassing entertainment aspects
2. personal relationships, such as seeking out information useful for the maintenance of personal relationships
3. personal identity, for example by watching similar others and seeking validation through this
4. surveillance, such as satisfying curiosity about what happens around them.

However, different media can satisfy a variety of different goals, and consequently UGT itself does not limit the types or number of gratifications.

In relation to the Internet and social functions of online interactions, broad motivations have emerged, including information exchange, consumption of information, socialising and general conversation, diversion and escapism, educational and information-seeking motivations and status-seeking motivations amongst others (Leung, 2013). Using UGT, Dolan et al. (2016) showed how social media contributions can be classified according to the gratifications sought by different users: ranging from positive co-creation behaviour to co-destruction behaviour.

Facebook specifically has been found to satisfy needs in relation to socialising, entertainment, self-status seeking and information (Park et al., 2009). Interestingly Leung showed that in terms of social and affection motivations, there is no difference between younger and older Facebook users (Leung, 2013). However, while research into gratifications provided by one social media outlet is useful, it is important to remember that the social media landscape is constantly changing – and made up of an overabundance of websites with different functionalities. As more and different functionalities become available, different motivations are likely to be satisfied. UGT suggests, in cases where individuals perceive newer technology to be superior to older technology, old technology becomes gradually displaced. For example, Ramirez and colleagues (2008), using UGT, showed the displacement effect of instant messaging, mobile phones and email on conventional landline telephones, and similar effects are likely to occur through the constant evolution of web-based technologies. For example, the currently mooted 'Internet of Things', where devices such as fridges auto-update their content, monitor and even predict consumer desires may ultimately replace traditional review sites through providing personalised suggestions of suitable food for the individual. An early experiment based on this technological vision can be seen by Amazon, who patented an 'anticipatory shipping' technology which predicts future orders of customers and begins shipping items to the customer before they have ordered them. The items will then remain in transit until they are ordered (Lomas, 2014).

## THINKBOX USES AND GRATIFICATIONS

Make a list of the media choices you made last night, including websites, television, games, etc.

List the types of uses and gratifications you have sought from each media choice and any alternative media choices you could have made.

Social Information Processing Theory

A very different theoretical approach focusing on the depth of social connections once online is **Social Information Processing Theory** (SIP). SIP is the most popular theoretical perspective when researching traditional social media networks, according to a survey of recent studies in marketing, advertising and public relations involving social media, by Khang and colleagues (2012).

SIP was developed specifically in response to the strong relationships being formed with online partners by American media-researcher Walther (1992). The strength of these relationships was originally surprising to many sociologists, as online communication contains significantly fewer relationship-developing clues beyond the textual message, most noticeably the absence of non-verbal cues in traditional online environments, for example during communication in online forums. SIP explains how individuals adapt to the lack of such clues and, over time, learn to overcome the lack of these cues, building strong and lasting relationships with others in a purely textual environment. A vital point to note is that SIP stresses that time is an important aspect of computer-mediated relationship formation. As Walther asserts, relationships based entirely on textual communication require significantly more time and constant, regular contact in order to form relationships than those based on face-to-face communication.

Comparing computer-based communication with traditional face-to-face communication, Walther found evidence of some online relationships surpassing traditional, face-to-face relationships in terms of emotional and affectionate attachment, a phenomenon he called 'hyperpersonal communication'. Such hyperpersonal communication is the result of four interrelated effects, facilitating a more socially desirable image of both sender and receiver, and affecting four areas of the traditional communication framework (e.g. sender, receiver, message and feedback).

Firstly, the receiver is likely to have an idealised perception of the interlocutor, particularly an over-interpretation of similarity. For instance, if people meet within the context of an online community, the information exchanged is likely to be confined to the shared interests between the sender and the receiver. Because of the strong focus of the communication, the receiver develops an exaggerated sense of similarity with the sender.

Secondly, the sender has usually full control over the image he or she wishes to portray, disclosing only traits that are perceived as socially desirable. This selective presentation is more difficult in a traditional face-to-face setting, where numerous other clues beyond the textual information interfere with the sender's desired portrayal of him/herself.

Thirdly, the computer-mediated communication is asynchronous, i.e. can be time-delayed, whereas face-to-face communication is nearly always synchronous. Consequently, a sender can reflect upon and edit messages readily before they are sent, whereas in traditional communication long reflection and editing is difficult and awkward.

Finally, in the absence of any non-textual cues, and combined with a pre-existing impression of the interlocutor, any communication 'loop' is likely to become a self-fulfilling prophecy. For example, if the impression of individual A is that she is extremely helpful and friendly, then individual B is likely to send a friendly message to individual A. Because of the friendly message individual A is likely to respond in a friendly manner, confirming the initial attribution of her as a friendly person, thus creating a self-fulfilling feedback loop.

SIP and hyperpersonal communication can, for example, explain why certain social media tools seemingly possess high credibility, for example, in the case of blogs. Where an individual subscribes to a blog through an RSS feed or email, the subscriber receives constant updates about new posts. As most blogs are thematically focused, over-attribution of similarity between the receiver and the blog author is likely to occur. Each blog post is likely to be edited prior to release, and singularly focused on a particular aspect of the author's life.

## SUMMARY

This chapter discussed the history of computer-based and mediated communication to the development of Web 2.0. While the notion of Web 2.0 is contested, it nevertheless represents a shift in prevailing thinking for Internet-based communications – moving website content and ways to engage with and create content from the owner to the user. Several theories showed how the Internet moved from fringe technology to popular communication medium to become a prevalent media choice for many users. However, these theoretical lenses can further guide future development and evaluation of technology, for instance, TAM can be used to evaluate website projects, UGT can be used to study motives for using and continuing to use specific social media tools and SIP can be used to study and guide social media activity, for example, blog content and interaction with readers.

## RESEARCH DIRECTIONS

This area already offers a substantial body of literature and theoretical models. Applying these theoretical frameworks to evolving new technology forms can offer fruitful avenues for future, mostly practitioner-based research, and ways to guide technological development. Theories presented in this chapter can also be used to study specific communities on the Internet, allowing for a more detailed analysis of motivating factors.

# RESEARCH HIGHLIGHT FACING FACEBOOK: IMPRESSION MANAGEMENT STRATEGIES IN COMPANY–CONSUMER INTERACTIONS

In their study, Lillqvist and Louhiala-Salminen (2014) examined communication strategies used to communicate with critical customers using organisational Facebook pages by two Finnish companies. Using discourse analysis as a tool and analytical lens, they investigated how company representatives responded to negative comments, and categorised the strategies used. The data for the study are three months' worth of discussion, occurring in late 2010 through to early 2011. In total they based the analysis on 82 company responses to 336 consumer posts covering 74 topics.

The researchers divided the strategies used to respond to critical posts into two broad categories, each covering three types of responses. Firstly, responses designed to uphold social acceptability. Three types of strategies were used: conventional politeness, in the form of greeting, thanking or apologising; moral discourse, where the company was presented as morally superior to the critical consumer; and diversion, where the company representative answered only part of the criticism or changed the topic.

Secondly, responses could be designed to promote credibility. Strategies to achieve this included showing category entitlement, for example by providing an authoritative answer based on the connection between the representative and the company; ridiculing, where the company representative brands a critical view as simplistic or unreasonable; and footing, where the company representative distanced him/herself from an official line of the company.

An interesting point that Lillqvist and Louhiala-Salminen noted was that representatives' answers in both companies vary in terms of writing style and strategies used, for example, only one company used ridiculing, whereas both companies relied heavily on conventional politeness.

Further, they also noted that in both cases, and probably in the general context of computer-mediated communication with companies, responses tended to be significantly less formal and more personalised than normally encountered in an official, business-like capacity. As responses tended to be similar to personal, day-to-day communication between individuals, Lillqvist and Louhiala-Salminen concluded that the role of company representatives is somewhat paradoxical: as representatives, they face the complexities of acting and responding as a company official and as an individual person at the same time – in an environment that encourages informal, personal communication.

Although Lillqvist and Louhiala-Salminen do not comment further on this, they also provide data regarding post frequency: the data showed that less than 1% of consumers who like the page actually take part in the discussions.

The complete article is available on the companion website of this book.

# CASE STUDY WELCOME BACK MAGGI!

Product recalls and safety bans are seldom events that companies look back at with pride, but in the case of Maggi's Instant Noodle in India, the company has every reason to be pleased how they handled the social communication of this event.

Nestlé India was forced to recall its bestselling, flagship Maggi 2-Minute Instant Noodle brand after a series of tests revealed that the noodles contained lead and MSG above the safety limit. Prior to the recall, Maggi Noodles had an astonishing 80% market share, which went down to 0% when the Indian food safety regulator banned all sales of the noodles. For a prestigious, international brand, being banned due to safety concerns is, unsurprisingly, not just a major blow but a full scale existential crisis – and could play out very badly on social media. Several brands before had faced significant opposition on social media, which effectively killed the brands and precluded a relaunch. Thus, in order to survive Maggi had to work hard to avoid social media becoming a toxic environment killing the brand in real life.

Maggi decided to adopt a proactive approach to its communication while the product was banned, using story telling. Maggi combined social media with traditional media to tell the story of people missing their favourite brand of instant noodles. In a series of short films all cumulating in the #WeMissYouToo hashtag, Maggi told the story of how core audiences are missing their favourite noodles each day. The films featured, amongst others, a young man having to order from take away menus, a couple fighting over who has to cook now and a mother being happy that the final tests revealed that Maggi was safe for her son to eat.

In November 2015, coinciding with the Diwali festive season, Maggi relaunched after almost five months of being absent from the shelves. The relaunch was celebrated with the #welcomebackMAGGI and a special deal: consisting of a box of 12 noodle packs together with a fridge magnet, calendar for the coming year and welcome back letter. The reaction on social media was astonishing: from politicians to actors all tweeting or posting on Facebook about their relief of the return of the noodle brand. The first batch of the special deal pack sold out within five minutes – and a year and a half after the scandal, which could have potentially killed the brand, the brand again recorded an impressive 57% market share in India.

## Questions to Consider

1. Do you think the project was a success?
2. How do you compare it to brand recalls of other brands – and their handling of the situation?
3. Think about the different audiences Maggi targeted (young men, young couples and mothers). Why would those audiences engage with the brand socially?
4. How do you explain the big welcome back when Maggi relaunched?

# FURTHER READING

Hennig-Thurau, T., Malthouse, E.C., Friege, C., Gensler, S., Lobschat, L., Rangaswamy, A. and Skiera, B. (2010) 'The impact of new media on customer relationships', *Journal of Service Research*, 13(3): 311–30.

Lanzolla, G. and Suarez, F.F. (2010) 'Closing the technology adoption-use divide: The role of contiguous user bandwagon', *Journal of Management*, 38(3): 836–59.

Tradewinds Harvard University (1996) 'Doing business on the Internet: Advertising', *Business Information Review*, 13(1): 33–8.

Weedon, A. (1996) 'The book trade and Internet publishing: A British perspective', *Convergence: The International Journal of Research into New Media Technologies*, 2(1): 76–102.

Williams, C.B. and Gulati, G.J.J. (2012) 'Social networks in political campaigns: Facebook and the congressional elections of 2006 and 2008', *New Media & Society*, 15(1): 52–71.

## REFERENCES

Alba, J., Lynch, J., Weitz, B., Janiszewski, C., Lutz, R., Sawyer, A. and Wood, S. (1997) 'Interactive home shopping: Consumer, retailer, and manufacturer incentives to participate in electronic marketplaces', *Journal of Marketing*, 61: 38–53.

Bagozzi, R.P. (2007) 'The legacy of the Technology Acceptance Model and a proposal for a paradigm shift', *Journal of the Association for Information Systems*, 8(4): 244–54.

Berners-Lee, T. (n.d.) developerWorks Interviews [Online]. Available at: www.ibm.com/developerworks/podcast/dwi/cm-int082206txt.html (accessed 15 January 2014).

Blumler, J.G. and McQuail, D. (1969) *Television in Politics: Its Uses and Influence*. Chicago, IL: University of Chicago Press.

Caywood, C.L. and Bauer, C.L. (1986) 'An electronic bulletin board system for the sales profession: A review and proposal', *The Journal of Personal Selling and Sales Management*, 6: 85–90.

Connolly, J.P. and Cameron, S. (1998) 'Fair dealing in webbed links of Shetland Yams: Shetland Times Ltd. v. Dr. Jonathan Wills and another', *Journal of Information Law & Technology*, 2 [Online]. Available at: https://warwick.ac.uk/fac/soc/law/elj/jilt/1998_2/connolly/ (accessed 27 November 2017).

Davis, F.D. (1989) 'Perceived usefulness, perceived ease of use, and user acceptance of information technology', *MIS Quarterly*, 13(3): 319–40.

Dolan, R., Conduit, J., Fahy, J. and Goodman, S. (2016) 'Social media engagement behaviour: A uses and gratifications perspective', *Journal of Strategic Marketing*, 24(3–4): 261–77.

Du, R.Y. and Kamakura, W.A. (2011) 'Measuring contagion in the diffusion of consumer packaged goods', *Journal of Marketing Research*, 48: 28–47.

Fishbein, M. and Ajzen, I. (1975) *Belief, Attitude, Intention, and Behavior: An Introduction to Theory and Research*, Addison-Wesley series in Social Psychology. Reading, MA: Addison-Wesley.

Godes, D. and Mayzlin, D. (2004) 'Using online conversations to study word-of-mouth communication', *Marketing Science*, 23(4): 545–60.

Gomez, F.C. (1998) 'Washington Post v. Total News, Inc.', *Berkeley Technology Law Journal*, 13(1): 21–34.

Grier, D.A. (1998) 'Politics, control, and computer networks: The Chinese Student Lobby of 1989', *Communications of the ACM*, 41: 137–45.

Grunig, J.E. (2009) 'Paradigms of global public relations in an age of digitalisation', *PRism*, 6: 1–19.

Hart, J.A., Reed, R.R. and Bar, F. (1992) 'The building of the Internet: Implications for the future of broadband networks', *Telecommunications Policy*, 16: 666–89.

Iyengar, R., Van den Bulte, C. and Valente, T.W. (2011) 'Opinion leadership and social contagion in new product diffusion', *Marketing Science*, 30: 195–212.

Kaplan, A.M. and Haenlein, M. (2010) 'Users of the world, unite! The challenges and opportunities of social media', *Business Horizons*, 53: 59–68.

Khang, H., Ki, E.-J. and Ye, L. (2012) 'Social media research in advertising, communication, marketing, and public relations, 1997–2010', *Journalism & Mass Communication Quarterly*, 89: 279–98.

Kindsmüller, M.C., Melzer, A. and Mentler, T. (2008) 'Online communities and online community building', in M. Khosrow-Pour (ed.), *Encyclopedia of Information Science and Technology*. Hershey, PA: IGI Global. pp. 2899–905.

Le Bon, G. (1896) *The Crowd: A Study of the Popular Mind*. London: T. Fisher Unwin.

Leiner, B.M., Cerf, V.G., Clark, D.D., Kahn, R.E., Kleinrock, L., Lynch, D.C., Postel, J., Roberts, L.G. and Wolff, S.S. (1997) 'The past and future history of the Internet', *Communications of the ACM*, 40: 102–8.

Leung, L. (2013) 'Generational differences in content generation in social media: The roles of the gratifications sought and of narcissism', *Computers in Human Behavior*, 29: 997–1006.

Lillqvist, E. and Louhiala-Salminen, L. (2014) 'Facing Facebook: Impression management strategies in company–consumer interactions', *Journal of Business and Technical Communication*, 28(1): 3–30.

Lomas, N. (2014) Amazon patents 'anticipatory' shipping: To start sending stuff before you've bought it [Online]. Available at: http://techcrunch.com/2014/01/18/amazon-pre-ships/ (accessed 18 January 2014).

MacKenzie, D. and Wajcman, J. (1985) *The Social Shaping of Technology: How the Refrigerator Got its Hum*. Buckingham: Open University Press.

O'Reilly, T. (2005) What is Web 2.0? Design patterns and business models for the next generation of software [Online]. Available at: www.oreilly.com/pub/a/web2/archive/what-is-web-20.html (accessed 6 November 2017).

Park, N., Kee, K.F. and Valenzuela, S. (2009) 'Being immersed in social networking environment: Facebook groups, uses and gratifications, and social outcomes', *CyberPsychology & Behavior*, 12: 729–33.

Press, L. (1992) 'RELCOM, an Appropriate Technology Network', *Proceedings of INET '92*, International Networking Conference, Kobe, Japan, 15–18 June. Reston, VA: Internet Society, pp. 259–67.

Ramirez, A., Dimmick, J., Feaster, J. and Lin, S.-F. (2008) 'Revisiting interpersonal media competition: The gratification niches of instant messaging, e-mail, and the telephone', *Communication Research*, 35: 529–47.

Rapp, A., Beitelspacher, L.S., Grewal, D. and Hughes, D.E. (2013) 'Understanding social media effects across seller, retailer, and consumer interactions', *Journal of the Academy of Marketing Science*, 41(5): 547–66.

Rheingold, H. (1993a) *The Virtual Community: Homesteading on the Electronic Frontier*, rev. edn. Cambridge, MA: MIT Press.

Rheingold, H. (1993b) 'A slice of my life in my virtual community', in L.M. Harasim (ed.), *Global Networks: Computers and International Communication*. Cambridge, MA: Massachusetts Institute of Technology. pp. 57–81.

Van den Bulte, C. and Wuyts, S. (2007) *Social Networks and Marketing*, relevant knowledge series. Cambridge, MA: Marketing Science Institute.

Venkatesh, V., Morris, M.G., Davis, G.B. and Davis, F.D. (2003) 'User acceptance of information technology: Toward a unified view', *MIS Quarterly*, 27: 425–78.

Walther, J.B. (1992) 'Interpersonal effects in computer-mediated interaction: A relational perspective', *Communication Research*, February, 19(1): 52–90.

Werman, R. (1993) *Notes from a Sealed Room: An Israeli View of the Gulf War*. Carbondale, NJ: Southern Illinois University Press.

# 5

# Gaming and Hybrid Platforms

## CHAPTER OVERVIEW

This chapter reviews the historical development of games as an alternative use of computer-mediated communication, entertainment and social networking, from the early beginnings as text-based Multi-User Dungeons to complete virtual worlds like Second Life. The chapter then reviews how marketers have adopted gaming technology for communication purposes, from distinguishable games in the form of adver-games with perspicuous product placements and games with in-game advertising to the gamification of consumption experiences, where game design principles are used to enhance the experience and to make it a social event.

## LEARNING OUTCOMES

On completing this chapter, you should be able to:

- describe the rise in popularity of games – from the early beginnings to virtual worlds and social games
- critically reflect how marketing communication can be inserted into games, and the relative advantages and disadvantages of advergames and in-game advertising
- explain, using appropriate theoretical models, the persuasiveness of game-based advertising
- discuss gamification of consumption, and how this can enhance the consumption experience.

## GAMING AND HYBRID PLATFORMS

Although computers were initially intended as sober business devices, it became clear swiftly that they could also be used to entertain the users. Consequently, the first computer-based games were produced. While early games were single-user activities, games later became ways to connect and engage audiences and consumers. We therefore briefly review the historical development of games and how games became a viable marketing tool.

### Early Video Games

It wasn't long after the first general purpose, programmable computer was switched on in 1946 that the embryonic technology got appropriated for gaming. In 1947, British computer pioneer Alan Turing became the first person documented to write a computer programme to play chess (Donovan, 2010). However, as computers were still in their infancy, the programme soon outgrew the available computing power. The development of a faultless computer chess game became the acme of video game aspirations in the early era of games research and development. These aspirations were serious enough to include the first academic paper discussing the possibility of computers as chess game devices in 1950 (Shannon, 1950), remaining even today one of the widest cited, most influential papers in the computer gaming literature.

However, as computers were initially not powerful enough to match humans when playing chess, more simple computer-based games emerged. In 1951, Nimrod, the first dedicated computer for game play, was displayed as part of the Festival of Britain. In 1952 Alexander Douglas, at the University of Cambridge, programmed the first 'video game' on a general purpose computer: OXO, a simple tic-tac-toe game, part of Douglas' thesis on human–computer interaction (Vaughan-Nichols, 2009). However, computer games such as OXO remained largely surreptitious, with mainstream computer research focusing on professional, especially mathematical, applications of the emerging technology. Around a decade later, three MIT students, Steve Russell, Martin Graetz and Wayne Wiitanen, created the first complex video game. In 1961, they developed Spacewar!, a modest point and shoot type game set in outer space (Graetz, 1981). As computers were prohibitively expensive in the 1960s, the game remained largely a diversion for computer researchers, appearing on many computers in research laboratories, principally in the US.

In the late 1960s, initial ideas for a computer-based games system for individual homes were first mooted. Originally, the system invented by Ralph Baer, and called a 'Brown Box', consisted of a console that could be used to play games using the increasingly popular television as a display. However, production was not viable due to high prices for the required components. It was only by the early 1970s that component prices had reduced enough to make production viable, and Magnavox Odyssey, the world's first commercial home video game console, was released.

The popularity and availability of consoles in homes and arcades characterised the rapid development of video games in the 1970s and early 1980s. A genuine 'video game mania' (Donovan, 2010: 81) engulfed the developed world, with rapid growth in types and genres of games available for the general public: from action games to vehicle simulations, playing video games became a favourite pastime. However, games consoles and video games in general remained largely offline activities, i.e. the games could be played together with other people in the same room, but early games consoles had no ability to connect to other consoles allowing a game to be played by several players simultaneously in different locations. Social gaming experience, at least for consoles, remained elusive until the mid-1990s.

## From MUD to Second Life and Virtual Worlds

Simultaneously with the rise in popularity of games consoles, personal computers became more versatile and affordable. In the late 1970s and early 1980s, computers allowed for both home-office and games functionality, blending both functions. For example, the Apple II computer, released originally in 1977, became one of the first personal computers blending the ability to play games with office functionality, with popular applications such as VisiCal, an early spreadsheet software.

With the emergence of more multipurpose computers, and relatively cheap ways of connecting remote computers in the late 1970s, early forms of online games appeared, either as an integral part of BBSs (see Chapter 4), or in the form of **MUDs,** short for Multi-User Dungeons. Because of technical limitations, especially bandwidth limitations of the networks, many of these were largely text-based, which made it possible to transfer game data relatively easily along limited capacity, early network lines.

One of the first of multi-user, online games was MUD – the Multi-User Dungeon game from which the genre took its name – created in 1978 by two computer programmers at the University of Essex in the UK. This game allowed for interactions between game players, either directly when players were simultaneously online, or through the design of characters and objects within the game context. The game therefore incorporated social aspects into the gaming experience. The game is essentially an early version of a **virtual world**, where players role-play against each other.

Due to the ability to simulate actions and personas while providing feedback to players, MUDs became popular not only as fantasy games, but were also designed for educational or purely social purposes, for example, virtual environments where the emphasis was more on players' discussions and interactive simulations with educational outcomes rather than playing a particular game (Haynes and Holmevik, 2001).

Merging social networking capabilities and game playing together was an important part of early virtual worlds experiences, and resulted in a rapid development in both educational and social contexts.

Based on the concepts of the first MUDs, early computer networks released their own versions of virtual worlds to entertain subscribers, moving away from purely text-based 'virtual realities' to increasingly two and eventually three-dimensional spaces in which game play took place. CompuServe, for example, launched WorldsAway in 1995. In this virtual world, subscribers could play and virtually interact with other subscribers using their own designed avatars representing them during game play. WorldsAway was itself based on a previous game, Habitat, launched in 1985 by the Canadian online service Quantum Link, originally specifically designed for Commodore 64 computers.

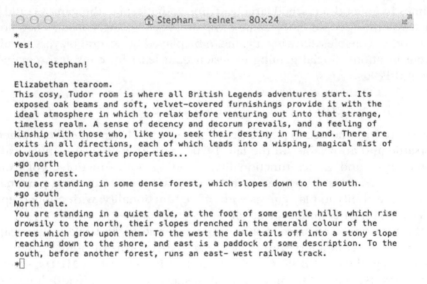

**Image 5.1**  MUD screen

In an educational context, Diversity University launched in 1993. Diversity U was the first virtual university 'game': it allowed the players to move around a virtual university campus, interact with other students and staff, give lectures and so forth, in a similar way to a 'real life' university (Harris and Wambeam, 1996).

With increasing network capacity, virtual worlds extended significantly in complexity and popularity. Because of the technological advancements, games became more realistic, popular – and some would argue addictive (Boyle et al., 2011).

A particular virtual world, Second Life, launched in 2003, has attracted both professional and academic interest – as well as marketer hype. Within Second Life, players (referred to as 'residents') create avatars, which can either be a lifelike representation of their real life persona, or can take any other shape or form as chosen by the player, allowing complete freedom of self-representation within the virtual world. The world itself is made up of different virtual neighbourhoods, representing anything from historical role-playing communities to virtual representation of 'real' life spaces (e.g. 'virtual Spain'). Residents can purchase virtual land of varying sizes, which can be furnished as required, including turning their properties into homes, workshops or other locations for fellow residents, such as community centres, shops or bars. Communication between residents is largely by text-based chat, although the option of voice chat has been available since 2007.

Second Life was unique in that it allowed, until 2013, 'residents' to hold exclusive copyright over all their creations in the virtual world. Because of this, residents can exchange and sell or buy content created by other users, effectively creating a purposeful virtual economy. The Second Life economy itself is based on exchanges of the virtual Linden Dollar, pegged at around L$270 to US$1. The currency can be converted freely between real life money, for example US Dollars, which in turn valued the Second Life economic activity in terms of GDP at around US$64 million in 2006, with a total of US$8.7 million being exchanged into L$ in April 2008 (Kaplan and Haenlein, 2009). Second Life has gained much interest, and hype, as a significant environment in which to conduct business transactions – and as a space with potential marketing impact. Examples of application in marketing include traditional advertising in the many virtual malls and on virtual billboards in Second Life, or more interactive scenarios where brands create virtual showrooms or outlets in which residents can purchase a company's goods. For example, the clothes firm American Apparel opened a virtual outlet in 2006 in Second Life. However, similar to when the World Wide Web began to emerge, simply transplanting established business models into a different technological environment proved challenging. The American Apparel branch was closed a year after opening in 2007 (Hansen, 2009). Similarly, Dutch banks ABN Amro and ING opened virtual branches in Second Life, but again closed them around a year later, failing to find an adequate business model that would translate into the virtual world (Burns, 2008).

A more successful model of using Second life was applied by 'aloft', the mid-price hotel range owned by Starwood hotels. They used Second Life to test the concept of 'aloft' branded hotels, and integrated feedback from virtual visitors into their design concepts when they launched in the real world about two years later (Jana, 2006).

Why most Second Life ventures have failed to engage the residents is subject to some debate. On the one side, some commentators suggested that ultimately virtual worlds are too complicated to access for users and difficult to maintain for companies. Consequently, companies have focused their marketing efforts on more accessible platforms, for example dedicated social networking websites such as Facebook (Howell, 2013).

Others have observed that one of the main weaknesses of Second Life (and other virtual worlds) is the lack of mobile integration, suggesting that gaming and social networking needs to be integrated between desktop computers and mobiles for consumers to be attracted (Burns, 2008).

However, although Second Life may have not fulfilled the economic expectations of some of the early corporate investors, the consequences of a potential for a reconstructed second life online remains a topic for discussion. This discussion includes the suggestion to view all of social media, including platforms such as Facebook, as a vast video game (Cirucci, 2013), in which reality and role-play merge to form a virtual whole. Seen as such, all of social media serve to create a constant hyperreality in which users operate – and which can be created and abandoned at will (see also the research highlight for more on hyperreality).

## THINKBOX HYPERREALITY AND VIRTUAL WORLDS

Think of when you have played a game involving a virtual world or simulation of some kind.

List the emotions you recall feeling. Which aspects of the game made you absorbed in the game? Which aspects destroyed the illusion of being in the virtual world?

### In-game Advertising and Advergaming

As games, other than just virtual worlds, became increasingly popular, marketers also capitalised on this new form of entertainment. Marketing activity centred on games came in two types: either as in-game advertising or as custom-designed **advergames** for particular brands.

**In-game advertising (IGA)** is essentially placing products or brands within the context of a game. Such **placements** can occur in a variety of different forms, for example, by placing branded storefronts in street-based games or by placing virtual advertising on the sides of the pitch in football games. In most cases the game will not depend on the advertising, and the game experience is not significantly changed by the IGA. However, in some cases, products have been placed as integral game components, for example, Facebook game developer Zynga included Cascadian Farm branded blueberries in its popular FarmVille game (Van Grove, 2010).

Contrary to IGA, advergames are a hybrid between advertising and game, defined as a 'form of branded entertainment that features advertising messages, logos and trademarks in a game format' (Mallinckrodt and Mizerski, 2007: 87). The aim of advergames is to entertain and engage website visitors or players on other devices in order to make an emotional connection between the game and the brand featured (Dahl et al., 2009). One of the earliest examples of an advergame was Chex Quest, released in 1996 by a cereal company. Originally, the game was given away with cereal boxes on a CD-ROM when purchasing Chex branded cereals. The promotion won several marketing awards and the game was credited with increasing the sales of Chex cereal by 295% (Christiansen, 2012).

In contrast to traditional video games with a long storyline or complicated rules, advergames are nearly always small and relatively simple-to-play games, which can be played within a few minutes. Therefore, the focus of advergames is on completing simple tasks, such as shooting bottles or solving simple puzzles. Further, advergames may include additional features linked to product purchase, for example some advergames allow for additional levels in a game to be unlocked by entering a code found inside a promotional product pack.

While in the beginning, such as in the case of Chex Quest, advergames were based on CD-ROMs, with increasing bandwidth, advergames became almost exclusively hosted on company websites, with some companies having dedicated websites for advergames only (e.g. www.postopia.com/ was a dedicated website operated by Kraft). In addition, many advergames are also available on mobile phones and on social networking sites.

Advergames are particularly appealing for advertisers, as they are frequently played many times over. This allows the player to become exposed and interact with the brand for extended periods of time, potentially significantly more than using traditional advertising. Although it is difficult to estimate how often advergames are played, some scholars have suggested that children play advergames up to 100 times per game, while adults spend up to 30 hours playing a particular advergame (Nelson et al., 2004).

Critics of advergames have highlighted that many of the games promote unhealthy food items and are poorly regulated in comparison to traditional advertising (Dahl et al., 2009). Researchers have further highlighted that many of the games attract not only casual gamers, but also seem to be directed towards children. Children in particular have been found to have only limited ability to recognise the persuasive intention of the games, raising serious ethical concerns (Panic et al., 2013).

Relatively little research has been carried out regarding the combined effect of linking games and networking sites. However, one study, looking at the effect of placing advergames on mobile social networking sites, has found a strong positive effect on word-of-mouth intention and a positive effect on brand attitudes (Okazaki and Yagüe, 2012), suggesting that placing advergames on a social network may be synergistically achieving both game-related outcomes, for example individual brand attitude change, and social media marketing objectives, for example creation of word of mouth.

## THINKBOX ADVERGAMES

Go to a website with a collection of advergames or download some games onto your mobile device. Try and play a few of them.

Are these games clearly identified?

Do these games clearly show that they are meant to be advertising?

Which social functions do these advergames have?

Think about what the likely influence is if you play these games. Try to describe even subtle influences.

What ethical problems can you imagine arise from the use of advergames as a marketing tool?

## Theoretical Models

Four theoretical frameworks – **Persuasion Knowledge**, **Social Cognitive Theory**, **Limited-capacity Model of Motivated Message Processing (L4MP)** and **Flow** – have been proposed as the main foundations for research into advergames and IGA (Terlutter and Capella, 2013). Flow and the L4MP are most clearly applicable to game-like environments. However, some of these theories, as argued by Cirucci (2013), may also be applied in the wider context of social media beyond game-like environments, for example, Social Cognitive Theory, and associated vicarious learning, can, conceivably not only take place when playing games, but also when observing behaviour of others in social networks. Similarly, persuasion knowledge is pervasive in all persuasion contexts, including advertisements, interpersonal communication as well as advergames or IGA. Accordingly, persuasion knowledge is discussed in Chapter 7 (Persuasiveness).

### Social Cognitive Theory

The central proposition of Social Cognitive Theory postulates that humans, especially, but not exclusively, children, learn by observing others. The theory complements Social Contagion (see previous chapter) and Classical Conditioning Theory, which assumes that people learn primarily by performing a particular task or behaviour and succeeding (or being rewarded) or failing (being punished). Bandura developed this theory based on his earlier work connected to Social Learning Theory (Bandura, 1977) by developing a model of three, reciprocal factors. The three factors of Bandura's model are cognitive, behavioural and environmental factors, each dynamically interacting and influencing the resultant behaviour. Social media, and particularly game play, influence directly all three behavioural influence factors.

Environmental factors include perceived socio-cultural norms and access to a supportive community. Socio-cultural norms have been shown to be influenced by marketing communications, for example, Chan and colleagues (2012) show that girls learn gender roles from advertising. Similarly, as discussed in Chapter 1 and in relation to Social Contagion, online communities can act as places with strong social bonding, conceivably amplified by reciprocal positive feedback as discussed by Social Information Processing Theory, and are places where contagion by cohesion will therefore arise.

Behavioural factors include skills, practice and self-efficacy that a given behaviour can be successfully accomplished. There is considerable evidence that children can learn skills and self-efficacy, for example by watching a particular action being performed (Knobloch et al., 2005), suggesting that behavioural factors can be learned by, for example, playing with products in the course of advergames.

Lastly, cognitive factors, which include knowledge, expectations and attitudes, are likely to be directly influenced by, for example, accessing discussion forums – or indeed through simulation in games. Games and simulation games used in social marketing for health education, so called 'serious games', for example have been shown to increase knowledge, attitudes and motivations to perform healthier behaviours (Connolly et al., 2012).

Currently, most research has focused on the application of Social Cognitive Theory to advergames and other online games, particularly for children, and exploring how the theory can be used to explain the efficiency and efficacy of these games. Future research could explore, for example, how adults are affected by playing various games – or indeed if Social Cognitive Theory can be applied to social media as a whole, and the consequences thereof.

## THINKBOX SOCIAL COGNITIVE LEARNING

Find a game designed to encourage a healthy behaviour. (Tip: go to www.foodafactoflife. org.uk/ for several healthy eating related games or www.smokefreekids.info/08game_clear_popup.htm for a quit smoking game.)

Think of how the game tries to convey the message.

Do you think people in 'at risk groups', for example smokers, would learn something through playing the game?

What effect do you think playing the game might have on the targeted groups?

### Limited-capacity Model of Motivated Mediated Message Processing (L4MP)

Limited-capacity Model of Motivated Mediated Message Processing (Lang, 2000), or L4MP for short, specifically addresses cognitive capacity issues for people to encode, store and retrieve information received. Once an individual is oversaturated with stimuli, information can no longer be successfully processed, and not successfully recalled. L4MP itself is an evolution of earlier work originating in the field of cognitive psychology, where researchers demonstrated the existence of an individual's limit of total attention capacity (Kahneman, 1973).

L4MP and limited cognitive capacity models have been tested considerably in the context of in-game advertising and product placement in games. As players limited cognitive capacity needs to be divided between the primary task (usually the game play) and the secondary task (paying attention to the commercial message), placement of the message is significant if the aim is to increase **brand recall**. Peripherally placed messages (i.e. advertising messages outside of the main game, such as in the case of Facebook advertisements surrounding the actual game space) are likely to result in significantly lower recall than brands or commercial messages placed directly inside the game. Game experience and involvement, i.e. the perceived level of difficulty or interest in the game, further moderates brand recall of brands placed inside games. Following the logic of L4MP, if a game is perceived as difficult or very demanding, then all cognitive resources will be allocated to the primary task of game play, leaving not enough cognitive resources available for the secondary task. However, this latter effect is only relevant for experienced gamers, as they are likely to learn how to 'weed out' unnecessary information (e.g. commercial messages). Inexperienced gamers do not know which aspects of the game to focus on, and are therefore likely to distribute their attention more evenly on all features in the game, including commercial messages (Lee and Faber, 2007).

A tactic of attracting game players' attention is placing products or advertisements that are incongruent with the game. This follows similar tactics used in product placements, though the use of incongruent placements is not uncontroversial. While placing of products or advertisements which are not congruent with the game being played result in increased brand recall (Lee and Faber, 2007), they are also likely to irritate the game player and activate persuasion knowledge. Activated persuasion knowledge in turn may lead to the deployment of persuasion coping measures that can result in the game players' development of negative attitudes towards the promoted brand (Van Reijmersdal, 2009) (see also Chapter 7 for a more extensive discussion of persuasion knowledge).

### Flow

Flow is a mental state where an individual is fully immersed in a task, feeling in complete control of the undertaking and consequently enjoying the experience (Csikszentmihalyi, 1998, 1990). Flow is the optimal point of game experience. It is situated between the unpleasant feelings associated with being over-challenged, and the player accordingly feeling anxious, frustrated or angry, and under-challenged, evoking feelings of boredom or dullness.

Research suggests that flow distracts from brands in the game leading to low brand recall (Schneider and Cornwell, 2005). However, despite the possibility of low recall, when players were 'in the flow', brand attitudes for in-game placed products were most favourably influenced (Waiguny et al., 2012).

Flow, like L4MP, doesn't only occur in game-like settings. Chaney and colleagues (2004) observed that both online chatting and game playing lead to lower recall rates for individuals 'in the flow'. However, it is important to note that recall is only one measure of marketing success. There is some suggestion, especially deriving from the literature on product placement, that while immediate recall may be difficult for players (or participants in or observers of other forms of entertainment), peripheral or unconscious brand exposure may still influence future behaviour and change long-term brand attitudes (Law and Braun-LaTour, 2004). This peripheral exposure effect is in part explained by the Elaboration Likelihood Model (see Chapter 3), as well as Mere Exposure Theory (Zajonc, 1968), which posits that even subconscious exposure to communication has the potential to change attitudes.

**THINKBOX L4MP AND FLOW**

Think of when you are playing a game – it may be helpful if the game has adverts surrounding it (e.g. on Facebook), or as part of the game.

> At what point do you enter a state of flow? Describe how flow feels different from other emotional states.

> How do you process surrounding or other messages in the game when you are in a state of flow?

> Can you recall any adverts?

## GAMIFICATION

Apart from clearly distinguishable 'games', like video games or advergames, the possibility of applying game-like principles to achieve a certain desired outcome, for example, a specific behaviour, has gained attention both with practitioners as well as academics in recent years (Van Grove, 2011). Commonly referred to as 'gamification', there are numerous success stories in the popular press regarding the application of gamification in marketing. For example, gamification ideas have been applied to tourism marketing. There, gamification has been found to be associated with a higher satisfaction rate amongst tourists and increased brand awareness (Xu et al., 2017). Similarly, gamification has turned fitness training into a virtual game 'played' with friends, and is a key success factor for many fitness platforms such as Nike+ (Zichermann and Cunningham, 2011).

The term 'gamification' emerged around the turn of the millennium, although it wasn't widely used until about a decade later. Although there are various definitions with marginal differences, all refer to essentially the inclusion of game-like elements in a non-gaming context to motivate people to behave in a certain way. A more marketing-specific definition is suggested by Huotari and Hamari (2012), particularly applied to service-oriented marketing. They refer to gamification as 'a process of enhancing a service with affordances for gameful experiences in order to support user's overall value creation' (2012: 19). Thus, their definition places greater emphasis on the possibility of enhancing a service experience specifically by encouraging co-creation with the customer. They further stress that an important aspect of gamification is the voluntary engagement by users as a means to create gameful experiences.

In practice, gamification relies on two core strategies to create a game-like experience. Firstly, gamified services include rewards for users completing specific tasks, for example, gamified services such as Nike+ offer badges for the fastest mile, longest run, etc. and a 'Nike-Fuel' energy counter to show rewards to users. Similarly, a profession network like LinkedIn uses gamification elements by displaying a progress bar to motivate users to complete their profile.

Secondly, competition with friends is a core strategy to get users engaged and keep them motivated. For example, using Nike+, a user can virtually 'run' against friends, and the application displays weekly and monthly leader boards comparing the individual users to their friends and other users in their age group.

In addition to these core strategies, gamification strategies can include adding specific rules about how a desired behaviour has to be performed, similar to rules encountered in classic games, or including narratives, for example to create a feeling of a 'virtual' game.

By using these strategies, companies or third parties can gamify a consumption experience. To develop gamification practices, it is important to focus on the extended consumption experience as discussed in Part 1. For example, while Nike+ products are essential to take part in the Nike+ experience, the game does not focus on selling Nike products. Rather, through the use of gamification techniques, Nike+ enhances the consumption experience of Nike+ compatible (and potentially other) products. True to the theory of gamification, Nike+ adds an additional service experience element to the consumption experience. Nike products, for example Nike sport shoes, can equally be used without taking part in the game. Thus participation in the 'Nike+ game' is voluntary, though enhances the extended consumption period of Nike products.

It is important to note that gamification can occur even if the underlying product or service is not actually providing the gamification. For instance, Foursquare, the location-based social network, gamifies consumption experiences by awarding badges and rewards for 'checking in'. Consequently, a consumption experience in a coffee shop can be gamified through checking in, although the coffee shop itself may not be an initiator of the gamification. For more on the 'gamification of life' through location-based networks, see the research highlight in Chapter 6.

## THINKBOX GAMIFICATION

Think of a business, for example a cinema or coffee shop.

Make a list of the behaviours that occur during consumption.
How can this business gamify each behaviour that occurs during consumption of their products?

## SUMMARY

This chapter has charted the history of gaming from the early video games to today's manifold game types, including virtual worlds, advergames and the related gamification of the consumption experience. Three theoretical models for explaining the potential of games to influence behaviour have been presented. Social Cognitive Theory focuses on learning through observing others or simulations, for example in the context of games; L4MP reminds marketers that humans only have a limited amount of cognitive ability and highlights that in cases of limited cognitive resource availability, some genitive function, such as activation of Persuasion Knowledge, may be inhibited; finally, Flow explains the unique emotions experienced by gamers at an optimal point of gaming experience.

## RESEARCH DIRECTIONS

The area of games and gamification offers several significant directions for future research, especially in the area of gamification and advergames. Both are relatively novel forms of marketing and therefore have little research connected to them. In the case of advergames, most research is focused on children, while little research has tried to look at the influence of advergames on adults. Further, social gaming experiences have so far received little attention, despite some social games becoming potentially significant marketing vehicles.

Similarly the area of gamification is largely unexplored and novel. Although there is some research in social marketing applications of gamification, more research in commercial settings promises interesting avenues for future research. In a different vein, as gamification uses game-like methods, but does not usually tend to involve full attention from the gamer, gamification research may further contribute to understanding how gamers are motivated to play games long term, but with low cognitive involvement at any one time (e.g. scenarios where both Flow and L4MP are unlikely to be applicable).

# RESEARCH HIGHLIGHT
## HYPERREALITY

Hyperreality is a core concept of post-modern philosophy, where a 'fake' reality becomes indistinguishable from the 'real' reality, or a situation where elements of reality and fake elements are blended in an indistinguishable way from each other.

French philosopher Jean Baudrillard introduced the term in the present-day meaning in the early 1980s (Baudrillard, 1981). He defined hyperreality, relatively strictly by the later application of the term, as 'models of a real without origin or reality'. In other words, a hyperreal image creates something with an actual meaning attached to it, although this image does not actually exist – or has never existed. For example, the image of Santa Claus has a widely acknowledged meaning and authenticity attached to the figure as representing Christmas and being the bearer of gifts, although, in reality, Santa Claus is a figment of the imagination and not a real person. However, and somewhat in contrast to the strict interpretation of the original definition, Santa Claus is loosely based on some historical figures, for example Saint Nicholas of Myra, and merged with characteristics of other fictional personas such as the Scandinavian Tomte or the British Father Christmas.

The two core strategies through which hyperreality is constructed are simulation and simulacrum. Simulacrum is something (or someone) that looks like a copy of a real existing thing or person, but has actually no original from which it is copied, i.e. it is a copy without original. Baudrillard defines a simulacrum as:

Simulation is no longer that of a territory, a referential being, or a substance. It is the generation by models of a real without origin or reality [...] It is no longer a question of imitation, nor duplication, nor even parody. It is a question of substituting the signs of the real for the real. (1981: 1–2)

*(Continued)*

Disneyland, for example, is a simulacrum, as it does not simulate any real existing place on earth. Rather, at least in its entirety, Disneyland has been designed to look realistic, and presents visitors with a version of the past that has no resemblance in factual history (see Eco, 1987 for a discussion of this). As such Disneyland has taken on an authentic meaning for visitors, although in reality it is not what it seems (i.e. it is just machines and building materials). Baudrillard and Eco have written extensively on Disneyland and the meaning it takes as a 'hyperreal world'.

A more subtle strategy to create hyperrealism is by means of simulation. In simulation, as per the definition of Baudrillard, original and 'fake' are blended to form a complete new, where the real and the fake become indistinguishable. For instance, shops and restaurants frequently blend original items (such as antiques) and fake items to create a brand space that appears to be real and authentic, although much of it is 'fake'. Take the example of Hard Rock Cafés around the world. Each branch uses real music-based memorabilia and blends these with a carefully designed interior to create the impression of a 'reality' of an American diner and music venue. Thus, you can experience a simulation of a 'real' American diner and music venue while sitting in the centre of Barcelona.

Hyperrealism has been used extensively in the wider marketing area, for example by designating certain brands as symbolising something when they are, in essence, not connected to this. For example, a luxury brand like Montblanc creates the impression of wealth and sophistication in the consumer, although, in reality, Montblanc is simply a brand of pens and accessories, and the impression of wealth is merely a simulation.

Similarly, experiential marketing techniques, including marketing of brands through events or sponsorship of events, used hyperreality tactics extensively to create brand spaces and portray desired images in the hope of creating impressions and brand associations in the mind of consumers. For example, Adidas uses the 'Predator Cup' experience as a way to promote their latest football wear to potential customers (see Wohlfeil and Whelan, 2006 for a discussion on the hyperreality created by this event). While with traditional techniques, experiential marketing is fairly limited in scope (i.e. limited by the number of participants etc.), with more advanced technology simulations and simulacrums can create ever more realistic impressions for an increasingly large audience. For example, virtual worlds, such as Second Life, can create simulations of real stories; games such as racing games can create simulations of real driving experiences. Through the use of simulacrums, customers can generate images of cars they desire, and test these cars even if the cars do not (yet) exist. For example, BMW allows customers to create their desired car, choosing a variety of different colours and options. Thus, customers are creating a hyperreal version of their future car.

In conclusion, creating hyperrealities, although not limited to virtual realities, has been substantially simplified by technological advancements. With electronic simulations, customers can start to experience products without actually possessing these products. Similarly, consumers can themselves construct hyperrealities where brands and products are created which have no equivalent or carry a different or no meaning in real life (e.g. within Second Life). Thus, the notion of hyperrealism, especially the disconnect between symbolic meaning of a product or service and actual meaning, has become more important in explaining consumption patterns in a digital world.

# CASE STUDY MCDONALD'S MONOPOLY

McDonald's Monopoly is a major annual sales promotion run by the fast food giant in several countries around the globe. It offers players the chance to win hundreds of thousands of prizes: from instant win food and drink items to large amounts of money, cars and other gadgets.

The game is played by purchasing a selected item of food from any of the participating restaurants. Each food item will come with either two or three stickers attached, hidden under a cover. One ticket will usually be a piece of property, mimicking the famous Monopoly game board, e.g. the sticker might represent a road on the original board. Once a player has collected all the properties of a specific colour, they become eligible for a win in that category.

Since 2005, in addition to the physical monopoly board, players can also play online: each pack of a food item contains an online play card in addition to the traditional piece. In 2016, McDonald's added a mobile game to the online game: players now need to scan their play cards with their mobile phone. The phone then reveals different prizes which can be stored or redeemed. The app also allows players to track all the properties collected on a virtual game board, to swipe to win prizes and to play 'chance cards' within the app. With augmented reality aspects and QR code scanning the app allows for a much more immersive game experience than the previous online games.

## Questions to Consider

1 Why do you think McDonald's offers both a real life and an online version?
2 What is the advantage of the online environment?
3 Discuss the ethical aspects of having to scan cards on snack food to enable playing.

# FURTHER READING

Buller, M.K., Kane, I.L., Dunn, A.L., Edwards, E.J., Buller, D.B. and Liu, X. (2009) 'Marketing fruit and vegetable intake with interactive games on the Internet', *Social Marketing Quarterly*, 15(sup1): 136–54.

Celtek, E. (2010) 'Mobile advergames in tourism marketing', *Journal of Vacation Marketing*, 16(4): 267–81.

Edwards, L., Swanson, M.A. and Ornelas, D. (2001) 'Health jeopardy: A game to market school health services', *The Journal of School Nursing*, 17(3): 166–9.

Zajonc, R.B. (2001) 'Mere exposure: A gateway to the subliminal', *Current Directions in Psychological Science*, 10(6): 224–8.

## REFERENCES

Bandura, A. (1977) *Social Learning Theory*. Englewood Cliffs, NJ: Prentice Hall.

Baudrillard, J. (1981) *Simulacres et Simulation*. Paris: Galilée.

Boyle, E., Connolly, T.M. and Hainey, T. (2011) 'The role of psychology in understanding the impact of computer games', *Entertainment Computing*, 2(2): 69–74.

Burns, V. (2008) Mindblizzard blog: ING and ABN flee Second Life [Online]. Available at: http://blog.mindblizzard.com/2008/02/ing-and-abn-flee-second-life.html (accessed 11 December 2013).

Chan, K., Ng, Y.L. and Williams, R.B. (2012) 'What do adolescent girls learn about gender roles from advertising images?', *Young Consumers: Insight and Ideas for Responsible Marketers*, 13(4): 357–66.

Chaney, I.M., Lin, K.-H. and Chaney, J. (2004) 'The effect of billboards within the gaming environment', *Journal of Interactive Advertising*, 5(1): 54–69.

Christiansen, P. (2012) 'Between a mod and a hard place', in E. Champion (ed.), *Game Mods*. Pittsburgh, PA: ETC Press. pp. 27–50.

Cirucci, A.M. (2013) 'First person paparazzi: Why social media should be studied more like video games', *Telematics and Informatics*, 30(1): 47–59.

Connolly, T.M., Boyle, E.A., MacArthur, E., Hainey, T. and Boyle, J.M. (2012) 'A systematic literature review of empirical evidence on computer games and serious games', *Computers & Education*, 59(2): 661–86.

Csikszentmihalyi, M. (1990) *Flow: the Psychology of Optimal Experience*, 1st edn. New York: Harper & Row.

Csikszentmihalyi, M. (1998) *Finding Flow: The Psychology of Engagement with Everyday Life*. New York: Basic Books.

Dahl, S., Eagle, L. and Baez, C. (2009) 'Analyzing advergames: Active diversions or actually deception. An exploratory study of online advergames content', *Young Consumers*, 10(1): 46–59.

Donovan, T. (2010) *Replay: The History of Video Games*. East Sussex: Yellow Ant.

Eco, U. (1987) *Travels in Hyperreality: Essays*. London: Pan Books in association with Secker & Warburg.

Graetz, J.M. (1981) 'The origin of Spacewar', *Creative Computing*, 7(8): 56–67.

Hansen, L. (2009) 'What happened to Second Life?' [Online], BBC News, 20 November. Available at: http://news.bbc.co.uk/1/hi/8367957.stm (accessed 11 December 2013).

Harris, L.D. and Wambeam, C.A. (1996) 'The Internet-based composition classroom: A study in pedagogy', *Computers and Composition*, 13(3): 353–71.

Haynes, C. and Holmevik, J.R. (2001) *High Wired: On the Design, Use, and Theory of Educational MOOs*, 2nd edn. Ann Arbor, MI: University of Michigan Press.

Howell, J. (2013) 'Whatever happened to Second Life?' [Online], BBC News, 21 June. Available at: www.bbc.co.uk/news/business-23000809 (accessed 11 December 2013).

Huotari, K. and Hamari, J. (2012) 'Defining gamification: A service marketing perspective', *Proceedings of the 16th International Academic MindTrek Conference*, Tampere, Finland, October 3–5, pp. 17–22.

Jana, R. (2006) 'Starwood Hotels explore Second Life first' [Online], *BusinessWeek*. Available at: www.businessweek.com/stories/2006-08-22/starwood-hotels-explore-second-life-first (accessed 11 December 2013).

Kahneman, D. (1973) *Attention and Effort*, Prentice-Hall Series in Experimental Psychology. Englewood Cliffs, NJ: Prentice-Hall.

Kaplan, A.M. and Haenlein, M. (2009) 'The fairyland of Second Life: Virtual social worlds and how to use them', *Business Horizons*, 52(6): 563–72.

Knobloch, S., Callison, C., Chen, L., Fritzsche, A. and Zillmann, D. (2005) 'Children's sex-stereotyped self-socialization through selective exposure to entertainment: Cross-cultural experiments in Germany, China, and the United States', *Journal of Communication*, 55(1): 122–38.

Lang, A. (2000) 'The limited capacity model of mediated message processing', *Journal of Communication*, 50(1): 46–70.

Law, S. and Braun-LaTour, K.A. (2004) 'Product placements: How to measure their impact', in J. Shrum (ed.), *The Psychology of Entertainment Media: Blurring the Lines between Entertainment and Persuasion*. Mahwah, NJ: Lawrence Erlbaum. pp. 63–78.

Lee, M. and Faber, R.J. (2007) 'Effects of product placement in on-line games on brand memory: A perspective of the limited-capacity model of attention', *Journal of Advertising*, 36(4): 75–90.

Mallinckrodt, V. and Mizerski, D. (2007) 'The effects of playing an advergame on young children's perceptions, preferences, and requests', *Journal of Advertising*, 36(2): 87–100.

Nelson, M.R., Keum, H. and Yaros, R.A. (2004) 'Advertainment or adcreep? Game players' attitudes toward advertising and product placements in computer games', *Journal of Interactive Advertising*, 5(1): 3–21.

Okazaki, S. and Yagüe, M.J. (2012) 'Responses to an advergaming campaign on a mobile social networking site: An initial research report', *Computers in Human Behavior*, 28(1): 78–86.

Panic, K., Cauberghe, V. and De Pelsmacker, P. (2013) 'Comparing TV ads and adver-games targeting children: The impact of persuasion knowledge on behavioral responses', *Journal of Advertising*, 42(2–3): 264–73.

Schneider, L.-P. and Cornwell, T.B. (2005) 'Cashing in on crashes via brand placement in computer games', *International Journal of Advertising*, 24(3): 321–43.

Shannon, C.E. (1950) 'Programming a computer for playing chess', *Philosophical Magazine*, 41(314): 256–75.

Terlutter, R. and Capella, M.L. (2013) 'The gamification of advertising: Analysis and research directions of in-game advertising, advergames, and advertising in social network games', *Journal of Advertising*, 42(2–3): 95–112.

Van Grove, J. (2010) FarmVille users plant 310 million virtual organic blueberries [Online]. Available at: http://mashable.com/2010/07/22/farmville-organic-blueberries/ (accessed 13 December 2013).

Van Grove, J. (2011) Gamification: How competition is reinventing business, marketing & everyday life [Online]. Available at: http://mashable.com/2011/07/28/gamification/ (accessed 20 January 2014).

Van Reijmersdal, E. (2009) 'Brand placement prominence: Good for memory! Bad for attitudes?', *Journal of Advertising Research*, 49(2): 151–3.

Vaughan-Nichols, S.J. (2009) 'Game-console makers battle over motion-sensitive controllers', *Computer*, 42(8): 13–15.

Waiguny, M.K., Nelson, M.R. and Terlutter, R. (2012) 'Entertainment matters! The relationship between challenge and persuasiveness of an advergame for children', *Journal of Marketing Communications*, 18(1): 69–89.

Wohlfeil, M. and Whelan, S. (2006) 'Consumer motivations to participate in event-marketing strategies', *Journal of Marketing Management*, 22(5–6): 643–69.

Xu, F., Buhalis, D. and Weber, J. (2017) 'Serious games and the gamification of tourism', *Tourism Management*, 60: 244–56.

Zajonc, R.B. (1968) 'Attitudinal effects of mere exposure', *Journal of Personality and Social Psychology*, 9(2): 1–27.

Zichermann, G. and Cunningham, C. (2011) *Gamification by Design: Implementing Game Mechanics in Web and Mobile Apps*. Sebastopol, CA: O'Reilly Media, Inc.

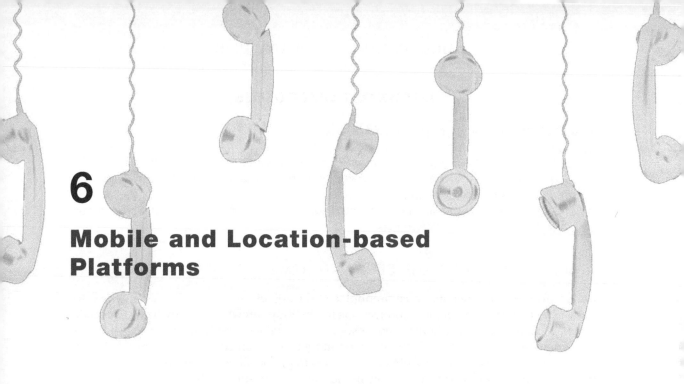

# 6

# Mobile and Location-based Platforms

## CHAPTER OVERVIEW

This chapter covers the rise of **mobile devices**, such as phones, tablets and phablets, and how **mobile social media** and **mobile marketing** make use of the opportunity for uniquely personalised and targeted communication. With their ubiquitous presence and expanding technical abilities, mobiles and tablets have started to rival computer-based social networking and are starting to equally challenge game console or computer-based gaming. Accordingly, as mobile phones and tablets are merging these functions into one, and are further complemented by location awareness and the availability of digital cameras, mobile devices offer a specific marketing and social networking context, which is further explored in this chapter.

## LEARNING OUTCOMES

On completing this chapter, you should be able to:

- understand the historical development of mobile phones and mobile computing
- reflect upon how mobile devices represent a unique marketing opportunity and how marketers can capitalise on this
- critically evaluate mobile marketing strategies, particularly in terms of the potential opportunities but also drawbacks.

## MOBILE AND LOCATION-BASED PLATFORMS

Mobile phones have become a commonplace and ubiquitous communication device for many people, enabling personal connections to anybody, anywhere, at any time. Especially in urban centres, mobile phones, and to some extent tablets and more recently **phablets,** have enabled the increase of the 'networked individual' – someone who is constantly connected, maintaining and establishing connections to people far away just as conveniently as instituting new connections with people in their immediate surroundings. Such connections can be known people in existing social networks or hereto unknown people, for example in the case of smart mobs (Rheingold, 2003) and people meeting through other forms of location-based social networking, like Gowalla, now part of Facebook, or Foursquare.

Connected to mobile devices, both mobile marketing and mobile social networking have become important features of contemporary marketing communications.

However, as mobile devices on the one hand offer the opportunity for uniquely personal, timely and location-sensitive communication, they also have the ability to cause irritation and annoyance. Consequently, while marketing on mobile phones is growing exponentially, it requires careful consideration on behalf of the marketer as to what consumers will and will not find acceptable.

To explore this area, this chapter first looks at the definitions of mobile marketing and mobile social media, followed by a discussion of how these platforms have evolved historically. From there, the theoretical foundations supporting the growth of mobile activities are examined, and how future research can explore this dynamic area further.

Given the complexity, diversity and flexibility of mobile devices, they offer a wide range of possibilities for marketers to interact with consumers, just as conveniently as for consumers to interact with other consumers. From simple advertising in applications or mobile advergames with social networking facilities to fully developed, mobile social networking platforms that leverage user-generated content as a means to market products and services to other users, the possibilities to engage with consumers on mobile devices are manifold and diverse. Within the mobile device area many applications are themselves branded or offer branded communication as content, consequently, the boundaries between commercial and non-commercial communication are widely blurred, possibly more so than on any other communication device.

Kaplan (2012) suggested a series of definitions to differentiate the two main buzzwords (mobile marketing and mobile social media) connected to mobile device-based marketing activity, both firm-generated and user-generated. According to his series of definitions, mobile marketing is 'any marketing activity conducted through a ubiquitous network to which consumers are constantly connected using a personal mobile device' (Kaplan, 2012: 130), that is, mobile marketing encapsulates branded applications or in-application advertising. Mobile marketing interlinks with mobile social media, which Kaplan defines based on his earlier definition of social media (Kaplan and Haenlein, 2010). Mobile social media is therefore defined as 'a group of mobile marketing applications that allow the creation and exchange of user-generated content'. It is important to note that Kaplan uses the term 'mobile marketing applications'. At first this seems unnecessarily restrictive, as some applications may not appear to have a primary marketing function. Rather, these applications appear as social media applications, which may incorporate obliquely marketing activity. For example, Facebook, either the mobile or desktop version, is not perceived by most of its users as first and foremost a marketing-focused application. The main focus of Facebook's activity could, however, be seen as primarily providing content that surrounds core marketing activity, such as suggested pages or sponsored updates. Particularly given the Facebook display logarithm discussed in Chapter 4, ensuring that all followers of a page see posted updates requires additional advertising spend, which in turn is the main source of income generation for Facebook. Similarly, OpenTable or Foursquare may at first appear to be primarily social media applications as they allow rating and finding of nearby restaurants or, in the case of Foursquare, also other places. However, in terms of marketing, they provide a potentially engaging platform where special deals and offers can be communicated to nearby users matching a certain profile, and they are therefore equally a marketing communication channel while at the same time serving as a social media platform. Moreover, both applications encourage users to generate content, such as reviews, and to exchange this content with other users in the vicinity.

The increase of mobile social networking has significantly impacted the presentation of Web 2.0 philosophy in everyday life. Whereas in the original definitions little thought was devoted to constant and on-going communication and participation, mobile social networking enables instantaneous user participation, perpetual folksonomy and geo-tagging on a previously unprecedented scale (Jaokar and Fish, 2006). With the use of an ordinary **smart phone**, mobile users can collectively rate and recommend places, tap into collectively generated knowledge, simultaneously connecting to each other, or staying connected irrespective of location.

To put this into perspective, it is useful to briefly review the historical developments of the various parts that have started to merge into current mobile devices: mobile phones and mobile computing.

## THINKBOX MOBILE SOCIAL MEDIA

Take a look at your smart phone or tablet. Find the various communication opportunities marketers currently have to communicate with you, or other sources of brand-specific communication. Remember to identify both user-generated as well as company-generated communication!

## The Development of the Mobile Phone

Mobile phones were first developed in the early 1970s, although it wasn't until the 1980s that they became commercially available. Originally, these phones could only be used to make and receive calls. In 1984 the possibility of sending and receiving short messages **(SMS)** was added to the **GSM** mobile phone communication standard, used in most countries. However, as the original GSM standards did not envisage much use of the SMS service, mobile phone providers therefore focused largely on providing voice communication, and no providers originally implemented text-based services. In line with this, with hindsight, flawed perception, it was not until 1992 when engineers working for the British Vodafone network started to experiment with SMS services by sending the very first text message (Shannon, 2007), leading to the first networks introducing text services a year later. Yet, many handsets originally were not equipped to send messages; rather they could only receive them. Despite this initial limitation, widespread adoption of the new service came in the following years. Consumers started to embrace the new technology, and SMS volume peaked in 2010 with around 6.1 trillion SMSs being sent. Since then alternative forms of text messaging, such as BBM, iMessage or WhatsApp, using the networks' data systems to transmit and receive text and multimedia messages, have challenged the comparatively costly SMS, although providing a very similar service as the original SMS.

Early mobile phones were equipped with only small displays and no phone company offered data services at anything near affordable rates. Consequently, mobile usage was generally limited to phone-based functions such as voice, and later SMS. However, with widespread adoption of mobile phones, marketers and entrepreneurs started to take advantage of the new channel to **reach** consumers. However, because of the technical limitations, early mobile phone commerce needed to avoid data communication, and rather focused on extending the mobile phone abilities. For example, the first commercially successful activity related to mobile phones was the selling of ringtones, and similar to ringtones, games also started to become available in the 1990s, although many of the early games were simple in design, taking account of the limited display abilities and processor power of early mobile phones. Both ringtones and games needed to be downloaded to Internet computers first before being installed on mobiles, as early data services made it slow to download significant amounts of data. Other services that were largely text based drove mobile commerce in the late 1990s, following the introduction of text-based services. Typical examples included jokes and news headlines delivered via SMS, which emerged in the late 1990s. These premium-rate SMS subscriptions enjoyed a brief phase of commercial success. With the introduction of **3G** mobiles, around the turn of the millennium, more data bandwidth became available and reasonably affordable. Therefore, other, richer media types, such as videos and more elaborate games, started to take advantage of the data capabilities. In line with UGT (see Chapter 4), these services quickly replaced the more cumbersome and expensive text services and ringtone and game offerings from the late 1990s.

However, even before 3G phones became available, there were several largely unsuccessful attempts during the 1990s to bring Internet connectivity to mobile phones, though all of these ultimately struggled to cope with the limited bandwidth. For instance, several companies offered premium web-to-SMS or email-to-SMS services. If an email was received, the email was then sent via SMS. Similarly, web pages could be requested to be sent using SMS. In the end, these services were severely limited because of the 160-character limit of SMS services and the text-only features.

Phone manufacturers and telephone companies did, however, work hard to make data services available. And in 1997, the way mobile data was transmitted and displayed started to be standardised across different mobile standards under the Wireless Application Protocol (WAP). Originally, **WAP** specifications involved content made available to users via a **push service**, combining the limited data and SMS – and based on its own proprietary mark-up language, which was different from general HTML used for websites. Consequently, the content available was greatly limited and dependent upon gateways that could rewrite websites into WAP accessible sites. This solution had the advantage that it was saving significant bandwidth because it didn't transmit most of the full-scale pictures or other media embedded in a web page. Rather, the service sent a scaled down version of whatever the user requested. However, coupled with the still high data charges and reasonably poor technical performance, the original WAP content was not successful commercially.

In 2002, the WAP standard was updated to version 2.0. However, the standard still remained largely underused, and certainly did not meet original expectations in terms of adoption and usage. Despite much hype around the potential for mobile commerce, much of the early WAP-based designs were heavily criticised for their poor usability, including the hasty application of web-based ideas (Ramsay and Nielsen, 2000), with too little attention being paid to the mobile environment in which the customer was using the site and the technical limitations of devices. Moreover, with increasingly available data bandwidth making the restriction on data-saving websites unnecessary, and following the introduction of devices capable of displaying most standard websites routinely, WAP began a rapid decline in the latter half of the 2000s.

Despite the technical limitations of the early mobile phones, mobile phones have become ubiquitous and highly personal devices and are used routinely beyond their original function as a voice communication device. As many mobile devices have started to take over functions originally performed by other devices, such as personal digital assistants and portable game consoles, they have significantly expanded their original functionality. For all intents and purposes, the usage of mobile phones for the original 'telephone' service is now only a fraction of actual usage, as users are increasingly using other services, such as data services and messaging functions.

## Mobile Computing

Concurrently with the development of mobile phones, the idea of mobile computers gained importance and widespread acceptance as the logical development of desktop-based systems. Originally, mobile computers were not networked devices, although increasingly, and mirroring the technological developments of mobile phones, mobile computing platforms became capable of being used as web-browsers and incorporated other functions, such as mobile gaming. The idea of mobile computing has been around since the early days of computers, however, technical limitations made the realisation of this vision a challenging task.

This early focus on multifunctional mobile devices can be gauged by their omnipresence in science fiction from the 1960s onwards. From the early 1960s *Star Trek* series to the 1968 film *2001: A Space Odyssey*, many science fiction portrayals included mobile computing devices, which incorporated personal digital assistant functions with other functions such as communication capabilities.

However, real world progress was slower. Around seven years after IBM pioneered the first 'laptop' computer in 1975, handheld, portable computing in the form of early personal digital assistants (**PDAs**) began when Psion launched a handheld computer device in 1984. The Psion II, though pioneering in terms of its vision, had a rather humble exterior, resembling a large handheld calculator. A further milestone in the development of mobile devices came in 1993 when Apple launched the Newton. At the time, the Newton was a ground-breaking device, often credited as the first implementation of tablet-style computing. Equipped with a large screen, similar to today's tablets, rather than relying on a keyboard, the Newton relied on a touch screen and handwriting recognition for input. And although development of the device was abandoned in 1998, the Newton was the first popular 'touch screen computer', a technology omnipresent in smart phones and tablets today. The Newton, although relatively short lived, attracted a cult-like following, which later on was used as the foundation for one of the most influential studies investigating online consumer groups (e.g. Muniz and Schau, 2005, who investigated the Newton brand community).

Many other manufacturers tried to launch, largely unsuccessfully, mobile tablet-like computers after Apple abandoned the Newton platform. The most successful company in the field was undoubtedly Palm Computing, which originally marketed their devices as personal digital assistants. Palm's first device, Zoomer, released in 1993, failed commercially. Nevertheless, later devices such as the Palm Pilot Series, released in 1996, enjoyed commercial success as digital diaries and note-taking devices, although they also incorporated limited gaming capabilities. Later devices additionally introduced support for Wifi and mobile data networks. Other manufacturers, such as Microsoft's PocketPC 2000 and Microsoft TabletPC, however, remained technically ambitious but commercially largely unsuccessful, attracting not more than a niche following.

It was not until 2010 through the introduction of the iPad **tablet computer**, based on the extant iOS operating system used in the iPhone, that mobile computing started to re-attract the attention of a mainstream audience. Significant developments in the availability and accessibility of mobile data networks, either via Wifi or 3G, and advancements in display technology and processor power, made these later devices more useful and user-friendly than original mobile computing devices. With other operating systems following suit, these tablet computers quickly gained a loyal following as a combined web-browsing, media viewing and gaming platform. With the introduction of smaller versions of tablet computers, in the form of phablets, tablet computers themselves are now starting to merge with smart phones as a unified device for all types of communications.

## Smart Phones

The idea of smart phones emerged, similar to the previously mentioned mobile computing devices, in the late 1960s as universal communicators. Yet, the first multifunction mobile phones were not developed until the 1990s, when advances in computing technology made it possible to combine personal digital assistants and mobile phones. However, by today's standards, these early devices were still relatively underdeveloped, with low resolution displays, often lacking cameras and lacking significant data options beyond simple WAP-based browsing.

The actual term 'smart phone' was first used in the marketing of the 1999 Ericsson R380, a device that combined personal digital assistant, similar to the Palm devices in circulation at the time, and telephone capabilities, including a touch-sensitive screen. It was considered revolutionary, as it managed to combine two functions while basically retaining the shape and weight of a traditional mobile phone.

Arguably the first mainstream major smart phones were later Blackberry models. The first model by the Canadian manufacturer RIM was launched in 1999. The original Blackberry 850 was, however, not a phone at all, but rather a pager-like device on which text-based emails could be displayed and answered. Palm, originally a dedicated personal digital assistant manufacturer, entered the market for smart phones with its Treo line in 2002. Palm remained largely unsuccessful, and when Blackberry entered the market in 2003 with their own device combining data and messaging services together with digital assistant functions, Palm's devices started to lose market share. Blackberry, not least through focused marketing, quickly developed the position of a status object amongst urban professionals.

Early smart phones, such as Palm's Treo and later Blackberry devices, were largely focused on a business market. Thus, they lacked entertainment applications beyond very basic games, focusing instead on email and messaging. This lack of focus on entertainment became the original niche for Apple, which entered the personal smart phone market when it launched iOS as a mobile operating platform for its range of iPhones in 2007. Apple positioned the iPhone from the start more as a phone with included entertainment and gaming devices, thus targeting the private user market. A year later using Google's operating system, Android-based phones become commercially available in 2008, competing directly in terms of functionality and market position with Apple's iOS devices. Windows Phone launched with significant delay in 2010, and to date remains a small player in the smart phone market.

Although the term 'smart phone' remains somewhat ambiguous, contemporary smart phones are best characterised as a combination of mobile computer, multimedia device and mobile phone, challenging in some aspects conventional desktop computing. For example, smart phones can be used to watch television streamed via mobile networks, as multiplayer game consoles and as eBook readers with integrated social networking functions.

Smart phones are rapidly replacing older technology, and have overtaken conventional mobile phones in most markets. In some countries more than two thirds of the population use smart phones, with the user base continually growing. For example, in 2013, 73% of the population in the United Arab Emirates relied on smart phones, 67% in Norway, 64% in Australia, 62% in the UK and 56% in the US and Canada (Fox, 2013). Converging smart phone and tablet technology, phablets are currently gaining increasing market share, combining the usability of a smaller tablet computer with the mobile networking capabilities of smart phones.

## Location-based and Other Enhanced Services

**Locative media** or location-based social media and mobile marketing require **GPS** or GSM-location functionality of the phone to 'locate' the user. This technology became widely available in both tablet computers and smart phones largely as a result of the introduction of 'Enhanced 911' services required by the US Federal Communications Commission. Enhanced 911 necessitates mobile phones to be located within a relatively small distance to enable emergency services to locate users who may be unable to identify their location. However, the location-awareness of mobile devices was quickly adopted for other uses, including the location-specific delivery of marketing communications and location-based social networking.

The first commercially available mobile platform using location-based services was the Palm VII mobile personal digital assistant, launched in 1999. Originally the functionality was restricted to retrieving local weather and traffic reports, and extremely costly, costing more than US$300 per MB (Kaplan, 2012).

Enhancing mobile Internet-based data with geographical data enables the blurring of the physical and the virtual world: the physical experience in the real world can be 'augmented' by location specific information. Such information can range in terms of information complexity. Relatively simple information involves guiding mobile users to the nearest branch of a coffee shop, for example through branded applications. Other uses allow suggestions of special offers from retailers in the vicinity to be displayed, as can be found on the location aware social networking application Foursquare. A further use is the more complex adoption of combining geo-enhanced information with other data sources, as in the case of so-called augmented reality applications. **Augmented reality** applications synthesise location-specific information together with supplementary information from other sources. For example, the Museum of London smart phone app allows users to view historical photographs of streets and read about historic events relevant to the current location (see Image 6.1).

**Image 6.1**   Augmented Reality Application, © Museum of London

Likewise, location-specific information can be used to create and communicate specific offers. For instance, a sales promotion can be made available to users in the vicinity of a restaurant or shop. Furthermore, such promotions can be time-specific, allowing flash promotions at certain times of the day to users who are nearby. Such a combination of location and time-specific marketing activities can be divided, according to Kaplan, into four distinct categories (see Table 6.1).

Combined with the availability of high-speed Internet capabilities, for example 3G, **4G** and Wifi, constant access to data networks enables individuals to capture, create and upload and share content at any time. Combining this ability with location-based services, such content can moreover be geo-referenced, and made available within existing social networks of non-present friends, for example by sharing a location with friends in the case of 'check ins' and also allowing for messages to be virtually 'deposited' for later visitors to a place. For example, review applications on smart phones, such as Qype, Yelp or Foursquare, allow users to leave tips for other people checking into a place.

**Table 6.1**   Mobile promotions

|  |  | Location-sensitive | |
|---|---|---|---|
|  |  | **No** | **Yes** |
| **Time-sensitive** | **Yes** | *Quick-timers* Twitter or other status applications, irrelevant of the location | *Space-timers* Foursquare or Gowalla where messages are space and time relevant (e.g. current location of friends) |
|  | **No** | *Slow-timers* Reading or consuming user-generated content such as YouTube or Wikipedia | *Space-locators* Location-specific messages relevant to other visitors (and not necessarily friends), such as reviews (Qype) |

*Source*: Kaplan, 2012

Although location-based social networking and marketing have made significant advancements in recent years, much of the location-specific information allows users to be located only within a distance of roughly around 50 metres. Thus users cannot be located with immediate certainty, for example if they are directly in front of a shop or display – or some metres away. However, technology such as **iBeacon**, introduced by Apple in late 2013, enhances GPS location specifically inside buildings, where GPS accuracy is comparatively low, to within a few centimetres. Envisaged future applications of the technology include providing customers with relevant information about products nearby, based on the location of their device. For example, users can be alerted when they are within a metre of their favourite products. Similarly, the technology also enables payments to be made via the phone without removing the phone or wallet containing credit cards, by sensing the closeness of the device.

**Image 6.2**   QR code for http://stephan.dahl.at/

Taking advantage of the camera inclusion in smart phones, **QR codes** have also gained attention as a feasible medium for marketers. Originally developed for manufacturers as a way to track parts during a production process, QR codes have become regularly featured in magazine advertisements and on billboards as a quick and convenient way to communicate website addresses. More imaginative use has allowed the QR codes to be used as 'virtual keys' to unlock specific content. Advertisers, for instance, can use QR codes on packages or on advertising to allow customers access to specific parts of a website with additional material.

While QR codes are mostly print or display based, the ability to 'listen' through the microphone of smart phones has also been used to create additional options for more engaging and interactive marketing. Based on technology originally developed by music-recognition software Shazam, marketers can now 'enhance' their television or cinema advertising. In these cases, the technology recognises the music or sounds used in the adverts, and similar to QR codes directs the user to a specifically designed part of a website.

Based on current technologies, Kaplan (2012) suggests a classification of mobile marketing activities based on two variables. Firstly the amount of consumer knowledge and secondly the initiator of the communication.

Based on this classification, mobile marketing activities can be classified as falling into one of four categories, with the recipients described as either 'victims', 'patrons', 'strangers' or 'groupies'. In the first two categories the company has a relatively high amount of knowledge about the recipients, for example based on the individual data connected to the mobile number. Thus companies can send marketing messages without consent,

**Table 6.2**   Mobile marketing activities

| | | Initiator of communication | |
| | | Company | Consumer |
|---|---|---|---|
| **Consumer knowledge** | High | *Victims* <br> SMS-based marketing campaigns other than opted-in | *Patrons* <br> Subscription-based services or opt-in messages |
| | Low | *Strangers* <br> Condensed episode of a TV series and/or exclusively produced to be viewed on mobiles (mobisodes) | *Groupies* <br> Exclusively QR code accessed content |

*Source*: Kaplan, 2012

therefore making the recipient effectively the 'victim' of the communication. Alternatively, consumers may opt into receiving specific communication, such as offers, i.e. acting as 'patrons' of the company.

For communication in the consumer-initiated, low consumer-knowledge quadrant, companies can make, for example, exclusive content available after a user has scanned a QR code. However, the company has ultimately no control over or knowledge of who scans the codes and accesses the information. Similarly, where a company inserts commercials into 'produced for mobile' episodes of television shows (or mobile exclusives), the advertising company has no knowledge over who is ultimately watching the commercials, i.e. the audience, similar to traditional advertising.

## Theoretical Considerations

Much of the research into mobile marketing remains nascent and scattered across various disciplines, with the research focusing on the adoption of various aspects of mobile technology. In this respect, the theoretical foundations of the research do not differ significantly from that of other technology adoption research. Consequently, theoretical models such as the Uses and Gratifications Theory, the Technology Adoption Model, or derivatives of these, including the Theory of Reasoned Action/Theory of Planned Behaviour, constitute the theoretical foundations of such research.

There is some suggestion that, broadly speaking, mobile device use is driven by similar motivating factors as general computer-based devices, with usefulness and ease of use being specifically important. For instance, Pagani (2004) showed through a series of focus group interviews, that third generation mobile device adoption was driven mostly by usefulness and ease of use, followed by price and speed considerations. These findings were largely similar to findings during the early stages of the popular growth of the Internet in the mid-1990s, and therefore show the similarity, as far as technological acceptance is concerned, and the ability of extant theoretical models to explain adoption.

However, for specific usage, Venkatesh and colleagues (2003) suggested in early research that there may be subtle differences between devices. Comparing motivators for visiting traditional websites and mobile device-based websites, the researchers found that content, in the form of relevant information and transactional abilities, ease of use and personalisation abilities were found to be relatively more important for mobile devices in relation to traditional websites. Conversely, for traditional websites, affective reactions towards the site, for example the 'feel' and design of the site, and promotion/advertising of the site were judged more important than for mobile device-viewed services. As Venkatesh et al. point out, some of these differences may be explained by mobile device display limitations, and as such may become less significant with more advanced technology.

A well-researched and controversial issue remains the attitude towards marketing on mobile phones. Early surveys trying to establish if mobile marketing represents a viable option for future marketing development showed remarkably high response rates. The American Direct Marketing Association in a survey conducted in 2008 showed that 70% of teenage and young adult mobile phone users responded to SMS messages. However, this response may come at a significant cost, as Shankar and Hollinger (2007) warned, much of mobile advertising is seen as intrusive, and may, therefore damage brand perception in the long term – even if customers respond initially. Similarly, in a 2012 survey of British mobile social media users, 62% reported that any brand interaction on mobile social media is perceived as intrusive, while only 23% said they liked to interact with a brand using mobile social media platforms such as Twitter (Bennett, 2012).

It is generally assumed that marketing communication that is perceived by the receivers as relevant is found to be useful, and indeed, has been found to be so in the context of mobile advertising (Chowdhury et al., 2010), although the question of frequency and novelty remains largely unexplored. Liu and colleagues (2012) have emphasised that a perception of information and entertainment and a high overall credibility of received mobile advertising are key factors predicting a positive response in a cross-cultural study of attitudes towards mobile advertising. However, they have also found that irritation is frequently occurring. The relative novelty of the medium, at least for now, is almost certainly a relative limitation of such findings. A consumer may find mobile or location-based commercial messages attractive when they occur only relatively infrequently – particularly so if these messages are novel or entertaining. However, if such messages, as for example in the case of iBeacon, amount to several messages in a short span of time, irritation is likely to result. This would, at least theoretically, explain Liu et al.'s finding of higher irritation rates in Japan than Austria. Mobile marketing has a longer history in Japan and is used more frequently. Consequently, mobile advertising may therefore be more novel for Austrian consumers, and curiosity could mask irritation.

As Shankar and Balasubramanian (2009) point out, mobile, personal, and specifically location-based advertising may be most suitable for messages designed to tap into the peripheral route to persuasion in relation to the Elaboration Likelihood Model (Petty and Cacioppo, 1986), previously discussed in Chapter 3. This highlights a potential difficulty of current technology, particularly as mobile advertising is based on alerts and notifications. These are likely to trigger central processing through engaging the consumer with the displayed message. On the one side these alerts are likely to have only minimal information requiring further, conscious action by the consumer to find out more if the individual is interested, which ELM would suggest is acceptable if the user is willing to elaborate on the message. On the other hand, in the case of the consumer not being interested, alerts require active dismissal. Subsequently, such alerts are likely to trigger persuasion knowledge and coping mechanisms (see Chapter 7). This, in turn, may inhibit the effectiveness of the communication or can lead to annoyance and a feeling of intrusiveness.

Unfortunately, due to the relative novelty of these marketing tools, specifically indoor-location-based services, such as those envisaged by iBeacon and similar services, there is, as yet, no data available as to how consumers will react to such notifications. However, from a theory-based perspective, current enthusiasm for these services may be exaggerated, as the likely feeling of intrusion would have to be counterbalanced by a perception of significant benefits. From a theoretical perspective, location-based advertisements that tap into the peripheral route of processing are likely to be more effective in the long run, though there is currently no technology or vision as to how this could be implemented. More subtle ways, such as tying marketing messages to social media-based messages, may be a way forward to avoid customer backlash, as in the case of creative use of location-aware services like Foursquare (see the research highlight and case study later in this chapter). However, these types of covert marketing messages may still pose significant ethical and perceptual problems.

Reacting to these potentials for irritation, a more subtle approach to mobile social media marketing is frequently advocated, for example in the four Is proposed by Kaplan (2012). The suggested four Is are:

1. *Individualisation* of messages so that they are taking user preferences and interests into account.
2. *Involving* the consumer through an on-going, engaging conversation.
3. *Integration* of marketing communication activities in the users' life in order to avoid irritation.
4. *Initiation* of user-generated content.

## THINKBOX IRRITATION VS. USEFULNESS

Make a list of which commercial messages you would find useful, and at what point would you find them intrusive or irritating. Classify your list using the Uses and Gratifications Theory. Explore how you would balance irritation with potential rewards.

## SUMMARY

This chapter has described the historical development of mobile devices and highlighted potential current applications of mobile technology for both marketing and social media usage. The converging technology, together with expanding technological possibilities, make mobile device-based social networking and marketing the potentially most significant growth area in the future. Particularly with the introduction of further data capabilities and further technical advancements, some futurists are already suggesting that the traditional PC (and games consoles) will soon be abandoned in favour of tablets, phablets, smart phones and ever more 'wearable' technology (Sabhlok, 2013). An early indication of this may be the mooted 'Internet of Things' (see Chapter 13). However, as this chapter discusses briefly, with more technical possibilities also come increasing challenges and ethical problems: from attitudes towards mobile marketing, irritation and potential consumer backlash to privacy and ethical concerns, which are further discussed in Chapter 12.

# RESEARCH DIRECTIONS

As this chapter has pointed out, mobile technology adoption and usage tend to be well researched and readily explainable with current theoretical frameworks. However, the novel aspects of marketing communications and social networking via mobile devices still remain largely under-researched. Potential future research directions include focusing on the life-span of these novel applications, for example by exploring specifically how does usage and attitude change over time? How can customer irritation be avoided? What concerns do users have, and what are the possible responses? Qualitative, quantitative and above all longitudinal research in this area, if conceptualised and made more widely applicable through the development of theories, can further guide future developments and research.

# RESEARCH HIGHLIGHT MOBILE GAMIFICATION

## 'Turning Life into a Game: Foursquare, Gamification, and Personal Mobility'

In his article, Frith (2013) describes how location-based mobile games impact on an individual's experience of the surrounding space, using the 'gamified' social networking app Foursquare as an example.

Foursquare merges social networking with location-based gaming: it has classic social networking capabilities, such as sharing of status messages amongst friends, and it also incorporates location-gaming aspects. These location-gaming aspects 'gamify' the experience of checking into locations, by, for example, rewarding check-ins with points or awarding 'mayorship' status of certain locations that individuals check into frequently.

The article analyses, through qualitative research based on 36 interviews conducted in the USA with frequent Foursquare users, how the engagement with the application changed the users' perception of the space around them, but also, to what extent and under which circumstances Foursquare-derived information was taken into account when making decisions about movement, i.e. did Foursquare users react to location suggestions and information about locations surrounding them.

The conceptual framework of the article is based on the notion of 'hybrid spaces', grounded on the work of de Souza e Silva (2006). As de Souza e Silva writes, hybrid spaces are spaces where social connections, digital information and physical spaces merge into a uniform whole. In hybrid spaces, individuals receive information which is both location- and person-specific, as in the case of Foursquare, where the application shows spaces around the individual, spaces where friends of the individual user have been and spaces the application suggests based on past spaces the user has checked in.

Key findings from the research show the effectiveness of gamification elements of the application. For example, Frith shows how users get competitive in order to obtain and retain mayorships of desirable places. Equally, some users are employing dubious means to obtain such rewards, for example, by checking in while being close by in order to accumulate the required check-ins to achieve mayorship status. Similarly, the application encourages users to seek out new places, for example when visiting a different city, and the opportunity to obtain 'badges' as a reward.

While the research itself does not talk about marketing opportunities connected to Foursquare, it nevertheless is an engaging insight into how Foursquare users are making decisions, and how these decisions are influenced through gaming elements (see also Chapter 5 on gamification). Marketers can learn directly from these insights, and use these tools to develop engaging platforms with low persuasion knowledge and where gamers can balance rewards vs. privacy.

The full article is available on the companion website of this book.

# CASE STUDY ABSOLUT UNIQUE ACCESS

WhatsApp is one of the most popular chat apps on mobiles around the world. Focused on one-to-one messaging with only limited group chat facilities, it is also a platform that has been traditionally very resistant to being used as a marketing tool. However, when the vodka brand Absolut launched a limited edition 'Unique' vodka in Argentina, WhatsApp became the central tool of the launch campaign.

Absolut vodka has long been associated with parties and nightlife, however, traditionally the brand has never 'spoken' directly to its customers. It changed this when it launched a new edition of vodka, and decided to celebrate the launch with one of the most exclusive parties ever held in Argentina. In fact, the party was so exclusive, that only two lucky winners were given tickets to attend.

In order to give away the tickets to the most suitable winners, Absolut created a fake doorman: Sven. Sven had a Facebook profile and, importantly, a WhatsApp number. Anyone who wanted to win one of the two tickets to the event had to convince Sven to let them in. By any means possible or imaginable.

*(Continued)*

The result? More than 600 hopefuls contacted Sven and started to chat with him. In order to convince Sven, many users sent pictures, created their own art works, started to sing, dance and some even made indecent proposals to Sven. Over 1,000 different images, videos and messages were sent over a period of three days before Sven made the final decision about whom he would allow to enter.

## Questions to Consider

1 Why would people contact Sven the doorman?
2 What is the likely effect of the campaign on the brand?
3 WhatsApp messages were one to one: how can the brand leverage this communication? What would be the ethical aspects of this?

# FURTHER READING

Hennig-Thurau, T., Malthouse, E.C., Friege, C., Gensler, S., Lobschat, L., Rangaswamy, A. and Skiera, B. (2010) 'The impact of new media on customer relationships', *Journal of Service Research*, 13(3): 311–30.

Schmitz Weiss, A. (2013) 'Exploring news apps and location-based services on the smartphone', *Journalism & Mass Communication Quarterly*, 90(3): 435–56.

Wood, D.M. and Ball, K. (2013) 'Brandscapes of control? Surveillance, marketing and the co-construction of subjectivity and space in neo-liberal capitalism', *Marketing Theory*, 13(1): 47–67.

## REFERENCES

Bennett, S. (2012) 62% of mobile users don't want social marketing messages from brands [Study] [Online]. Available at: www.mediabistro.com/alltwitter/mobile-social-marketing_b22903 (accessed 22 January 2014).

Chowdhury, H.K., Parvin, N., Weitenberner, C. and Becker, M. (2010) 'Consumer attitude toward mobile advertising in an emerging market: An empirical study', *Marketing*, 12: 206–16.

De Souza e Silva, A. (2006) 'From cyber to hybrid mobile technologies as interfaces of hybrid spaces', *Space and Culture*, 9: 261–78.

Fox, Z. (2013) The 15 countries with the highest smartphone penetration [Online]. Available at: http://mashable.com/2013/08/27/global-smartphone-penetration/ (accessed 22 January 2014).

Frith, J. (2013) 'Turning life into a game: Foursquare, gamification, and personal mobility', *Mobile Media & Communication*, 1(2): 248–62.

Jaokar, A. and Fish, T. (2006) *Mobile Web 2.0: The Innovator's Guide to Developing and Marketing Next Generation Mobile Apps.* London: Futuretext.

Kaplan, A.M. (2012) 'If you love something, let it go mobile: Mobile marketing and mobile social media 4x4', *Business Horizons*, 55: 129–39.

Kaplan, A.M. and Haenlein, M. (2010) 'Users of the world, unite! The challenges and opportunities of social media', *Business Horizons*, 53: 59–68.

Liu, C.-L., Sinkovics, R.R., Pezderka, N. and Haghirian, P. (2012) 'Determinants of consumer perceptions toward mobile advertising: A comparison between Japan and Austria', *Journal of Interactive Marketing*, 26: 21–32.

Muniz Jr, A.M. and Schau, H.J. (2005) 'Religiosity in the abandoned Apple Newton brand community', *Journal of Consumer Research*, 31: 737–47.

Pagani, M. (2004) 'Determinants of adoption of third generation mobile multimedia services', *Journal of Interactive Marketing*, 18: 46–59.

Petty, R.E. and Cacioppo, J.E. (1986) *Communication and Persuasion: Central and Peripheral Routes to Attitude Change.* New York: Springer.

Ramsay, M. and Nielsen, J. (2000) *WAP Usability, Déjà Vu: 1994 All Over Again.* Fremont, CA: Nielsen Norman Group.

Rheingold, H. (2003) *Smart Mobs: The Next Social Revolution.* Cambridge, MA: Basic Books.

Sabhlok, R. (2013) Death of the PC: Time to kiss your computer goodbye? [Online]. Available at: www.forbes.com/sites/rajsabhlok/2013/08/13/death-of-the-pc-time-to-kiss-your-computer-goodbye/ (accessed 23 January 2014).

Shankar, V. and Hollinger, M. (2007) 'Online and mobile advertising: Current scenario, emerging trends, and future directions', Marketing Science Institute, Special Report, 07–206.

Shankar, V. and Balasubramanian, S. (2009) 'Mobile marketing: A synthesis and prognosis', *Journal of Interactive Marketing*, 23: 118–29.

Shannon, V. (2007) '15 years of text messages, a "cultural phenomenon"' [Online], *New York Times*. Available at: www.nytimes.com/2007/12/05/technology/05iht-sms.4.8603150.html?pagewanted=all&_r=0 (accessed 23 January 2014).

Venkatesh, V., Ramesh, V. and Massey, A.P. (2003) 'Understanding usability in mobile commerce', *Communications of the ACM*, 46: 53–6.

# PART 3

## Understanding Content in Social Media Marketing

This third part of the book focuses on the content of marketing-relevant messages in the social media sphere.

Each of the chapters examines a different aspect of message content, starting by exploring why social media messages are perceived as persuasive, and which factors influence persuasiveness. The first part of Chapter 7 looks at persuasiveness from the perspective of the receiver of persuasive messages, exploring the processes that produce persuasion. The second part of the chapter then complements the first part by examining how marketers can generate more persuasive messages, for instance using models such as the Functional Triad and the 7S framework, and which factors increase persuasiveness of the various messages that are circulating on the multitude of social media sites and applications.

The next chapter in this section addresses the much hyped concept of **engagement**, and critically examines the meaning and role of this often believed gauge of behavioural intention. Chapter 8 considers the potential problems arising from the currently very broad definition of 'engagement' being used by practitioners, and discusses the role of interim measures of social media effectiveness, trying to close the **attitude–behaviour gap**.

Finally, the third chapter in this section addresses the most influential type of messages: messages related to brands, products or services, created by and shared amongst seemingly non-commercial individuals – or **word of mouth (WOM)**. WOM remains the most persuasive type of marketing-relevant message. However, while WOM is by no means new, social media sites have greatly enhanced the reach and spread of WOM messages. Chapter 9 therefore examines different types of WOM, some of which emerged as a result of social media functionality, such as location-based social networking, and further considers how WOM can be encouraged and which aspects influence perceived WOM credibility.

# 7

# Persuasiveness

## CHAPTER OVERVIEW

This chapter explores concepts of social media persuasiveness by considering various interlinked theories used to explain the sometimes intensified persuasion attributed to social media messages, particularly in the case of user-generated or celebrity-endorsed messages, but also occasionally in the case of organisation-generated messages.

## LEARNING OUTCOMES

On completing this chapter, you should be able to:

- understand how individuals process persuasive messages and potential reactions towards these messages
- critically discuss the role of coping mechanisms
- explain the role of technology as a mediating factor to enhance persuasiveness
- appreciate some of the psychological processes underlying the heightened credibility of user-generated and celebrity-generated messages.

## SOCIAL MEDIA PERSUASIVENESS

While previous chapters have hinted at the processes involved in persuading in the context of social media, this chapter examines this process from different angles. The first part of this chapter looks at three interconnected theories of persuasion processing, that is, persuasion from the perspective of the receiver. Both the Elaboration Likelihood Model (ELM) and the **Heuristic–Systematic Model (HSM)** explain what happens when an individual is confronted with a 'persuasion attempt', such as a sales proposition or a brand-originated message. The third model, the **Integrated Model of Persuasion**, integrates aspects of both theories into a coherent whole. While both ELM and HSM were developed in the 1980s, and therefore before the rise of social media, they are still, nevertheless, applicable when trying to understand what happens to individuals when they evaluate received persuasive messages, for example in the case of a sponsored tweet, a picture posted by a brand they follow on Facebook, or in the case of a friend talking about a brand.

The second part of the chapter looks at how persuasion can be achieved more effectively from the perspective of the persuader, and which factors influence persuasion effectiveness.

## Elaboration Likelihood Model

The Elaboration Likelihood Model has already been discussed in Chapter 3 in the context of anthropomorphic human-brand relationships found in the social media environment. However, it is worthwhile to consider the model briefly in the context of overall persuasion activity in a social media context, as both central and peripheral processing are likely to be triggered, and ELM is widely used to research persuasiveness in social media. Chu and Kamal (2008), for example, used ELM to explain differences in how blog-readers reacted to posts from bloggers they followed. They explained that blog-readers who trust the bloggers they read, elaborate less about the message content. That is to say, those readers tended to engage in a less critical manner with the blog content they were presented with. Conversely, in the case of less trusted bloggers, readers were more likely to use central elaboration to judge message credibility. In other words, readers paid more attention to the argument that the bloggers were making.

Apart from blogging activity, social media exposure itself contains a significant amount of brand exposure, from products in pictures of friends to brand-generated social media content. Therefore, and similar to traditional forms of product placement, in a social media context, these product placement-like brand occurrences can appear in such a way that they are triggering peripheral or central processing. For example, persuasive messages can be placed so that they encourage interaction – for instance in the form of sharing a picture on Facebook, commenting on a status update, etc. In these cases social media interaction with consumers is likely by the central route, i.e. the consumer engages in elaborative activities with the presented product message.

Conversely, product placements within a social media context can be subtler, and are not likely to encourage interaction or engagement with a particular message. In those cases, elaboration, similar to traditional advertising, is likely to be peripheral, with persuasion resulting from classical conditioning or mere exposure. For example, photos and updates on social networking websites can show the product in the background, without making any product-related claims or arguments, even if the message is brand-generated.

## Heuristic–Systematic Model

The Heuristic–Systematic Model of Information Processing (Chaiken et al., 1989) offers, similar to the ELM, a two 'passage' view of how individuals process persuasive communications. Most researchers see the ELM and the HSM as closely related and complementary, although there are subtle differences.

The HSM suggests that information is processed in one of two ways: either by following relatively simple decision rules (**heuristics**) or by engaging with the message content in a systematic form. Heuristic processing occurs in cases of low motivation or ability to process a message. In these cases, information is processed based on pre-formed evaluation rules to establish message validity. For example, if a source is generally accepted to be right (for instance, the person holds the heuristic that experts are always right), and motivation or ability to process a message is low, then any information originating from an expert is considered trustworthy and believable without significant elaboration or engagement with the message.

Conversely, in the case of high motivation and/or ability to process a message and/or in the absence of established supportive heuristics, individuals are more likely to elaborate on the message by evaluating message content and attempting to ascertain source credibility in order to establish message validity.

The HSM and the ELM share the fundamental notion that individuals process persuasive messages either systematically and carefully (systematic or central processing) or, under certain conditions, individuals rely on simple clues to evaluate a message (heuristic or peripheral processing).

The key difference between the ELM and the HSM is that the HSM assumes that both systematic and heuristic processing can occur simultaneously with the focus on establishing message validity. The ELM, by contrast, designates that message content is examined either centrally or peripherally, with no indication that both forms of processing can occur simultaneously.

## Integrated Model of Persuasion

In the late 1990s, Meyers-Levy and Malaviya (1999) integrated elements of the ELM and the HSM to form an Integrated Model of Persuasion. However, rather than simply integrating existing frameworks, they also added two new parts to the extant framework. Firstly, Meyers-Levy and Malaviya added an 'experiential' processing path in addition to the heuristic (peripheral) and systematic (central) paths found in the preceding models. Secondly, they argued that after a message has been evaluated via one of these processes, a judgement evaluation stage completes the processing of information.

Experiential processing is distinct from low cognitive (heuristic or peripheral) processing and high cognitive (systematic or central) processing in that the act of merely subconsciously engaging in processing triggers sensations or feelings. As such, advertising exposure may result in attitude change even when no attention to the message is being paid. This effect has also been studied by other researchers (e.g. Chartrand, 2005), who have likened such processing to an automatic process that evades conscious deliberation. As such, experiential processing of a message is similar to the well-established mere exposure effect (Zajonc, 1968), which states that individuals acquire, over an extended period of time, a preference for objects based on their familiarity with them. For example, if someone sees a particular brand name frequently, the individual develops a perceived familiarity with the brand. Because of this familiarity, that person will also develop a preference for that brand over brands that the individual may be less familiar with (Zajonc, 2001).

This effect is largely subconscious, and, subsequently, experiential processing requires minimal cognitive resources, in contrast to heuristic (peripheral) processing, which requires modest but significant cognitive resources to evaluate the message and systematic (central) processing that requires large amounts of cognitive resources.

The second difference from previous models presented by the Integrated Model of Persuasion is the addition of a 'judgement correction stage' immediately following processing of persuasive communication through one of the three processes described above. The judgement correction occurs on an on-going basis following exposure to persuasive communication, constantly adjusting a person's current view of a product, service or brand. Meyers-Levy and Malaviya (1999) suggest that this on-going adjustment is driven by the desire of individuals to hold equitably accurate views free of bias. Therefore, following a persuasion episode, once people have cognitive resources available to engage in such a judgement process, adjustment to the initial evaluations will occur.

Although there is only limited research to illustrate the judgement adjustment in the case of social media, from a traditional web perspective, this process has been highlighted as a stimulating avenue for future research (Sadarangani and Gaur, 2004). Theoretically, given the hypothetically closer and more continuous contact between consumer and brand in social media settings, for example if the person is following a brand on Twitter, focusing research on the workings of, and how to achieve desired outcomes from, the judgement correction stage appears timely and topical.

While the Integrated Model as a whole remains less studied than the traditional models of ELM and HSM, the model has received significant empirical support, although many of the studies were not directly related to social media. However, as Rauschnabel and colleagues (2012) point out in their study of brand postings on Facebook, there appears to be significant overlap between design features which invoke ad-liking in print and in a social media context. Consequently, the Integrated Model, and similarly other models originally developed for print advertising, are likely to be equally valid in the case of brand-generated social media posts, like for instance Facebook page updates.

## THINKBOX ELM, HSM AND THE INTEGRATED MODEL

Looking at three brand pages on Facebook, evaluate how consumers are likely to process the represented information in the last few updates. Carry out this analysis using the ELM, the HSM and the Integrated Model. Then compare results and the applicability of each model.

## OTHER FACTORS INFLUENCING PERSUASION

While the previous section concentrated on factors enhancing the persuasiveness of social media, the framework of persuasion knowledge takes a neutral stance, focusing on the effects which occur as a result of an individual realising that a persuasion attempt is taking place.

### Persuasion Knowledge

During the 1990s, Friestad and Wright argued that many researchers focus on what makes messages persuasive, but ignore how recipients of persuasion attempts react to such incidences. This reversal of the focus resulted in the **Persuasion Knowledge Model** (Friestad and Wright, 1994), which focuses on explaining the coping mechanisms employed by consumers in response to marketers' persuasion tactics (see Figure 7.1).

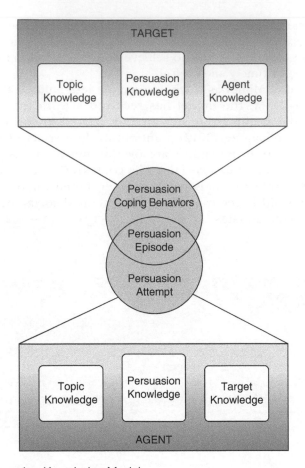

**Figure 7.1**   The Persuasion Knowledge Model

The central premise of the model is that consumers, being constantly exposed to multiple persuasion attempts, over time develop certain coping strategies. In doing so, consumers become better able to respond to such attempts, and learn to adapt their behaviour accordingly.

The model consists of two primary actors. Firstly, the 'target', i.e. the person or persons for whom the persuasion is intended, such as a consumer. Located opposite the target is the creator of the persuasion message, identified as the 'agent', for example, marketers, a sales person or a company responsible for a marketing campaign. The agent engages in a certain strategic behaviour hoping to persuade the target. The term 'persuasion attempt' describes this action, which can take multiple forms, for example it can be an advertisement, a sales talk or presentation or indeed a sponsored tweet or a company's page update.

The target may recognise some part (or all) of this persuasion attempt as intended to influence him/her, i.e. as part of a persuasion attempt by the agent. The target-recognised part of the attempt is labelled 'persuasion episode', which includes the recognised message and additionally the target's perception of how and why the agent has designed, constructed and delivered the recognised message. It is important to stress that any such episode may encompass multiple encounters, for example, it may consist of a combination of several sales presentations, online advertising and traditional media advertising occurrences.

The targets respond to a persuasion attempt by employing 'persuasion coping behaviours'. These coping behaviours are neutral in value, i.e. the model explicitly does not assume that targets will always react negatively or positively to a perceived persuasion, depending on the evaluation of the persuasion episode.

Three knowledge structures influence the agent's persuasion attempts – and the target's coping behaviours. For the agent, these three structures are:

1. topic knowledge, i.e. knowledge about the content of the message that is the subject of the persuasion attempt
2. target knowledge, such as knowledge or beliefs about the traits, goals, attitudes and competencies of the target
3. persuasion knowledge itself, which is a cognitive resource helping to 'construct and deliver' (Friestad and Wright, 1994: 3) a persuasion attempt.

For the target, the three knowledge structures consist of:

1. topic knowledge
2. agent knowledge, such as the knowledge and beliefs about how the agent will deliver a persuasion attempt
3. persuasion knowledge, i.e. the schemata used to recognise, manage and cope with a persuasion episode.

The target's activation of persuasion knowledge relies on three factors: firstly previous experience, secondly the target's cognitive ability and finally motivation.

As experience with previous persuasion episodes enhances persuasion knowledge, relatively new forms of persuasion attempts may not be recognised as persuasion episodes. For example, in the early days of email, many people did not immediately recognise spam messages as persuasion attempts, something that is today virtually unthinkable. Similarly, when Twitter introduced sponsored tweets, there were considerable concerns about how followers on Twitter could recognise commercial or sponsored tweets as a persuasion episode (c.f. Sherwin, 2013).

Although activated persuasion knowledge is frequently characterised as inherently negative for the marketers' effort to reach consumers, Friestad and Wright stress that persuasion coping behaviour can actually be both negative and positive, depending on the target's evaluation of the persuasion episode. The key evaluation criterion for consumers is the desire to retain control over the outcome of the persuasion attempt. Particularly, targets try to align coping strategies in order to optimise their personal goal achievement, i.e. if a customer (target) is trying to get some office work done quickly, an email which offers a solution to solve the current task more efficiently is evaluated positively – irrespective of the consumer being aware that the message is most likely designed to elicit a purchase (and hence recognised as being a persuasion episode). In a similar vein, a study looking at charitable donations found that activated persuasion knowledge increased donation rates – because people who donated pursued the goal of charitable giving. Subsequently, the persuasion episode was evaluated favourably as the persuasion message was goal congruent for the targets.

Conversely, if a target is trying to catch up with friends on a social networking site and a sponsored status update attempts to sell office furniture, such an attempt is likely to be evaluated as incongruent with the current goal. In this case, activated persuasion knowledge can lead to target irritation, which in turn gets incorporated into agent and topic knowledge. Thus, over time, the target may learn that persuasion attempts by that company (agent) or using that medium are irritating, and evoke consistently negative coping behaviours. This effect can be seen in the case of variation in click-through rates for keyword-search ads. As Yoo (2009) showed, click-through rates for these types of ads reduce significantly when persuasion knowledge is activated, i.e. the ads are recognised as a persuasion episode by the targets. Specific to social media, Boerman et al. (2017) showed that disclosure of sponsored content leads to activated persuasion knowledge and consumers distrusting the sponsored post – at least if the poster is considered a celebrity. The result is that activated persuasion knowledge results in a reduced word-of-mouth activity for posts that disclosed that they are sponsored.

Although activated persuasion knowledge is not always negative, it clearly provides a potential barrier for persuasion. Therefore, it may not be surprising that many marketing professionals, rather than taking the risky approach by activating persuasion knowledge, prefer not to activate persuasion knowledge (i.e. incidences where the target is not recognising the incident as a persuasion episode). As Nyilasy and Reid (2009) found, many practitioners recognise persuasion knowledge as inherently negative and talk about a 'mutation of effects', suggesting that consumers will become resistant to persuasion attempts over time. Following from this, many practitioners try to develop novel ways to 'cut through and engage' the consumer, with social media offering relatively novel ways of trying to connect with consumers.

A different technique for reducing persuasion knowledge activation is engaging targets' mental resources, for example, a study examining people's involvement in a movie with frequent product placement showed that consumers who were highly involved in the movie plot had lower levels of activated persuasion knowledge than people who were less involved by the movie's plot (Matthes et al., 2007). Similarly, when playing advergames online, Waiguny and colleagues (2012) showed that gamers who use more cognitive resources, for example by playing a technically challenging game, have lower activated persuasion knowledge than gamers who are not engaged by a game.

A more controversial way of reducing persuasion knowledge is to try and hide the persuasive intent of the communication by not clearly attributing the source. Social media can be problematic in this context, as it offers the agent new ways of reaching out to the target. For instance, the target may not recognise the persuasive nature of the communication, which may be intentional or unintentional on the part of the agent, resulting in a potential boomerang effect when found out. Both Sony (Megagames, 2006) and Wal-Mart (Gogoi, 2006) faced strong criticism for using blogs written by paid writers to promote their products, so called fake blogs (or flogs).

In the Wal-Mart case, the flog was supposed to be a blog written by two Wal-Mart enthusiasts, who blogged about their experiences shopping at the store's branches while travelling across the US. While the couple did indeed travel across the US, no attribution was originally made to Wal-Mart who paid for their travel.

Similarly, Sony apologised about a website that contained supposed discussions from teenagers as to why they wanted a PlayStation for Christmas.

In a similar example, McDonalds was one of the first high profile companies to use 'promoted tweets' to announce that the previously discontinued McRib burger was to be reintroduced to the menu for a short period of time (Heine, 2010). In this case, no attempt was made to hide the authorship of the company. However, the tweet was mocked on Twitter, rather than Twitter users retweeting the original tweet as was originally hoped.

A contested area is when and how persuasion knowledge develops. As can be seen from the above examples, unfamiliarity with a medium is likely to result in little or no persuasion knowledge. Similarly, age and cognitive development play a role. However, when and how children develop persuasion knowledge remains subject to debate, and is likely to be media channel specific, for example in the context of traditional advertising, most children can recognise persuasive communication as such by the ages of seven or eight (Moses and Baldwin, 2005). However, when playing advergames, children at the same age seem to not recognise the persuasion intention and have not developed coping mechanisms (Mallinckrodt and Mizerski, 2007). For a more extensive discussion, especially about the ethical and legal aspects of targeting children, and other potentially vulnerable groups, see the discussion in Chapter 12.

## Online Persuasion Theories

While the ELM, the HSM and the Integrated Model focus on the reception of persuasive messages, other theories have examined more closely how technology can act as a tool to encourage persuasion, particularly from a design point of view. Fogg's Functional Triad and Dahl's 7S framework are both closely related – and set out a number of principles which can help to design more persuasive applications.

### Functional Triad

Technology can adopt various roles, each with their own ability to lead to persuasion in the view of the users when interacting with it. Fogg (1999), in very early research into how technology can become a persuasion agent, categorised the three roles and described them as the **Functional Triad** of Computer Persuasion (see Figure 7.2).

Technology can be mapped against each of these dimensions of persuasive technology, depending on which function (or functions) it serves. For example, a calculator increases the ability to perform arithmetic functions; an advergame can act as a virtual environment providing (virtual) experiences with a brand; and social media interaction can create authentic social relationships. While Fogg describes the functional triad as neither 'intellectually deep or conceptually difficult' (Fogg, 1999: 28), this simple typology has been successfully used to design and implement technology-guided persuasion in a variety of contexts. It is especially popular in serious games design and when designing applications related to health and behaviour change persuasion, such as in the context of social marketing. For example, the triad has been used to design applications and other technology-led initiatives to persuade people to eat healthily, engage more in exercise and other lifestyle changes (Torning and Oinas-Kukkonen, 2009) and even to avoid texting while driving (Miranda et al., 2013).

As a simple-to-use tool, the Functional Triad can guide intervention design and help technology designers categorise and enhance technology for behaviour change.

## 7S

Complementary to the Functional Triad is the **7S Framework**. The framework is centred on mobile applications, and developed on the basis of game design principles, complemented with user insights and analysis of successful applications from the health and social marketing sector. Although the context of the framework is quite specific, the principles can be applied across a range of persuasion attempts using social media, including beyond mobile applications.

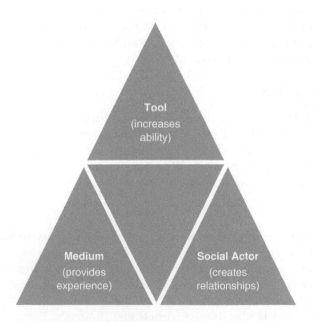

**Figure 7.2**   Functional Triad of Computer Persuasion

*Source*: Fogg, 1999

At the centre of the framework are seven design principles:

1. Simplification
2. Sign-posting
3. Self-relevance
4. Self-supervision
5. Support
6. Suggestion
7. Socialisation

### Simplification

Simplification requires the presentation of simple rules to engage the consumer – this could be simple rules to follow for desired behavioural outcomes or making it simple to engage with content, for example by making it easy to share, ask for clear steps to follow, etc. The rational for ensuring simplicity lies in the fact that people are likely to become irritated or bored if a simple task is presented with too much detail. Taking the example of a coffee maker, a manufacturer can send an update reminding customers to use one teaspoon of coffee per cup, without further elaboration on why this is the optimal quantity.

### Sign-posting

Links from social media sites can encourage followers to find out more about the background of simplified tasks, that is, sign-posting is useful to justify and elaborate on the concepts presented as simplified rules. The 7S implicitly assumes that this is an optional process usually followed by users once they have engaged with the simplified rules. For instance, a person may start on a particular diet without understanding why or how the diet is supposed to work. However, once engaged and following the simplified rules, the individual may seek further information, which should be optionally available. For example, the coffee maker manufacturer from the above example can link to a web page explaining in more detail how to measure the right amount of coffee, how the amount of coffee can influence the cream, etc., and show how the suggested amount of coffee results in the best coffee. Making the information available following the establishment of a behaviour has also been found to encourage more positive attitude formation (Torning and Oinas-Kukkonen, 2009).

### Self-relevance

Enabling the user to customise the user experience creates a more personalised experience, enabling the provider to provide tailored messages, shown to enhance engagement and retention (Noar et al., 2007). Moreover, tailoring and customisation reduces reactance and creates 'buy-in' and has been found to be overall positively evaluated by most users, despite privacy concerns (Sundar and Marathe, 2010) in the case of customised commercial messages. Several researchers have explained this phenomena by pointing to an increase in perceived control over the communication process by the receiver, which in turn has been previously linked to more positive consumption experiences (Chandran and Morwitz, 2005).

Customisation does not mean full individualisation, but rather that small components of the user experience are individualised, such as choosing wallpaper or enabling the user to upload an avatar. Customisation also reduces reactance by engaging cognitive resources.

However, while customisation of online advertising has been found to increase intention to interact with a customised advert, Bright and Daugherty (2012) suggest that the perception of receiving a customised advert may result in a less positive attitude towards the ad.

Depending on the context, customisation can be easily achieved by simple means, such as using the name in communications or giving limited control over themes, avatars or other tools, which may ultimately represent a possibility of self-representation and implied self-relevance for the consumer.

### Self-supervision

Self-supervising is designed to allow the user to see their individual progress towards a specific goal. Typical examples of self-supervising can include charts or other graphical elements that enable the tracking of progress, images that users can compare, or even applications that allow users to practise a specific behaviour, even if the individual is unlikely to perform such actions. For example, Stella Artois developed an iPhone app to allow users to 'pour', using their phone, a 'perfect pint'. For our coffee maker example, self-supervising could consist of pictures of well-crafted coffee to compare and rate his/her performance, or it could also include daily coffee charts, allowing the customer to see how many coffees he/she has drunk, made or shared, etc.

### Support

Support allows a person to receive (generally positive) feedback on their efforts, for example, the coffee maker manufacturer could encourage customers using social media to upload pictures of their perfect cup of coffee. In this case, positive support encourages learning through operand conditioning (Skinner, 1938) and such feedback is a vital component of advancing adult learning and is strongly motivational (Sluis-Thiescheffer et al., 2011).

### Suggestion

Suggesting further improvements, or helping with mishaps, particularly coinciding with positive reinforcement, helps to establish constant goal setting, and therefore more persistent behavioural pattern construction. Suggestions can come in the form of setting goals for the next action or suggesting longer term goals. A key aspect of the model is that suggestions should come in a timely fashion, ensuring that a consistent behaviour pattern is built, for example, social networks can be used to remind people of special, seasonal promotions.

### Socialisation

The final aspect of the 7S framework emphasises social media integration as a powerful way of allowing users to share success and achieve social supervision and peer support. This has long been recognised as a successful motivator (Hogan et al., 2002), which increases user engagement and fosters long-term involvement (Schubart et al., 2011).

For example, social communities and friends can provide additional motivation, a type of 'social reward' or 'external reward'. Leveraging virtual social support, particularly for socially desirable behaviours or brand engagements with socially desirable brands, can be a powerful motivator and reinforcement, similar to a positive surveillance practice of Bentham's classic Panopticon (Bentham, 1791).

The 7Ss can also be mapped back to the Functional Triad, for example, sign-posting, suggesting and simplifying can be seen as elaborations on the tools category of the Functional Triad, socialising and support map onto the social actor category and self-supervision links to the medium category. Similar to the Functional Triad, the 7S Framework is neither particularly conceptually difficult nor intellectually deep, though it is a useful tool, and arguably a simple checklist, to evaluate and guide mobile application design. While the focus is clearly on application design and personalised communication, some features can, however, be replicated in non-application, social media environments, for instance, sign-posting and simplifying can be used to design messages posted on brand or organisational pages or as status updates.

## THINKBOX FUNCTIONAL TRIAD AND 7S

Select two commercial health-promoting applications, such as Nike+ or DailyMile, two commercial applications such as advergames and two non-profit or governmental applications promoting a desired behaviour. Compare them using the Functional Triad and the 7S framework.

## POSITIVE FACTORS INFLUENCING PERSUASION

Social media persuasion depends heavily on influencing social perceptions by influencing social norms; the factors that are particularly supportive of successful persuasion are similar to those further discussed in the eWOM chapter. However, in addition to word of mouth, peers do not generate all persuasive forms of communication and a significant amount of persuasion attempts in the social media context are firm generated, such as status updates and postings to Facebook followers. Therefore some additional factors should be taken into consideration: credibility of the communication and the product as a core construct, together with perceived similarity and the possibility of outside endorsement of any messages.

### Credibility

Tseng and Fogg (1999) in their earlier work related to computer persuasion, classified **credibility** into four types: presumed, reputed, surface and experienced.

*Presumed credibility* is perceived credibility arising out of previously formed heuristics, such as assumptions and stereotypes. For example, computers by their very nature are assumed to be highly credible and perform tasks with fewer mistakes than humans. This can be used to explain, according to Tseng and Fogg, why some people assign more credibility to computer-presented material than human-originating material, i.e. a suspension of disbelief in cases of computer-presented information. In a similar way, people may assume that unwanted spam email is always trying to sell inferior products, and therefore, the presumed credibility of email of unknown origin may be rather low.

*Reputed credibility* is based not on simple heuristics, but rather on received reports about the credibility of someone or something. These may be perceived objective reports, such as reputed credibility based on magazine articles, or based on user-generated reports, for example based on reports from a review website.

*Surface credibility* on the other hand is based on intrinsic features, for example, by consumers examining the features of a website or evaluating the perceived credibility of claims made by an organisation on their social media stream. As such, surface credibility is very much 'judging the book by its cover' (Tseng and Fogg, 1999: 42).

The last, and arguably strongest, form of credibility is *experienced credibility*, where users rely on specific experience with the organisation to form judgements about communication they receive from the organisation. For example, a previously satisfied customer of a restaurant is likely to attach high credibility to any future communication, for instance when receiving a newsletter promoting future events.

**Table 7.1**   Four evaluations of credibility

|  | User perceives product as credible | User perceives product as not credible |
| --- | --- | --- |
| **Product is credible** | Appropriate acceptance | Incredulity error |
| **Product is not credible** | Gullibility error | Appropriate rejection |

However, as humans are prone to assign credibility erroneously, there is the possibility of potential erroneous rejection of computer-based persuasion, which in turn may require strategy adjustment for social marketing strategies. Tseng and Fogg (1999) classify the evaluation of credibility based on the quadrant shown in Table 7.1. For example, a company marketer who enters virtual communities and overtly markets the company's product may trigger (an incorrect) rejection based on presumed credibility – as simple heuristics are used to classify such an 'intrusion' as a spamming attempt. Therefore a strategic adjustment needs to be made to avoid this incredulity error from occurring again.

## Perceived Similarity

Perceived expertise, suggesting advantage in terms of knowledge rather than similarity of experience, has conventionally been found to be a positive influence on recipients' attitudes and behaviour (Hass, 1981). However, more recently this view has been challenged by Paek and colleagues (2011), suggesting that, at least for young consumers, in a world dominated by user-generated content, perceived similarity – rather than expertise (and potentially seniority) – is more persuasive.

Perceived similarity is the extent to which message recipients identify with a message, based on the perception that the message is a reflection of their own experiences – or originates from a sender who is similar to the receiver. For instance, young consumers have been found to assign more credibility to reviews of new products in blogs and user-generated reviews, rather than relying on expert advice from more experienced sources, such as consumer organisations or expert reviewers. Three classical and well-established theoretical frameworks have been used to explain this phenomenon (Paek et al., 2011). Firstly, Kelman's *source attractiveness model* (1961), which suggests that message receivers identify more closely with people they perceive as being similar to themselves. If they are perceived as similar people, then this has a positive effect on the evaluation of messages – a 'someone-like-me' effect.

Secondly, *social influence theory*, which posits that because of an underlying desire for conformity to similar people, especially in the case of younger audiences, young people tend to think and behave in ways similar to others around them (Moscovici, 1985). Consequently, perceived similarity has a higher influence on younger consumers than it may have on older consumers.

Thirdly, *reference group theory* (Sherif and Sherif, 1964) postulates that perceived similarity is the main factor for recipients of messages to recognise the sender as belonging to their reference group. Messages coming from a member of the reference group are in turn more likely to influence attitudes and behaviour (Paek et al., 2011).

Based on these conceptual notions, the relative persuasiveness of user-generated content can be explained, even when such user-generated content is contradicting expert advice.

## Parasocial Relationships

A further factor that has been shown to enhance credibility in online (and offline) settings are celebrities endorsing or seen to be using a product. Celebrities, particularly those who engage in social media, are considered the new 'prime time' and are significant opinion leaders, for example when posting about brands or entertainment options (McClelland, 2011) with endorsement considered more effective than comparable Facebook ads or Twitter updates (Lueck, 2012). This influence on social media can be measured, for example, in the Adly Influence Index (www.adly.com), which publishes rankings of celebrities based on their influence on Twitter.

Classic **Parasocial Interaction Theory** has been suggested as a possible explanation for the phenomenon of Twitter and Facebook endorsement popularity. Parasocial Interaction Theory was developed in the 1950s by Horton and Wohl (1956), and defines specific communication circumstances, where communication is perceived by the recipient as 'immediate, personal and reciprocal', although the sender does not share these assumptions. For example, by following a celebrity's Twitter or Facebook updates, fans create a strong illusionary relationship and develop a sense of intimacy with the sender. However, this relationship and communication by the celebrity are ultimately strongly mediated and one-sided, resulting in a relationship where the recipient has in-depth knowledge of the sender, while the sender has almost no knowledge of the recipient (Hartmann and Goldhoorn, 2011).

Gleich (1997) showed that this type of illusionary parasocial interaction with individuals via computer-mediated communication can be perceived as comparable to actual social relationships for recipients. As Kassing and Sanderson (2009) show, the rise of social media-based interactions has greatly facilitated the rise of **parasocial relationships**, while Lueck (2012) demonstrated that these types of relationships can be activated to create persuasive advertising, for example sponsored tweets or product placements in celebrity-shared pictures can trigger the persuasive effects attributable to parasocial relationships. In Lueck's study this effect was particularly strong for female recipients, although this may be because Lueck's study focused on a female celebrity.

Even with this limitation in mind, social media-mediated communication has without doubt increased the possibility of parasocial relationships occurring, particularly if social media relationships are enduring, as suggested by Social Information Processing Theory (see Chapter 4). Consequently, the framework is useful to explain the effectiveness of endorsements beyond traditional product placement models.

## SUMMARY

This chapter has explored the reasons for the persuasiveness observed in social media contexts. A number of theoretical explanations have been proposed, which singularly or combined are able to explain this observation. In particular, the ELM, the HSM and the Integrated Model of Persuasion can be used to explain persuasion processing. Persuasion Knowledge is a widely used theoretical model to explain coping strategies of both the target (or receiver) of persuasive communication as well as the sender. The chapter further presented two social media-specific frameworks: the Functional Triad and 7S Framework for social media persuasion, before briefly considering the conceptual basis of why user-generated and social media-based relationships are frequently found to be as persuasive if not more so in some cases than real-life relationships, particularly in the context of perceived similarity and the formation of on-going parasocial relationships.

## RESEARCH DIRECTIONS

Future research directions regarding persuasion centre on the increasingly blurred environment of entertainment or social messages and commercial messages, in particular, activation of persuasion knowledge, effects of activation and non-activation predominantly for younger consumers. Similarly, on-going persuasiveness and effects of persuasive, potentially personalised, messages at different stages of decision making will offer fruitful avenues of future research. For instance, future research can focus on providing more evidence of effective persuasion frameworks leading to sustainable behaviour change in social marketing.

# RESEARCH HIGHLIGHT BRAND IMAGE

Lim and colleagues (2012) examine the difference between the brand of the city of Las Vegas as portrayed in advertising or marketer-generated communication and in user-generated content in the form of YouTube videos. Using a content analysis based on 107 user-generated videos and 91 marketer-generated videos, the authors demonstrate that the consumer image for Las Vegas emphasises different aspects related to the 'Sin City', in particular focusing on adult entertainment. Conversely, marketer-generated videos focus more on the wider experience of visiting the city, including night-life attractions, gaming and more general entertainment options available.

Lim and colleagues argue that marketers need to engage more with consumers to achieve a more coherent brand image. In the case of Las Vegas, the marketer-generated brand of 'What happens in Vegas, stays in Vegas' could be, say the authors, undermined by consumer-generated, different brand images with potentially higher credibility. The authors consequently advocate that marketers should embrace social media users with high levels of output, and encourage them to produce more quality output in the form of brand-coherent messages.

The full article is available on the companion website of this book.

# CASE STUDY EBAGS

eBags is one of the largest and most successful online retailers of suitcases and bags, based in Colorado. While the backbone of their business seems very traditional, selling bags and suitcases, the company has embraced technology to deliver added value to their customers – and persuade customer to continue buying from them.

One of the most innovative ways to distinguish itself from their competitors was the launch of the eBag app. The app offers conventional shopping functionality, including special offers, but also offers more functionalities than a conventional shopping

*(Continued)*

app. The most distinctive feature of the app is the ability to perform a 'visual search', where the consumer can take a picture of the bag he or she likes, and the app then searches for the closest possible match. A different feature is a Tinder-style 'like or dislike' function, where users can tell the app which bags they like. The app then suggests special deals and bags based on their preferences.

The company also sells 'connected' luggage tags, which work exclusively via the app. The users register their bag details and addresses using the app, and if the bag gets misplaced, the details can be retrieved by scanning the QR code of the luggage tag.

## Questions to Consider

1   How has eBags distinguished itself from the competitors?
2   Visit the eBags website and use one of the persuasion frameworks to analyse the luggage tag.
3   How and why would people install an app specifically to purchase bags? What mechanisms and persuasion techniques does eBags use to convince people?

# FURTHER READING

Filieri, R. and McLeay, F. (2013) 'E-WOM and accommodation: An analysis of the factors that influence travelers' adoption of information from online reviews', *Journal of Travel Research*, 53(1): 44–57.

Kruikemeier, S., van Noort, G., Vliegenthart, R. and de Vreese, C.H. (2013) 'Getting closer: The effects of personalized and interactive online political communication', *European Journal of Communication*, 28(1): 53–66.

Lim, Y., Chung, Y. and Weaver, P.A. (2012) 'The impact of social media on destination branding: Consumer-generated videos versus destination marketer-generated videos', *Journal of Vacation Marketing*, 18(3): 197–206.

## REFERENCES

Bentham, J. (1791) *Panopticon: Or the Inspection House*. London: T. Payne.

Boerman, S.C., Willemsen, L.M. and Van Der Aa, E.P. (2017) '"This post is sponsored": Effects of sponsorship disclosure on persuasion knowledge and electronic word of mouth in the context of Facebook', *Journal of Interactive Marketing*, 38: 82–92.

Bright, L.F. and Daugherty, T. (2012) 'Does customization impact advertising effectiveness? An exploratory study of consumer perceptions of advertising in customized online environments', *Journal of Marketing Communications*, 18: 19–37.

Chandran, S. and Morwitz, V.G. (2005) 'Effects of participative pricing on consumers' cognitions and actions: A goal theoretic perspective', *Journal of Consumer Research*, 32: 249–59.

Chartrand, T.L. (2005) 'The role of conscious awareness in consumer behavior', *Journal of Consumer Psychology*, 15: 203–10.

Chu, S.-C. and Kamal, S. (2008) 'The effect of perceived blogger credibility and argument quality on message elaboration and brand attitudes: An exploratory study', *Journal of Interactive Advertising*, 8: 26–37.

Fogg, B.J. (1999) 'Persuasive technologies', *Communications of the ACM*, 42: 26–9.

Friestad, M. and Wright, P. (1994) 'The persuasion knowledge model: How people cope with persuasion attempts', *Journal of Consumer Research*, 21(1): 1–31.

Gleich, U. (1997) 'Parasocial interaction with people on the screen', in P. Winterhoff-Spurk and T.H.A. van der Voort (eds), *New Horizons in Media Psychology: Research Cooperation and Projects in Europe*. Opladen: Westdeutscher Verlag. pp. 35–55.

Gogoi, P. (2006) Wal-Mart vs. the blogosphere [Online]. Available at: www.nbcnews.com/id/15319926/ns/business-us_business/t/wal-mart-vs-blogosphere/ (accessed 1 September 2013).

Hartmann, T. and Goldhoorn, C. (2011) 'Horton and Wohl revisited: Exploring viewers' experience of parasocial interaction', *Journal of Communication*, 61: 1104–21.

Hass, R.G. (1981) 'Effects of source characteristics on cognitive responses and persuasion', in R.E. Petty, T.M. Ostrom and T.C. Brock (eds), *Cognitive Responses in Persuasion*. Hillsdale, NJ: Erlbaum. pp. 141–72.

Heine, C. (2010) 'McRib Is Back' promotion turns into a Twitter roast [Online]. Available at: www.clickz.com/clickz/news/1869732/mcdonalds-mcrib-Twitter-cooks-salty-comments (accessed 23 August 2013).

Hogan, B.E., Linden, W. and Najarian, B. (2002) 'Social support interventions: Do they work?', *Clinical Psychology Review*, 22: 381–440.

Horton, D. and Wohl, R.R. (1956) 'Mass communication and para-social interaction: Observations on intimacy at a distance', *Psychiatry*, 19: 215–29.

Kassing, J.W. and Sanderson, J. (2009) '"You're the kind of guy that we all want for a drinking buddy": Expressions of parasocial interaction on floydlandis.com', *Western Journal of Communication*, 73: 182–203.

Kelman, H.C. (1961) 'Processes of opinion change', *Public Opinion Quarterly*, 25: 57–78.

Lim, Y., Chung, Y. and Weaver, P.A. (2012) 'The impact of social media on destination branding: Consumer-generated videos versus destination marketer-generated videos', *Journal of Vacation Marketing*, 18(3): 197–206.

Lueck, J.A. (2012) 'Friend-zone with benefits: The parasocial advertising of Kim Kardashian', *Journal of Marketing Communications*, 21(2): 91–109.

Mallinckrodt, V. and Mizerski, D. (2007) 'The effects of playing an advergame on young children's perceptions, preferences, and requests', *Journal of Advertising*, 36(2): 87–100.

Matthes, J., Schemer, C. and Wirth, W. (2007) 'More than meets the eye', *International Journal of Advertising*, 26: 477–503.

McClelland, S. (2011) 'Twitter: The making of elites who influence', *Intermedia*, 39: 8–9.

Megagames (2006) Sony fake PSP blog busted [Online]. Available at: http://megagames. com/news/sony-fake-psp-blog-busted (accessed 23 August 2013).

Meyers-Levy, J. and Malaviya, P. (1999) 'Consumers' processing of persuasive advertisements: An integrative framework of persuasion theories', *Journal of Marketing*, 63: 45–60.

Miranda, B., Jere, C., Alharbi, O., Lakshmi, S., Khouja, Y. and Chatterjee, S. (2013) 'Examining the efficacy of a persuasive technology package in reducing texting and driving behavior', in S. Berkovsky and J. Freyne (eds), *Persuasive Technology*. Berlin: Springer. pp. 137–48.

Moscovici, S. (1985) 'Social influence and conformity', in G. Lindzey and E. Aronson (eds), *Handbook of Social Psychology*. New York/Hillsdale, NJ: Random House/L. Erlbaum Associates. pp. 341–412.

Moses, L.J. and Baldwin, D.A. (2005) 'What can the study of cognitive development reveal about children's ability to appreciate and cope with advertising?', *Journal of Public Policy & Marketing*, 24: 186–201.

Noar, S.M., Benac, C.N. and Harris, M.S. (2007) 'Does tailoring matter? Meta-analytic review of tailored print health behavior change interventions', *Psychological Bulletin*, 133: 673–93.

Nyilasy, G. and Reid, L.N. (2009) 'Agency practitioner theories of how advertising works', *Journal of Advertising*, 38: 81–96.

Paek, H.-J., Hove, T., Jeong, H.J. and Kim, M. (2011) 'Peer or expert? The persuasive impact of YouTube public service announcements producers', *International Journal of Advertising*, 30: 161.

Rauschnabel, P.A., Praxmarer, S. and Ivens, B.S. (2012) 'Social media marketing: How design features influence interactions with brand postings on Facebook', in M. Eisend, T. Langner and S. Okazaki (eds), *Advances in Advertising Research* (Vol. III). Wiesbaden: Springer Gabler. pp. 153–61.

Sadarangani, P.H. and Gaur, S.S. (2004) 'Being more effective on the world wide web: A communication model', *IIMB Management Review*, 16: 36–47.

Schubart, J.R., Stuckey, H.L., Ganeshamoorthy, A. and Sciamanna, C.N. (2011) 'Chronic health conditions and Internet behavioral interventions: A review of factors to enhance user engagement', *Computers Informatics Nursing*, 29: 81.

Sherif, M. and Sherif, C.W. (1964) *Reference Groups: Exploration into Conformity and Deviation of Adolescents*. New York: Harper and Row.

Sherwin, A. (2013) '#ad: Tweeting celebrities warned to reveal commercial interests following Coronation Street Dispatches sting' [Online], *The Independent*. Available at: www.independent.co.uk/news/people/news/ad-tweeting-celebrities-warned-to-reveal-commercial-interests-following-coronation-street-dispatches-sting-8690864.html (accessed 22 August 2013).

Skinner, B.F. (1938) *The Behavior of Organisms: An Experimental Analysis*. Oxford: Appleton-Century.

Sluis-Thiescheffer, R., Bekker, M., Eggen, J., Vermeeren, A. and De Ridder, H. (2011) 'Development and application of a framework for comparing early design methods for young children', *Interacting with Computers*, 23: 70–84.

Sundar, S.S. and Marathe, S.S. (2010) 'Personalization versus customization: The importance of agency, privacy, and power usage', *Human Communication Research*, 36: 298–322.

Torning, K. and Oinas-Kukkonen, H. (2009) 'Persuasive system design: State of the art and future directions', in *Persuasive 2009: Proceedings of the 4th International Conference on Persuasive Technology*. New York: ACM Press. p. 30.

Tseng, S. and Fogg, B.J. (1999) 'Credibility and computing technology', *Communications of the ACM*, 42: 39–44.

Waiguny, M.K., Nelson, M.R. and Terlutter, R. (2012) 'Entertainment matters! The relationship between challenge and persuasiveness of an advergame for children', *Journal of Marketing Communications*, 18(1): 69–89.

Yoo, C.Y. (2009) 'The effects of persuasion knowledge on click-through of keyword search ads: Moderating role of search task and perceived fairness', *Journalism & Mass Communication Quarterly*, 86: 401–18.

Zajonc, R.B. (1968) 'Attitudinal effects of mere exposure', *Journal of Personality and Social Psychology*, 9: 1–27.

Zajonc, R.B. (2001) 'Mere exposure: A gateway to the subliminal', *Current Directions in Psychological Science*, 10: 224–8.

# 8

# Engagement

## CHAPTER OVERVIEW

This chapter critically assesses the concept of engagement, closely linked to social media marketing activity. The chapter focuses on explaining the assumed role of engagement in closing the attitude–behaviour gap of consumers, and defines different types of engagement. The chapter also examines audiences most likely to perform engagement actions, and the implications this has for designing engagement-based strategies, before briefly considering threats associated with potentially negative engagement in the form of **culture jamming**.

# LEARNING OUTCOMES

On completing this chapter, you should be able to:

- critically discuss the term 'engagement' and what it means
- typify different types of engagement
- discuss how engagement may be seen as a proxy for behaviour, and which assumptions this is based upon
- assess likely audiences of engagement and the influence of these on the design of engagement strategies
- critically reflect on the potential for reactance and negative forms of engagement.

## ENGAGEMENT

Professionals like to portray 'engagement' as central to the online experience, especially in the context of social media, where 'engagement' can take a wide variety of different forms, from simple exposure to actions involving brand-generated messages, to liking, sharing and commenting on brand-owned Facebook pages and recommending these pages to friends.

Prior to the rise of social media many of the activities now broadly covered under the term 'engagement' were impossible. Marketing had to rely heavily on advertising, with the disadvantage of advertising being often disconnected from the purchasing experience (e.g. television adverts which are temporally removed from a targeted individual's shopping experience) – or marketers had to engage in sales promotion tactics at the point of purchase. Marketers faced a 'black box' situation: they had little control over, or at least access to data about, what happened in the minds of consumers between the contact in the form of an advert on television, and, for instance, the purchase of the advertised product the next day when visiting a supermarket.

With more opt-in communication opportunities, including always-on technologies and constantly connected individuals, a variety of engagement actions potentially connect exposure to commercial messages and purchasing by relying on an on-going, interactive communication process that nudges the individual to perform a desired behaviour (such as purchasing a product). The anticipation is that, following exposure to an advertisement, viewers engage in a series of mini-steps, such as viewing a brand page on a social network, liking a brand or seeking to read reviews, which can be tracked and monitored, and provide evidence of customer progression from intention to actual purchase. Consequently, rather than facing a 'black box' situation as described above, engagement has become touted as visible and measurable actions which have filled the significant void for marketers during key decision-making processes, and this may explain the popularity of the concept – particularly for practitioners.

However, before looking at the evidence of how effective engagement is, it is first necessary to define engagement.

## Definition of Engagement

The term 'engagement' has become a significant buzzword in the marketing industry, being used often in very different contexts. There is also a noticeable divide between practitioners and academics: practitioners have claimed that engagement is central to online experience, while scholars have largely relied on alternative, more precise, measures of online experiences (Mollen and Wilson, 2010).

Because of the wide usage of the term engagement by professionals, implying anything from looking at an advertisement to purchasing a product, it is easy to see that it is almost impossible to create a uniform and precise definition of what is meant by the term.

From an academic vantage point, scholars have criticised the lack of a clear boundary between what is 'engagement' and similar concepts widely used in academic research. For instance, academic concepts such as 'participation' (Brodie et al., 2013), which involves a deliberate behaviour, such as liking or sharing of content created by marketers, or 'involvement' (Mollen and Wilson, 2010), which is a measure of an emotional relationship, are widely researched concepts which collectively incorporate some aspects of what practitioners refer to as 'engagement'. Despite this clear focus, and probably because of the popularity with practitioners, the **Advertising Research Foundation (ARF)** created a specific task group to more closely define the term. The result was, what the ARF calls, a deliberately broad definition of 'engagement'. The ARF and two other professional bodies – the Association of National Advertisers and the American Association of Advertising Agencies – now use this definition, defining engagement as: 'turning on a prospect to a brand idea enhanced by the surrounding context' (ARF, n.d.). This definition has, however, been criticised as overly broad, and with possible reach beyond the social media or even online environment. For instance, based on the definition, traditional advertising could, if it occurs in the right context, be seen as a form of engagement. The ARF has further clarified that engagement is the consequence of customer co-creation, resulting in a more personal and deeper brand meaning. Again, while social media makes co-creation significantly easier, it remains unclear how engagement is then differentiated from 'participation', as Brodie and colleagues (2013) suggest. The arising problem is that such broadness leads to confusion and makes measurement impossible, as empirical evidence suggests that what is commonly referred to as engagement is, in fact, a distinct concept. For instance, someone sharing a funny advertisement on a social networking site does not mean that the person is also engaging with the brand – or indeed even considering purchasing the product. The engagement can happen purely because of the entertainment value of the product, for instance in the case of foreign adverts being shared on social media because they are funny or entertaining.

While a concrete definition of engagement remains elusive, it is nevertheless possible to derive a working definition based on the actions understood to encompass engagement – the term is most frequently used to describe an active process of interaction between a brand or brand-generated message and a consumer, for example, in the form of liking a status update. Whether or not this liking results in actually clicking a 'Like' button could be subject to debate. Arguably even without a behavioural outcome, the brand-generated message and the consumer have interacted, if only in a small and fleeting way. Consequently, engagement could be described as a meaningful interaction, suggesting that it is centrally processed, and the consumer elaborates at least fleetingly on the received message.

**THINKBOX DEFINING ENGAGEMENT**

Make a list of how you 'engage' with brands online.

Can you identify what constitutes engagement?

Can you define the concept of engagement based on the list?

The core idea of engagement implies that active forms of engagement diminish the attitude–behaviour gap and establish a more enduring relationship between brand and customer. The effectiveness of increased interactivity in building relationships has been widely acknowledged in the field of relationship marketing (Egan, 2011). However, the implied effect as a way to decrease the attitude–behaviour gap deserves some more explanation. It is therefore useful to briefly review the conceptual foundations and practical implications of this gap.

## Attitude–Behaviour Gap

The attitude–behaviour gap is a widely recognised phenomenon describing situations where consumers have a positive attitude or even intention to perform a specific behaviour, however, ultimately fail to do so. The attitude–behaviour gap is also sometimes referred to as the **value–action gap** or making reference to specific behaviour, for example the green gap in the context of environmental behaviours (Black, 2010). The attitude–behaviour gap is particularly well researched in areas where individuals hold generally highly positive views of a particular behaviour; however, they tend not to follow up on these views. For instance, a great deal of research has been conducted in areas such as pro-environmental behaviour, health behaviour and charity-related giving and volunteering intentions. However, the attitude–behaviour gap is unquestionably not limited to non-profit or charitable areas, as, for example, individuals may hold positive attitudes towards a brand or behavioural intentions to purchase a product but fail ultimately to do so.

The attitude–behaviour gap is further explicitly acknowledged as part of the **Theory of Reasoned Action** (Fishbein, 1979) and the later **Theory of Planned Behaviour** (Ajzen, 1991), which is in turn the basis of the Technology Acceptance Model (see Chapters 2 and 4). For instance, the attitude–behaviour gap can be observed in technology adoption or usage, for example when individuals have the intention to update their profile on LinkedIn in preparation for entering the job market, but continue to put this behaviour off.

### Theory of Reasoned Action/Theory of Planned Behaviour

The Theory of Reasoned Action (TRA) was originally developed in the 1970s by psychologists Icek Ajzen and Martin Fishbein (Fishbein and Ajzen, 1975), to explain the frequently weak correlation between attitude measures and actual performance of behaviour. In its original form, the TRA explained behaviour as a result of a behavioural intention, which itself is the result of perceived social norms and an individual's attitude towards the behaviour.

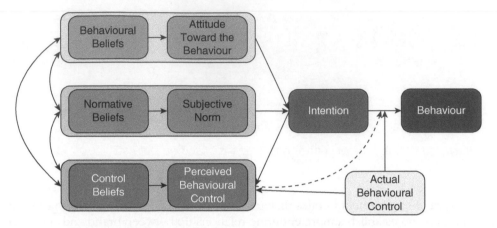

**Figure 8.1**   Theory of Reasoned Action

*Source*: Fishbein and Ajzen, 1975

Copyright © 2016 Icek Ajzen. Retrieved with permission from https://people.umass.edu/aizen/tpb.diag.html

The social norms are the perceived behavioural norms based on environmental and social factors. These factors are largely extrinsic, for example peers, friends, spouse or family. For instance, when seeing many friends performing a particular behaviour, an individual is likely to perceive this behaviour as a social norm, for example, when many friends use WhatsApp to communicate, then relying on WhatsApp for communication can be positively perceived as a behavioural norm. The attitude towards the behaviour on the other hand is the personal perception of the behaviour, consisting of beliefs about the behaviour. For instance, a person may find communication via WhatsApp useful or may believe that communication using this channel will result in improved social connections. Consequently, when both subjective norm and attitude are positive towards the behaviour, the individual is likely to form a positive behavioural intention.

The original TRA was later adapted to become the Theory of Planned Behaviour (TPB). The new model does not make substantive changes to the TRA, but it incorporates 'perceived behavioural control' (Ajzen, 1991). Perceived behavioural control is comparable to Bandura's self-efficacy (Bandura, 1997), which itself is part of Social Cognitive Theory (see Chapter 5), and explains the personal belief of how successfully an individual thinks he or she can take appropriate actions in response to a given situation. For example, if a person has significant experience of setting up websites successfully, then this person is likely to have a high perceived self-efficacy. If a person, on the other hand, has never attempted to create a website, he or she may hold much lower self-efficacy beliefs.

The attitude–behaviour gap occurs most notably after a behavioural intention has been formed; however, in some cases the gap may occur prior to the behavioural intention.

Traditional marketing communications had no tools to attempt to narrow the gap beyond increasing positive attitude or trying to influence the perception of social norms. In the context of social media various types of engagement, such as liking or interacting with a brand posting, are popularly assumed to be indicators of the individual consumer progressing towards performing the behaviour. For instance, if a person subscribes to the

Twitter feed of a brand, popular marketing assumptions are that the person will be more likely to purchase the brand (and potentially repurchase). Consequently, engagement has been popularly likened to an in-between intention and behaviour proxy, although some academic researchers have cautioned against this.

## Timing of Social Media Engagement

When assessing the actual value of engagement behaviour, and whether it can be used as a proxy for actual behaviour or as a way of gauging that the attitude–behaviour gap is narrowing, it is crucial to determine where in the purchasing process the engagement behaviour occurs – and who engages. For instance, in cases where the engagement behaviour occurs after the formation of attitudes but before purchasing, then engagement (or intermediary) measures would be a good way to demonstrate social media effectiveness.

### DAGMAR/AESAR Model

Based on research into micro-blogging, such as Twitter, Zhu and Zhao (2012) argue for an adoption of the **DAGMAR** model (Colley, 1961) traditionally used in advertising. Similar to DAGMAR, the proposed **AESAR** model is a linear model of the advertising (or in this case social media) comprehension process, highly similar to the **AIDA** (Attention, Interest, Desire, Action) model developed around the first decade of the twentieth century.

DAGMAR (Defining Advertising Goals for Measured Advertising Results) assumes that a consumer moves through four phases, and that advertising can influence the move from the initial phase through to the final phase. The four stages of the DAGMAR model are: Awareness, followed by Comprehension, followed by Conviction and finally Action.

Similar to DAGMAR, AESAR divides the social media comprehension and engagement process up into five parts: Awareness, Engagement, Sentiment, Action, and Retention. It thus adds retention after the action has occurred, while specifying that engagement comes prior to sentiment building. If engagement occurs prior to brand sentiments being formed, then this would suggest engagement precedes the processes described in the Theory of Reasoned Action/Theory of Planned Behaviour. This may be plausible in the case of advertising, where the recipient has no control over the message received, or in the case of 'sponsored' social network activity (see also section on mere virtual presence, pp. 170–1); however, the authors do not explain how such engagement can occur prior to the formation of attitudes (or sentiments) but after the establishment of awareness. The assumption for micro-blogging sites, and potentially other forms of engagement, is that consumers are likely to follow a brand or even retweet brand-originating messages prior to forming attitudes about the brands. In the absence of empirical evidence provided with the model, the assumption that such engagement activities precede emotion/sentiment forming appears problematic and prima facie is only applicable in very limited circumstances. Rather, it is considerably more likely that consumers engage with a brand online once an attitude has been formed, which may be after at least one consumption experience, for example by tweeting how they experienced the product or service. Similarly, although consumers can like a Facebook page, and subsequently receive brand-originating messages, prior to a purchase of a product or service, it would be most likely that the consumer already holds a positive view of the brand. Consequently, the consumer then seeks to confirm the held views by liking the page – rather than aiming to establish or change attitudes.

Thus, the purchasing status of consumers plays a crucial role when considering who is most likely to engage. Nelson-Field and colleagues (2012), while not explicitly addressing engagement behaviour, compared the customer base of Facebook fan pages with that of traditional advertising. The study is based on self-reported purchase data from Facebook fans, compared to panel data from advertising viewers. Comparing data for a chocolate brand and a soft-drink brand, they conclude that the fan base on Facebook is heavily skewed towards heavy buyers of both brands. Heavy purchasers made up, on average, 60% of the fan base and an equally relatively large (28%) proportion of moderate purchasers of the brand were fans. Consequently, such opt-in, organic or non-paid engagement with the Facebook fan base is nearly wholly likely to reach an existing customer base. As self-reported non-buyers accounted for merely 3% of the sample, this would suggest that in at least 97% of the cases attitudes towards the brand had already been formed. Further, virtually everyone following the Facebook updates recalls having purchased the brand at least once in the preceding 12 weeks. The study did not evaluate if the remaining 3% of the fan base had already formed attitudes towards the brand, and were considering purchasing the brand in future (e.g. would have formed a behavioural intention). While the study did not immediately address engagement, the results are nevertheless a significant caution when interpreting engagement (and follower activity), especially if the assumption is that engagement reaches non-brand users. Subsequently, it seems more cautious to assume that engagement occurs amongst people with well-established attitudes, and existing behavioural intentions that are also acted upon. Consequently, as Nelson-Field et al. point out, while some marketing practitioners would like to assume that communication with a fan base is equal to communication via traditional advertising, the empirical evidence from their study suggests otherwise.

Despite these limitations, the popularity of the term engagement in practitioner circles is, nevertheless, mirrored by an increasing interest in academic circles. This includes, for example, the listing of customer and consumer engagement as one of the key research priorities by the Marketing Science Institute (MSI) in 2010, which explicitly states that firms see engagement as a key driver for 'creating, building, and enhancing customer–firm relationships and (ultimately) improving business performance' (Marketing Science Institute, n.d.: 4).

**THINKBOX** TIMING OF ENGAGEMENT

Return to the list from the previous ThinkBox. For three brands you follow or like on social media, list when you started to follow/like the brand and which interactions you have had recently. Have these interactions changed the way you relate to the brands?

## TYPES OF ENGAGEMENT

While there is agreement that engagement is more powerful than simple awareness (Rappaport, 2007), there is debate as to what types of engagement exist. Van Doorn and colleagues (2010) for example, conceptualise customer engagement predominantly as specific customer behaviours. Conversely, Bowden (2009) emphasises cognitive and emotional aspects of consumer engagement. From a practitioner perspective, the ARF distinguishes two types of engagement – **emotional engagement** and **behavioural engagement**. Practitioner-based literature usually describes emotional engagement as more easily achievable but less powerful than behavioural engagement, although such a distinction is debateable as, for example, emotional engagement may include customer loyalty, which is likely to be a significant driver of repeat purchases, and relatively hard to achieve, while behavioural engagement may consist of not much more than opening a promotional email, with no resultant purchase intention (MarketingNPV, 2008). Authors from the academic domain have further challenged this simple dichotomy. Hollebeek (2010) and Brodie and colleagues (2013) describe engagement in terms of three engagement types. While acknowledging both emotional and behavioural engagement, these authors identified a further dimension of engagement, which they termed cognitive engagement. Cognitive engagement is characterised by sustained cognitive processing or cognitive absorption (Brodie et al., 2013: 107). Thus, the notion of cognitive engagement clarified that engagement activities are centrally processed. However, sustained cognitive processing can be argued to be an antecedent to emotional or behavioural engagement as, for instance, a person is more likely to follow a brand on Twitter after having thought about the brand. A further complication when considering cognitive engagement is that it is more complex to measure – for example measuring the level of engagement and elaboration of consumers while visiting websites is relatively tricky. Thus, while cognitive engagement is a likely construct, the lack of measurement possibilities and the absence of any cognitive measures in the professional field make it hard to utilise this form of engagement.

Contrary to cognitive engagement, emotional and behavioural engagement measures are, however, widely used in practitioner-based research, and it is therefore useful to briefly examine the two types of engagement.

### Emotional Engagement

Emotional engagement occurs when a consumer makes a conscious, or, some would argue even a subconscious, connection with a brand. This can be, for example, as a result of advertising, seeing a Facebook 'suggested post', a sponsored tweet or a different type of marketing stimuli. Emotional engagement does not result in any immediately visible and therefore measurable behaviour, but rather it influences subtle precursors of potential later behaviours, for example, emotions and attitudes towards the brand. The main focus of emotional engagement is consequently how the customer feels about a brand, rather than ways in which the customer interacts (on a visibly behavioural level) with a brand.

From an academic and market-research point, social media has not changed the way emotional engagement is measured, or conceptualised. Rather, it appears that the term is used to combine several well-established concepts which have been traditionally used as proxies to predict behavioural intentions and/or behaviours. Traditional market research practices, such as **brand recognition** or brand recall studies, association techniques, customer satisfaction surveys or measurements of brand image provide well-established and tested frameworks for measuring the success of emotional engagement. Similarly, brand liking and similar concepts often used in academic discourse are clearly types of emotional engagement, and are well established and discussed in the literature.

However, while emotional engagement is widely recognised as a precursor to behavioural intention and eventual behaviour, it is not a direct measure of actual behaviour. As previously discussed, many people hold positive attitudes towards environmentally friendly products – yet substantially fewer people buy them. This phenomenon, known as the attitude–behaviour or intention–behaviour gap, is widely researched and debated (c.f. Fishbein and Ajzen, 2005 for a summary), for example in the context of the Theory of Planned Behaviour and Theory of Reasoned Action.

Thus, it can be concluded that the term emotional engagement is neither novel nor does it describe a new concept. Rather the term describes a mixture of established concepts with well-tested and widely used measurements available.

## Behavioural Engagement

Because of the attitude–behaviour gap, behavioural engagement is commonly regarded as a more valuable type of engagement than emotional engagement, i.e. there is a logical argument to assume that small, different behavioural engagements could be seen as an interim measure of marketing effectiveness, showing how the consumer is being 'nudged' towards action.

Interactive media, and particularly social media, has offered a myriad of possibilities for behavioural engagement that were previously unknown, and it has removed significant barriers for more traditional behavioural engagements. For example, it is now significantly easier to contact a shop, for example by using email, than it would have been before the widespread use of the Internet. Similarly, potential customers can interact directly with online advertising – for example by liking or sharing adverts posted on a social networking site, a behavioural engagement that is only possible due to the technical possibilities offered by social media sites.

However, as interactive and social media allows for a wide variety of behavioural engagements (see Table 8.1 for some simple examples) this leads to conceptual and measurement problems.

Given the wide variety of possible behavioural engagements, they are unlikely to be a coherent whole, and based upon similar antecedents. Rather, the list of possible engagements appears to be a direct link to traditional loyalty concepts; for instance, the types of behavioural engagements detailed in Table 8.1 could be linked to the 'Ladder of Loyalty' (Christopher et al., 2002). The ladder of loyalty is a simple representation of six loyalty stages, ranging from prospect, i.e. someone who may purchase a product or service, to advocates and partners, who engage in referral behaviour and actively foster a relationship with a company. As most behavioural engagement actions are easily measurable, behavioural engagement measures simplify previously more complicated market research. By measuring click-through rates in email communication, for instance, a company can measure the amount of prospects. Similarly, by observing mentions of a brand in blogs and via other social media tools, an organisation can evaluate how large their pool of advocates is likely to be. However, for behavioural engagements in social media, such as liking and retweeting, considerably higher levels of loyalty are required (see also the discussion about Facebook fan communities on p. 166). Therefore, it is important to remember that the vast majority of highly engaged individuals are less likely to require further incentives to purchase, but marketers should focus on providing social media fans with appropriate messages, tools and skills to act as brand advocates to people with currently low engagement levels. The most prominent example of such tactics would be encouraging word of mouth, which is the subject of the following chapter.

**Table 8.1** Types of behavioural engagements

| Action | Intensity | Loyalty stages |
| --- | --- | --- |
| Opening a newsletter or promotional email | Low intensity interest | Prospects |
| Clicking on an ad | | |
| Reading product reviews about the product online | Medium intensity interest | |
| Visiting a company website | | |
| Watching promotional material on company site | High intensity interest | |
| Requesting more information | | |
| Visiting online stores to check out prices | Purchasing | Clients |
| Visiting a real life store | | |
| Buying a product or service | | |
| Rating the product online | Advocacy | Advocate |
| Blogging about the product | | |

## Engagement Outside the Brand Sphere

While much of the professional discussion about engagement prioritises direct engagement with brand-originated communication, such as advertising or promotional emails, or branded products, a large part of the academic research has focused on the engagement with brands in areas that are not brand-owned. This more closely echoes the MSI definition of engagement as 'customers' behavioural manifestation toward a brand or firm *beyond purchase*, which results from motivational drivers including: word-of-mouth activity, recommendations, customer-to-customer interactions, blogging, writing reviews, and so forth' (Marketing Science Institute, n.d.: 4). Particular inspiration for much of the work has come from a focus on virtual communities, which, while some may without a doubt be owned by a specific brand, the vast majority of online communities are neither aligned to a particular brand nor owned by a specific brand. For example, while there is a specific Apple online community (discussions.apple.com), many others, for example, MacRumors (with over 800,000 members) complement Apple's own online community. Similarly, computer website CNet (http://forums.cnet.com/) has an active community with thousands of different topics, with the discussions spanning different hardware manufacturers, including, but certainly not limited to, Apple.

The importance of online communities to understand customer behaviour has already been discussed in detail in Chapter 1, including the various roles that participants take when engaging with other consumers in virtual communities in Chapter 2. An important difference with the professional attention on engagement focused on brand-owned communication channels though is the consistent finding from academic studies that consumers do not primarily engage in communities because of brand loyalty (as frequently claimed or assumed by professionals), but rather that social motivations play a significantly more important role. As Wiertz and de Ruyter (2007) point out, even in firm-hosted online communities, members' predominant motivation for participation is a perceived commitment to the community – not the brand. This view is mirrored by Woisetschläger and colleagues (2008), although in the latter research a positive brand image of the community sponsor is also found to be related to community participation, albeit less so than more social factors such as identification with the online community, satisfaction with the community, and degree of influence within the community.

The consistent academic findings that wider social factors, rather than simple brand-related factors, drive engagement leads to the more sobering view, from the perspective of a brand manager, of brand-owned communities. Creating engagement requires non-commercially driven, objective participation, comprising sharing of knowledge, education and co-creation with customers. This suggests, as discussed in Chapter 2, that a theoretical base for customer engagement can be found in the concepts related to relationship marketing and the service-dominant logic view of marketing.

## THINKBOX TYPES OF ENGAGEMENT

Think of five recent brand-related online engagements. Classify them into behavioural or emotional engagement. Discuss the influence each type of engagement has on you and your perception of the brand (positive and negative)!

## Mere Virtual Presence

Engagement in social media also frequently triggers third parties to be exposed to brand imagery or brand-originated messages; for example, in the case of an individual sharing a brand-created picture amongst friends or instances where friends see that a person has liked a brand page on Facebook. In the latter case, the profile picture of the brand page is displayed to friends of the original follower, i.e. individuals who have not actually followed but are prospective followers of the brand. In a similar way, Facebook advertising and Twitter suggested tweets allow for the display of sponsored updates to recipients that are not currently following or liking a brand. Depending on the choice of the advertiser, these advertisements can include the names of friends of the recipient who are currently likers or followers of the brand, i.e. those who have previously interacted with the brand (e.g. the advert states that John Smith likes brand XYZ).

Naylor and colleagues (2012) refer to the effect of these displays as mini-connections or **mere virtual presence** and examined under which conditions the existing fan base should be revealed as a motivation for further individuals to like a page. Based on a series of studies, the authors show that in cases where the existing fan base is homogenous and similar to the targeted audience, and in cases where the fan base is heterogeneous but includes fans similar to the targeted audience, the fans should be revealed. In the latter case, however, the research suggests that only those fans that are similar to the targeted audience should be shown to the recipients of the adverts.

In cases where the fan base is homogenous but different from the targeted audience, for example if a company is trying to grow into new market areas, or in cases where their fan base is heterogeneous but doesn't include fans similar to the targeted audience, the fan base should not be revealed.

This would suggest that mere virtual presence could hypothetically be related to social norms in the Theory of Reasoned Action/Theory of Planned Behaviour. It also suggests that displays of friends' actions may have a wider, peer-referent aspect which complements mere exposure theory as a theoretical model explaining attitude changes resulting from passive mini-connections, such as in the case of a friend's brand-related actions.

## NEGATIVE ENGAGEMENT AND CULTURE JAMMING

An often ignored, but greatly feared form of engagement is negative engagement on social media. Negative forms of engagement can be in the form of frustration from genuine customers unleashing negative comments on social media sites – or it can be in the form of social activism taking over social media marketing campaigns for their causes, so called 'culture jamming', particularly linked to campaigns trying to elicit engagement actions. Many organisations have fallen victim to negative forms of engagement. Waitrose, the upscale British supermarket chain, for example, launched a Twitter campaign asking followers to complete the sentence 'I shop at Waitrose because... #WaitroseReasons'. In response, many Twitter users ridiculed the supermarket, suggesting it was the best place to shop for gold-laced toilet paper – or to avoid poor people (Smithers, 2012). Many other organisations had similar experiences when engaging in social media campaigns, including the New York Police Department, which got inundated with pictures of brutal arrests when asking for pictures to highlight positive police work (Tran, 2014), or investment bank JPMorgan, whose campaign #AskJPM backfired with more than two-thirds of around 8,000 responses within a period of six hours making negative comments (Burn-Calander, 2013).

A potential explanation for these actions can be found in **Reactance Theory**, a widely used theoretical framework in social psychology and health-related social marketing.

## Reactance Theory

The theoretical foundations of Reactance Theory date back to the 1960s and have been observed frequently in relation to health-related social marketing campaigns, for instance, in the case of campaigns aiming to reduce alcohol consumption, but achieving a 'boomerang' effect (Ringold, 2002). However, reactance is by no means restricted to health and social marketing, and reactance has also been linked to growing anti-consumption behaviour (Chatzidakis and Lee, 2013), such as culture jamming.

Reactance Theory (Brehm, 1966) states that direct or potential threats perceived as limiting freedom of an individual have the potential to lead to reactance. In cases of reactance, individuals become motivated by the perceived threat itself and assert their freedom and attempt to regain control of their perceived threatened freedom. Engaging in threatened behaviour, or reacting in a way contrary to the behavioural outcome is then seen as a means of re-establishing personal freedom. For instance, in the case of health-related marketing campaigns, individuals can choose to engage in a behaviour that is portrayed as unhealthy, even though they may be aware that such behaviour may have negative consequences for themselves. Likewise, in the case of culture jamming, taking over Twitter messages is unlikely to lead to widespread negative perception amongst individuals who, for example, shop at Waitrose, or any change in the pricing strategy of the supermarket chain or the targeted demographic.

## THINKBOX REACTANCE

Analyse the updates of the brands from the previous ThinkBoxes and find out if they are trying to elicit engagement in some form. Discuss their potential for negative engagement or the threat of culture jamming. How can brands react in case of negative engagement?

## SUMMARY

This chapter has looked at the notion of engagement, an often debated, but not very well defined idea of consumers interacting with brand-related messages. Engagement types can be broadly categorised as either behavioural engagements, where individuals actively interact with brand-related messages, for instance liking the message, commenting or sharing it; or, alternatively, engagement can be emotional, for instance, through exposure to a message without actual physical interaction. Implicit in the notion of 'engagement' is that engagement actions are intermediate steps towards customers performing a desired behaviour, such as purchasing, repurchasing or recommending a brand. Within the context of the Theory of Reasoned Action or Theory of Planned Behaviour, engagement actions are therefore likely to be found surrounding the behavioural intention – either as small steps towards forming a behavioural intention, or preceding behavioural intention formation, nudging the individual closer to the desired behaviour.

Although alternative timings have been suggested, for example prior to attitude formation, it is likely that significant engagement occurs after attitude formation. However, mini-connections (or emotional engagements) through third-party engagements, for example sharing of friends' brand-related engagement, may have an impact prior to awareness or attitude formation, as postulated by mere virtual presence theory.

A question when considering the value of engagement must, however, be the targeted audience. It is likely that customers who are already loyal or relatively loyal carry out most engagement actions, particularly behavioural ones. Thus, the question must be how engagement can be used to create a wider diffusion of brand-originating messages.

Finally, the chapter raised the issue of the potential for negative engagement and reactance, which, on an individual level, can also manifest itself in the form of negative word of mouth, discussed in the next chapter.

## RESEARCH DIRECTIONS

The wide-ranging definitions and multitude of different emotional and behavioural engagement types, some of which have been extensively researched in traditional media context, hinder research into engagement. Specific types of engagement, particularly behavioural engagement actions, do offer potential for future research and theory building. As behavioural engagement was impossible with traditional advertising methods, more research in this area can lead to a deeper understanding of this novel phenomenon. Professional research can also benefit from exploring how different types of engagement can be used to create a ripple effect from loyal and engaged customers to those currently not in the fan base.

## RESEARCH HIGHLIGHT
## ENGAGEMENT

In their study, Huang and Dunbar (2013) examine the interactions between patients and hospitals on Twitter and Facebook pages. The theoretical framework for their study is based on Social Exchange Theory (Homans, 1958), which they use as a way to

*(Continued)*

evaluate fan base and follower interactions. Social Exchange Theory posits that all social relationships are formed on the basis of a cost-benefit analysis – individuals try to maximise benefits and risks of social interactions in an exchange-like function, similar to the main proposition of the Uses and Gratifications Theory. The difference is that for UGT the focus is mainly on the user, while Social Exchange Theory considers both users and suppliers.

Huang and Dunbar examine a sample of 172 Facebook pages and Twitter sites from hospitals in the US. For each Facebook page and Twitter site, the authors coded the 25 most recent posts by fans.

For Facebook, the results show that visiting and liking a Facebook page is the most common form of engagement, with only approximately 10% of the fan base engaging with the posts in the form of 'liking', 2.5% posting on the page and only a minute amount of fans recommending the page.

For Twitter, the authors do not show any comparable data because of the differences in types of engagement. However, Huang and Dunbar point out that businesses make up around 50% of hospitals' followers.

The study exemplifies the problem of making comparisons across different social networks. As various networks offer different types of engagement, some of which are difficult to measure, for example retweets, it is difficult to make suitable comparisons. Despite this limitation, Huang and Dunbar conclude that Facebook is used by hospitals more as a platform to interact with visitors, while Twitter is used mostly to broadcast information.

The full article is available on the companion website of this book.

## CASE STUDY GRANNIES ON FACEBOOK

In Romania, Vodafone, the UK-based, multi-national mobile telecoms operator, decided to leverage the power of its 4G network and smart phones to help solve a social problem: loneliness of elderly people. Many elderly people live alone or become disconnected from friends, family and society. This has been a growing problem in many societies, including Romania, where around 40% of people over the age of 65 live alone.

Themed as a 'social experiment', Vodafone taught two 'grannies' how to use social media, using their network and smart phones. The two women, referring to themselves as the 'Bunici de duminica' or 'Sunday Grannies', moved in together after their respective husbands died, as they had been feeling increasingly isolated from the world around them. One of the key traits that both shared was their love for food, and so they continued cooking as if they were living with an extended family. This resulted in the key idea of the experiment: could they use social media to engage with other people around them – and make their flat a bustling social hotspot again? The result: the 'Sunday Grannies' invented Sunday lunch menus, cooked them and shared them on their own Facebook page. They also started to invite students, who often missed home cooked meals, to have Sunday lunch with them – and shared this. The result was that they became immensely popular: their Sunday lunches attracted nationwide media attention, visits from celebrities and the two grannies even started to sell some of their products in supermarkets. From a social media perspective, the Facebook page became the second most liked paged in Romania, attracting over 400,000 likes.

Soon, the success of the 'Sunday Grannies' became a success to thousands of other elderly people living alone in Romania. Vodafone responded to this by launching an app where people from all around the country could organize pop-up lunches.

With more than 380 million media impressions, the campaign became one of the most successful campaigns ever run in Romania. The campaign also contributed to a tripling of social media adoption by seniors, with a 20% increase in Facebook accounts by people over 65 in Romania.

## Questions to Consider

1  How do rate the engagements that Vodafone created?
2  How did Vodafone avoid reactance in this social experiment?
3  What do you think are the benefits of such a campaign? What are the potential negatives?

# FURTHER READING

Bernhardt, J.M., Mays, D., Eroğlu, D. and Daniel, K.L. (2009) 'New communication channels: Changing the nature of customer engagement', *Social Marketing Quarterly*, 15: 7–15.

Neiger, B.L., Thackeray, R., Van Wagenen, S.A., Hanson, C.L., West, J.H., Barnes, M.D. and Fagen, M.C. (2012) 'Use of social media in health promotion: Purposes, key performance indicators, and evaluation metrics', *Health Promotion Practice*, 13(2): 159–64.

Verhoef, P.C., Reinartz, W.J. and Krafft, M. (2010) 'Customer engagement as a new perspective in customer management', *Journal of Service Research*, 13(3): 247–52.

## REFERENCES

Ajzen, I. (1991) 'The theory of planned behavior', *Organizational Behavior and Human Decision Processes*, 50: 179–211.

ARF (n.d.) Defining engagement initiative [Online]. Available at: http://thearf.org/research-arf-initiatives-defining-engagement (accessed 17 September 2013).

Bandura, A. (1997) *Self-efficacy: The Exercise of Control*. New York: Worth Publishers.

Black, I. (2010) 'Sustainability through anti-consumption', *Journal of Consumer Behaviour*, 9: 403–11.

Bowden, J.L.-H. (2009) 'The process of customer engagement: A conceptual framework', *Journal of Marketing Theory and Practice*, 17: 63–74.

Brehm, J.W. (1966) *A Theory of Psychological Reactance*. New York: Academic Press.

Brodie, R.J., Ilic, A., Juric, B. and Hollebeek, L. (2013) 'Consumer engagement in a virtual brand community: An exploratory analysis', *Journal of Business Research*, 66: 105–14.

Burn-Calander, R. (2013) The top 10 corporate social media disasters [Online]. Available at: www.businessinsider.com/the-top-10-corporate-social-media-disasters-2013-11 (accessed 28 April 2014).

Chatzidakis, A. and Lee, M.S. (2013) 'Anti-consumption as the study of reasons against', *Journal of Macromarketing*, 33: 190–203.

Christopher, M., Payne, A. and Ballantyne, D. (2002) *Relationship Marketing: Creating Shareholder Value*, rev. edn. Oxford/Burlington, MA: Elsevier Butterworth-Heinemann.

Colley, R. (1961) *Defining Advertising Goals for Measured Advertising Results*. New York: Association of National Advertisers.

Egan, J. (2011) *Relationship Marketing: Exploring Relational Strategies in Marketing*. New York: Prentice Hall.

Fishbein, M. (1979) 'A theory of reasoned action: Some applications and implications', in H. Howe and M. Page (eds), *Nebraska Symposium on Motivation, 1979*. Lincoln, NE: University of Nebraska Press. pp. 65–116.

Fishbein, M. and Ajzen, I. (1975) *Belief, Attitude, Intention, and Behavior: An Introduction to Theory and Research*, Addison-Wesley Series in Social Psychology. Reading, MA: Addison-Wesley.

Fishbein, M. and Ajzen, I. (2005) 'The influence of attitudes on behavior', in D. Albarracín, B.T. Johnson and M.P. Zanna (eds), *The Handbook of Attitudes*. Mahwah, NJ: Erlbaum. pp. 173–222.

Hollebeek, L.D. (2010) 'Demystifying customer brand engagement: Exploring the loyalty nexus', *Journal of Marketing Management*, 27: 785–807.

Homans, G.C. (1958) 'Social behavior as exchange', *American Journal of Sociology*, 63(6): 597–606.

Huang, E. and Dunbar, C.L. (2013) 'Connecting to patients via social media: A hype or a reality?', *Journal of Medical Marketing: Device, Diagnostic and Pharmaceutical Marketing*, 13(1): 14–23.

MarketingNPV (2008) How do you measure engagement? Start by defining it in the right context [Online]. Available at: www.marketingnpv.com/content/how-do-you – measure-engagement-start-defining-it-right-context (accessed 18 September 2013).

Marketing Science Institute (n.d.) 2010–2012 research priorities [Online]. Available at: www.msi.org/research/index.cfm?id=271 (accessed 18 September 2013).

Mollen, A. and Wilson, H. (2010) 'Engagement, telepresence and interactivity in online consumer experience: Reconciling scholastic and managerial perspectives', *Journal of Business Research*, 63: 919–25.

Naylor, R., Lamberton, C. and West, P.M. (2012) 'Beyond the "Like" button: The impact of mere virtual presence on brand evaluations and purchase intentions in social media settings', *Journal of Marketing*, 76(6): 105–20.

Nelson-Field, K., Riebe, E. and Sharp, B. (2012) 'What's not to "Like?" Can a Facebook fan base give a brand the advertising reach it needs?', *Journal of Advertising Research*, 52: 262.

Rappaport, S.D. (2007) 'Lessons from online practice: New advertising models', *Journal of Advertising Research*, 47: 135–41.

Ringold, D.J. (2002) 'Boomerang effects in response to public health interventions: Some unintended consequences in the alcoholic beverage market', *Journal of Consumer Policy*, 25: 27–63.

Smithers, R. (2012) 'Waitrose Twitter hashtag invites ridicule' [Online], *The Guardian*. Available at: www.theguardian.com/business/2012/sep/19/waitrose-Twitter-hashtag (accessed 28 April 2014).

Tran, M. (2014) '#myNYPD Twitter callout backfires for New York Police Department' [Online], *The Guardian*. Available at: www.theguardian.com/world/2014/apr/23/mynypd-Twitter-call-out-new-york-police-backfires (accessed 28 April 2014).

Van Doorn, J., Lemon, K.N., Mittal, V., Nass, S., Pick, D., Pirner, P. and Verhoef, P.C. (2010) 'Customer engagement behavior: Theoretical foundations and research directions', *Journal of Service Research*, 13: 253–66.

Wiertz, C. and de Ruyter, K. (2007) 'Beyond the Call of Duty: Why customers contribute to firm-hosted commercial online communities', *Organization Studies*, 28: 347–76.

Woisetschläger, D.M., Hartleb, V. and Blut, M. (2008) 'How to make brand communities work: Antecedents and consequences of consumer participation', *Journal of Relationship Marketing*, 7: 237–56.

Zhu, J. and Zhao, A. (2012) 'A model framework for measuring enterprise micro-blogging marketing results', paper presented at the 12th International Conference on Engineering and Business Management.

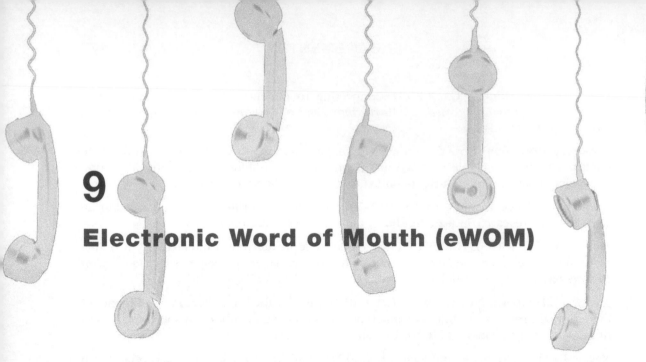

# 9

# Electronic Word of Mouth (eWOM)

## CHAPTER OVERVIEW

Word of mouth is central to many social media marketing activities, as user-generated and brand-related messages are a highly valued and strongly encouraged outcome of social media engagement, particularly as recommendations amongst friends are the most trusted source of brand-related information. This chapter looks at word of mouth from various perspectives. Firstly the chapter defines what word of mouth is, and how it is essential to, but differentiated from, related terms such as **viral marketing** or **buzz marketing**. The chapter further explores why individuals engage in word-of-mouth activity, suggesting ways in which WOM activity can be encouraged, which factors influence the perceived credibility of the message and finally what effect positive and negative messages have for organisations.

# LEARNING OUTCOMES

On completing this chapter, you should be able to:

- critically discuss word of mouth and delineate the term from associated terminology
- discuss the motivators for engaging in word of mouth, and the different motivators for positive and negative word of mouth
- critically evaluate the effectiveness of word of mouth, including the effect of negative word of mouth.

## WORD OF MOUTH

The previous chapter already hinted at word of mouth as the most valued outcome of engagement, i.e. a scenario where brand users are becoming, in an ideal case, brand ambassadors and endorse the product amongst their social network. In fact, word of mouth (WOM) has long been recognised as an efficient and effective marketing tool, even before the adoption of the Internet or social media – or even widespread mass-media usage. Against a backdrop not only of high prices of traditional marketing techniques, but also of clutter and oversaturation in many marketing communication environments, such as television or magazine advertising, WOM is seen as a significant precursor for both future purchasing intentions and actual purchase behaviour (Chevalier and Mayzlin, 2006; East et al., 2008) for new customers, while also increasing loyalty amongst existing customers (Wangenheim and Bayon, 2004). Specifically online, WOM has been claimed as highly effective in influencing purchasing decisions and brand equity (Cheung et al., 2009; Hennig-Thurau et al., 2004; Steffes and Burgee, 2009), even amongst relative strangers. Social media in particular, through the creation of what has been termed 'unprecedented intimacies' (Montgomery and Chester, 2009: 17) between some population segments and brands offers new possibilities for WOM-based marketing, encouraging WOM to take place as well as ensuring that WOM activity is widespread.

## Definition of WOM

Traditionally, WOM communication has been defined as 'person-to-person communication between a perceived non-commercial communicator and a receiver concerning a brand, product, or a service' (Arndt, 1967). While this traditional definition is still applicable in essence, social media has changed WOM communication from a customarily interpersonal environment, i.e. between people usually familiar with each other, to a considerably wider activity, where many or all participants may be unfamiliar with each other, or may only know each other through previous virtual interactions. For example, while traditionally WOM activity was mostly restricted to friends and family, through social media, negative or positive comments about a brand can potentially reach hundreds and thousands of recipients, most of whom may be unknown.

While traditional, i.e. face-to-face WOM (**tWOM**) activity is reasonably well defined and easily distinguishable, as per the original definition above, the multitude of electronic communication channels that are used to spread electronic WOM (**eWOM**) has dramatically increased the variety of different types of WOM, the researchability of WOM and stimulated researchers to look at different electronic WOM (eWOM) 'platforms'. These platforms have greatly facilitated spreading of messages, for example by providing reviews, such as in the context of posting reviews on websites (Lee and Youn, 2009), eWOM occurrences in online forum discussions (Brown et al., 2007) and, arguably as a precursor to social media, amongst Usenet newsgroup users (Godes and Mayzlin, 2009). However, the term eWOM has also been used more widely to describe information exchange amongst friends using SMS texts on mobile phones (Okazaki, 2009), that is, sharing of brand-related messages amongst people who are well known to each other, but by electronic means. In the latter case, the ease of being able to forward messages using electronic means, such as SMS, has been linked to an increased volume of eWOM. This in turn has contributed to the interest in generating and researching eWOM.

## Types of eWOM

In the context of social media, WOM recipients can be roughly classified into four broad categories, from social (familiar) settings to review (unfamiliar) settings.

In *social* environments, WOM activity engages mostly 'friendship' networks, such as in the case of discussions on Facebook user pages. Such activity is therefore most likely directed towards and read by people who are reasonably familiar with the WOM creator.

In *hybrid* environments, such as online communities, although participants may not know each other personally in real life, participants tend to interact extensively with each other for an extended period of time. Thus participants are likely to have established social ties well beyond the information passed on through WOM, and tend to interact with relatively high levels of familiarity.

In *broadcasting* environments, WOM originators and creators are likely to have some form of familiarity; however, unlike in online communities, familiarity in these environments is likely to be largely one-sided. For example, bloggers have less familiarity and interaction with each individual reading their blog posts, although blog followers may have some level of familiarity with the bloggers. Similarly, the bloggers will have an abstract sense of who their readers are, although probably less so than in online communities.

On the opposite pole, in *review* environments, WOM recipients and creators may be entirely unknown to each other, and both parties may never engage in any further exchange beyond passing on information contained in the review post. There are a wide variety of platforms fostering WOM exchanges between virtually unknown persons, for example, in the case of review websites such as TripAdvisor. Similarly, location-based social networks such as Foursquare encourage users to submit tips that are then seen by subsequent users checking into a particular location, but apart from sharing the location they may not have any other familiarity with the originator of the message.

**Table 9.1** Types of eWOM

| High levels of familiarity | | | Low levels of familiarity |
| --- | --- | --- | --- |
| Social | Hybrid | Broadcasting | Review |
| e.g. Facebook | e.g. Online communities | e.g. Blogs | e.g. TripAdvisor |

A key difference between eWOM and traditional forms of WOM is the longevity of messages, i.e. once a message has been posted it remains visible for an extended period of time – whereas traditional WOM tends to be short lived. Similarly, whereas for traditional WOM the sender and receiver are usually in the same place at the same time (i.e. speaking face to face), the eWOM sender and receiver are neither in the same space, time – or both. This separation of the WOM message from both space and time, coupled with the longevity of the communication, allows the information to be received by multiple consumers on multiple occasions. For example, consumers who are reading tips on location-based social networking sites, such as Foursquare, are in the same space, but not in the same time. Similarly, members of an online community reading product reviews from other members are neither in the same space nor the same time as the author of the review.

A further difference between traditional and eWOM, arising from the longevity and mostly public observability of the message, is the possibility to measure intensity, spread and the content, for example if the eWOM is positive or critical. Traditional WOM, particularly in private, face-to-face settings, was practically immeasurable as no records of communications were generally available. Data for eWOM, on the other hand, is widely available, and can therefore be measured by market research providing both quantitative and qualitative insights into the communications.

The final difference is that companies can often respond directly and publicly to eWOM. TripAdvisor, for example, allows hotel and business owners to comment on user comments directly.

These characteristics, which distinguish eWOM from traditional WOM, have also given rise to some marketing techniques based on WOM-generation, which are briefly discussed in the next section.

## Associated Terminology

There are a number of terms associated with WOM-based marketing activity. Many of these terms are often used interchangeably, and it is therefore useful to define and delineate the terms to avoid confusion.

The term *viral marketing* has been in existence since the late 1990s, and essentially refers to the practice of passing along marketing messages. Originally the term was coined by two venture capitalists to describe a specific campaign by Hotmail (Porter and Golan, 2006). During the 1990s, the free mail service appended advertising messages in the form of a signature to emails sent via the service. The advert spread, like a virus, amongst social networks simply by everyone in the network interacting with each other (i.e. emailing).

Thus, practically surreptitiously, Hotmail users spread these adverts amongst their contacts. In this case, no WOM about the product was involved in the viral marketing, as the sender had no control over which adverts were appended to the emails.

However, viral marketing is not only used to describe stealth-like marketing activities, but can also refer to cases where friends pass on a promotional message; for instance, a YouTube advert or other product recommendation intentionally passed amongst friends. Phelps and colleagues (2004) used the term to describe consumers passing on email messages with promotional content. Similarly, Porter and Golan (2006) describe activities where specific advertising-like messages are being passed along social networks as viral advertising, defining this term as 'unpaid peer-to-peer communication of provocative content originating from an identified sponsor using the Internet to persuade or influence an audience to pass along the content to others' (2006: 29).

Somewhat controversially, and going beyond spreading of messages intentionally or unintentionally through social networks, Shirky (2000) suggested that 'viral marketing' encompasses consumer-to-consumer discussion of products by electronic means, thus suggesting that viral marketing can be used synonymously with eWOM. Despite this suggestion, few academics and practitioners would use these terms interchangeably, rather referring to viral marketing or advertising specifically in the case of marketer-originating materials being passed along social networks in the hope of achieving an epidemic-like distribution of the material. Conversely, eWOM, while brand-focused, does not make primary use of marketer-originated materials. Rather eWOM relies on user-generated brand messages being passed along social networks as well as potentially amongst unknown users, for instance in the case of review websites.

Another, more recent WOM marketing related term is *buzz marketing*, referring to the creation of buzz (in the form of WOM activity) for a product or service, usually as a result of a planned activity (Dye, 2000). Buzz marketing does not exclusively focus on marketing by electronic means; rather, it aims to create product-related buzz by engaging a wide variety of different spokespersons and contexts. For example, Buzzagent Jono, a company specialising in buzz marketing, encourages people, pre-selected on the basis of apparent opinion leadership, to speak face to face to friends as part of a campaign. However, many campaigns also entail a significant amount of social media-directed activity. This activity can be either from the company itself, i.e. by using blogs or other social media activity (Winer, 2009) – or it can be similar to the conventional buzz marketing amongst friends, created by targeting bloggers, or other perceived opinion leaders, online to spread a message, for example, by sending items for review to bloggers, or offering discounts to Foursquare users checking into a place. Buzz marketing consequently does not primarily rely on marketer-generated materials to be passed along, but entices user-generated, brand-related messages to be spread through the increase of WOM. Buzz marketing is, however, a marketer-planned activity, which distinguishes it from organically arising WOM activity.

**Referral marketing** denotes the practice of encouraging individuals to directly suggest a product to friends. Referral marketing activity typically offers an incentive to the referrer or the referrer and referee, for example a reduced subscription rate or monetary reward, in exchange for a successful referral. Sugarsync, a cloud storage company, for example, offers rewards to users who encourage friends to sign up to the service by increasing the referrer's online storage capacity. Consequently, referral marketing specifically refers to marketer-driven attempts to create WOM activity through the use of incentives for the sender (and sometimes the receiver). As such, referral marketing is similar to viral marketing in that it uses social networks to spread the message. Nevertheless, it is different from viral marketing in that it offers specific incentives for engaging in WOM-related activity. As most referral marketing campaigns use marketer-generated templates and materials, such as pre-formatted recommendation emails, it is different in this aspect from buzz marketing, which relies predominantly on user-generated messages.

As can be seen from the preceding terms, a large variety of specialist marketing activities focus on creating or increasing WOM activity. It is therefore important to review the underlying mechanics of the effectiveness of WOM before examining the components of WOM and specific cases of WOM, such as positive and negative WOM and how WOM messages are assessed by the receivers.

## THINKBOX WOM, VIRAL AND BUZZ

Think of organic WOM, viral marketing and buzz marketing. Make a list of positive and negative aspects of each, both from a consumer perspective and from an organisational/brand-related perspective.

## Effectiveness of WOM

A highly contentious issue is the claimed effectiveness of WOM – with some sources attributing astounding rates of effectiveness, while others are more cautious. Either way, the ultimate effectiveness of WOM is difficult to estimate, though Dye (2000) claims two thirds of the US economy is directly influenced by WOM activity, and approximately 70% of Internet users claim to trust electronic WOM (Accenture, 2010). While there is broad agreement amongst both practitioners and academics that WOM is effective at influencing purchasing behaviour, the magnitude of the influence is dependent on distinctive aspects of the circumstances in which WOM activity can occur. For example, WOM activity has long been associated with influencing consumer response to advertising campaigns (Arndt, 1967), mediating the influence of these campaigns, that is, positive WOM activity coinciding with advertising heightened the effectiveness of campaigns, while negative WOM activity lowered the effectiveness. In social media terms, seeing updates about a brand from friends is likely to increase attention to advertising from the same brand, thus increasing the effectiveness of the advertising campaign. It is also important where the WOM originates from. For example, specifically in the context of social media, positive eWOM that is generated by other users has been found to have a positive effect on brand attitudes and brand equity. However, brand – or marketer-generated eWOM only increased brand attitudes (Schivinski and Dabrowski, 2016).

In the same way, post-purchase WOM has been associated with creating a 'ripple effect' for traditional marketing communication activity. The effects of the initial communication activity, for example an advertising campaign, are prolonged and proliferated by purchasers' WOM activity beyond the duration of the campaign (Hogan et al., 2004). For instance, if someone has bought a new phone, and consequently shares the information about the phone with friends through social media, such sharing will increase and prolong the original campaign.

Two-step Flow Theory and Social Network Theory explain the effectiveness from a theoretical angle.

## Two-step Flow Theory

Two sociologists, Katz and Lazarsfeld (Katz, 2006), developed the **Two-step Flow Theory** (**TSFT**) (sometimes called Multi-step Flow Theory) in response to the rise of mass media in society, to explain how the dissemination of information from media to the general public works. The theory recognises that personal ties are more influential than media messages in influencing behaviours, attitudes and values. However, media messages are also effective, yet, are likely to reach the individual mediated through other individuals. The TSFT states that opinion leaders, i.e. influential individuals, when exposed to media messages are the first to react to these messages. These opinion leaders then introduce the messages into their social networks. Thus, the theory stresses, the general public is unlikely to react to mass media messages, but the public will react, in turn, to messages transmitted by opinion leaders. Therefore, opinion leaders play a crucial gatekeeper-like role in gathering, reacting to and disseminating information to their 'opinion followers', and become an essential part of influencing the general public.

TSFT therefore postulates that advertising, directed at opinion leaders, is followed by WOM activity initiated by the targeted opinion leaders, concurring with the ripple effect observed by Hogan et al. (2004) for traditional media. However, Lopez and Sicilia (2013) show that in the context of social media, campaigns can be successful if there is a campaign to create WOM activity prior to advertising campaigns. This latter finding does not necessarily contradict TSFT, but rather supports the importance of targeting opinion leaders to engage in WOM activity. In the case of targeting them prior to a traditional media advertising campaign, the effect of the WOM activity is likely to occur concurrently with the advertising campaign. As Arndt (1967) has shown, concurrent positive WOM activity enhances advertising effectiveness. Conversely, if opinion leaders are targeted during traditional advertising campaigns, then WOM is likely to occur during the campaign and, because of the ripple effect, after the campaign.

## Social Network Theory

The idea of different levels of influence, i.e. opinion leader and opinion follower, was developed further into what is now commonly referred to as **Social Network Theory** (**SNT**). SNT postulates that individuals (and organisations) are connected through a network of relationships, referred to as 'ties'. These ties can be either strong or weak in nature. Strong ties are connections between individuals with a strong personal (or organisational) bond, for example close friendships or people who have frequent and prolonged contact. Strong ties are also most likely to be formed in homogenous groups, i.e. they are amongst individuals who are very much alike.

Conversely, weak ties are developed between individuals with less powerful friendships, such as loose acquaintances. Weak tie connections can spread across a wide variety of different, i.e. heterogeneous, groups.

SNT also identifies the importance of opinion leaders and opinion followers. Opinion followers form strong ties, but are less skilled at forming (or do not have access to) weaker ties. The result is that followers most likely operate largely within the networks where they have strong ties. These networks are made up of people similar to each other, i.e. an environment where opinions are similar. On the contrary, opinion leaders are more likely than followers to form both weak ties, usually with members of other groups, and strong ties, which ascribe them influence within their own social group, made up of opinion followers. This ability to 'network' with other social groups (i.e. groups based on weak ties) consequently exposes the opinion leaders to different ideas. Such ideas are then interpreted and reintroduced into networks where the opinion leaders have strong social ties. Therefore, SNT claims that opinion leaders act as connectors between different groups helping to diffuse ideas amongst a wide range of groups.

However, in the context of social media, most WOM passes between connections with weak ties, i.e. individuals with virtually no strong connections, such as on review sites (Chatterjee, 2001). However, contrary to traditional face-to-face settings, there is evidence that online reviews, despite weak ties, pose similar credibility as WOM originating from individuals with strong ties (Steffes and Burgee, 2009). Given these contradictory findings, the concept and significance of **tie strength** requires some further examination.

**THINKBOX** TIE STRENGTH

Think of product recommendations you have recently seen, either because you have searched for them specifically (e.g. on review sites) or because someone you follow on social media has made them. Make a list of how you evaluate the recommendations. What makes the recommendations trustworthy?

## Tie Strength

The importance of tie strength for social media-based WOM is subject to some debate, in particular as tie strength is widely regarded as greatly significant for the success of traditional WOM, while in the context of eWOM the research findings are contradictory. Previous research, based on email messages, has found that messages received from individuals with strong personal ties are most likely to be shared, and therefore focusing on networks with strong ties holds the highest probability of generating messages which may be passed on (Huang et al., 2009). In a similar manner, but based on a social media environment, van Noort and colleagues (2012) suggested that marketers should encourage individuals to forward messages to those they have strong ties with, rather than focusing on generating as much forwarding or sharing as possible. This is somewhat counterintuitive to most marketing campaigns that focus on generating as many messages as possible. However, van Noort et al. found that if messages were forwarded to individuals with loose ties, those messages were often perceived as spam and for that reason disregarded. Consequently, focusing on passing messages amongst strong tie networks in favour of relying on as many messages as possible is essential, in particular in a context, such as social networking sites, where users are already highly sceptical of advertising (Kelly et al., 2010) and have a low threshold for identifying and discarding potential spam messages.

However, as previously noted, although some WOM activity on the Internet is confined to directly suggesting or forwarding messages between friends, a significant part of WOM activity takes place between complete strangers, yet has been found to be as credible as between individuals with strong ties. This results in the somewhat paradoxical situation of a U-shaped credibility curve: credibility of eWOM activity is highest when received by strangers and by individuals with whom the receiver has close ties. Yet, credibility is lowest in cases where the sender and receiver have relatively loose ties.

A possible explanation of this seeming inconsistency is that, although tie strength is important, it is not the decisive factor when individuals establish credibility of a message. Rather, as van Noort et al. (2012) argue, the perceived intent of the sender influences the likely response. A receiver sees a message as most convincing when either the sender is perceived as having no immediate connection (and therefore no attributable intent) to convince the receiver – or where a sender is well known, and therefore the intentions can be estimated. In cases where the intent is not easily estimated, for example, between individuals with loose ties, messages may be perceived as less credible. Therefore, the perceived intention of the communication may be the key factor for understanding how WOM receivers assess credibility of perceived messages, a view that assents with the workings of persuasion knowledge theory (see Chapter 7 for a full discussion). Essentially, van Noort et al. suggest that persuasion knowledge-related coping mechanisms get triggered by relatively unknown people engaging in WOM activity, for example acquaintances. Conversely, persuasion knowledge is low for situations where the interlocutor is either a close friend or a complete stranger.

## Evaluation of Credibility of WOM Messages

There is, however, still relatively sparse research regarding which factors enhance eWOM message content credibility specifically, particularly amongst people who are not personally known to each other (e.g. review sites). However, the mere availability of a review mechanism on e-commerce websites, i.e. environments where communication amongst consumers is encouraged, has been found to encourage trust (Awad and Ragowsky, 2008).

Cheung and colleagues (2012), drawing on the Elaboration Likelihood Model (see Chapter 7), show that consumers use a combination of both central and peripheral clues.

They found the most important predictor of review credibility is the quality of the main argument, a central clue. Argument quality is, however, moderated by peripheral clues, such as perceived reviewer credibility and consistency of the review argument as well as perceived balance, i.e. presentation of both pro and con arguments in the review. Product familiarity has likewise been highlighted as influential for WOM credibility in online environments. Zhu and Zhang (2010) demonstrate that WOM in the form of online reviews for video games is more influential for lesser known games than for well-known games. While this is positive for positive WOM, the authors also point out that in cases where a product is relatively unknown, a single negative review may have a damaging effect on sales.

### Warranting Theory

A theoretical foundation for the evaluation of eWOM messages is provided by **Warranting Theory**. Warranting Theory is based on the warranting principle proposed by Walther and Parks (2002) and is itself connected to Social Information Processing Theory (see Chapter 4). The warranting principle stipulates that receivers of messages attach greater credibility to messages that cannot be easily manipulated by the person (or organisation) discussed in the message. For example, where a customer review is not easily manipulated by a retailer, then this review is seen as significantly more credible than a statement on the retailer's website. In cases where recipients of a message have access to statements originating from the subject of a message (for instance, a statement on a website) and perceived independent reviews, individuals will attempt to compare these statements. This process is called 'Social Triangulation' by Walther.

Applying Warranting Theory to online settings, Utz and colleagues (2012) show that, for example, even for online stores with a high credibility, consumer reviews are regarded as significantly more credible than the store reputation alone, confirming and complementing the findings by Awad and Ragowsky (2008), that the simple presence of consumer reviews on e-commerce websites creates perceived trust.

Similarly, Willemsen and colleagues (2012b) have found that the warranting principle can explain why self-disclosure as an expert in product reviews posted online leads to a perceived reduction in trustworthiness by readers of such reviews. These types of disclosures are fairly common in reviews, for example where someone states that they are working in a particular field and therefore have a wealth of experience in working with a product they are about to review. Only where secondary data is available about the trustworthiness of the self-proclaimed expert, for example through ratings of the expert by other users, are message recipients likely to rate the messages as trustworthy.

## Motivators of WOM and eWOM

A significant body of research has suggested a variety of motivators of WOM, both traditional as well as online. Motivators can be broadly classified into three overall categories: product-, message content- and relationship-related antecedents (Dahl and Eagle, 2012). See Table 9.2 for a full list of antecedents.

The relationship-related antecedents cannot typically be influenced directly by marketers, although there is research suggesting that reminding or requesting customers to tell others about a product can result in increased WOM activity. For instance, referral marketing is based on this principle; however, it is usually coupled with the offer of an incentive. The other motivators, i.e. antecedents related to the message content and the product itself, are more easily controlled by the marketer and can serve as guidance as to how to encourage WOM and whom to encourage to initiate WOM conversations.

The most extensive study of specifically product-related traditional WOM activity was carried out in 2008 by de Matos and Rossi. In their meta-analytic review of 125 studies, they identified satisfaction, loyalty, quality, commitment, product trust and perceived value as important drivers of WOM activity. Of these, satisfaction and loyalty were the most significant triggers of WOM activity, confirming previous research findings (Ladhari, 2007). Additionally, Moldovan and colleagues (2011) and Okazaki (2009) suggested that product originality has become a salient motivator, which is specifically noticeable in the case of online WOM, for example, sharing of brand-related messages in social networks as a means to 'show off', or the sender asserting influence by implying access to specifically trendy or novel products or ideas.

**Table 9.2**  Product-, message content- and relationship-related antecedents

| Category | Individual constructs |
| --- | --- |
| Product | Loyalty |
| | Commitment |
| | Perceived value |
| | Product originality |
| | Quality |
| | Trust product |
| | Satisfaction |
| Message features | Credibility |
| | Usefulness |
| | Emotional response to message |
| Relationship to receiver | Tie strength |
| | Homophily |
| | Opinion leadership |
| | Specific request for help |
| | Personal trust |

*Source*: adapted from Dahl and Eagle, 2012

Dahl and Eagle (2012) compared motivators for traditional and electronic WOM, and found that, although both types of WOM share similarities, there are distinct differences which are important for marketers. While existing loyalty triggers both forms of WOM, social (such as interpersonal trust) and situational factors are important drivers of traditional WOM. However, when sharing information about products using social networks, novelty aspects of products were found to be strong triggers of WOM. This finding gives further support to the significance of product originality as a major antecedent to the occurrence of, specifically, eWOM. Moreover, this finding is consistent with previous findings investigating factors causing messages to become viral (Dobele et al., 2007), but suggesting that novelty not only triggers viral messages, but is also a driver for less dynamic WOM activity.

Focusing further on motivators for engaging in online communities, Hennig-Thurau and colleagues (2004) show that expected social benefits from the online community, incentives (such as prizes and discounts) as well as altruistic motives (concern for others and personal extraversion or desire for positive self-enhancement) are the key drivers for eWOM activity. The research further stresses the importance of social aspects as significant drivers of WOM activity, similar to the previously observed salience of social factors as motivators to engage in online communities in the first instance (see discussion in Chapter 8, and Wiertz and de Ruyter, 2007; Woisetschläger et al., 2008). All the same, the importance of social motivators may be site-purpose specific. Munzel and Kunz (2014) show in their analysis of a hotel review site that altruistic motives, i.e. sharing of positive experiences or warning others of negative experiences, outrank social motives for contributors. As the study was based on a review site, the importance of altruistic motives may, however, be readily explained given the site's specific focus on providing reviews rather than a social environment in which to discuss, for instance, travel plans. Consequently, site-specific context and functionality play a potentially significant role in the motivations, which suggests that marketers trying to encourage eWOM must not restrict their thinking purely to motivators, but also take into consideration where they want the WOM activity to occur. For instance, if marketers want to encourage WOM activity on review sites, messages such as 'Let other travellers know', where other travellers are likely to be unknown to the sender of the message, are likely to be more successful. Conversely, if the marketer wishes to encourage WOM activity in specific social networks of customers, then messages such as 'Tell your friends how you discovered this trendy place' are likely to be more effective.

Clarifying the differential motivators for different types of WOM, Alexandrov and colleagues (2013) challenge the assumption that all forms of WOM, electronic and traditional, are the same for both positive and negative WOM. In their study they show that senders engage in WOM as a result of different motives, depending on whether the **valence of WOM** is positive or negative. For positive WOM (i.e. recommending something to friends) the main motivation for senders stems from the need for self-enhancement. This means that a sender is trying to boost his/her self-image by engaging in positive WOM, for instance, by voicing opinions that others are likely to agree with, or that show the sender in a positive light. A further intention is to bond with other, like-minded individuals and compare oneself favourably with one's peers. Conversely, negative WOM is motivated by the need for self-affirmation, for example, as a means to restore a damaged self-image, with less emphasis on comparison to peers but driven by a desire to help others – arguably more altruistic motives – for example by helping others, including unknown people, to avoid a potentially negative experience.

Apart from altruistic motives, people further engage in negative WOM as a means to vent their frustration, as a means to achieve emotional relief after a negative experience and to restore cognitive balance (Hennig-Thurau et al., 2004). Additionally consumers use negative WOM as a means to empower themselves vis-à-vis an organisation that has delivered an unsatisfying experience (Willemsen et al., 2012a).

The intention to post either negative or positive messages has been found to be influenced by the personality of the poster. Shin and colleagues (2013), relying on the Regulatory Focus Theory (Higgins, 1998), which posits that people are either promotion or prevention focused, found that prevention-focused individuals have stronger intentions to post a (negative) review following a negative service experience. Conversely, promotion-focused individuals have stronger intentions to post a (positive) review following a positive service encounter. Further, both types of individuals are more likely to post a review if their own experience is different from the previously portrayed experience in existing reviews, that is, an inconsistent service experience increases the WOM activity intention.

The importance of differentiating between positive and negative WOM, not only from a motivational perspective, has been the subject of significant further research, which is discussed in the next section.

## THINKBOX MOTIVATORS

Think of product reviews or recommendations you have given – either on review sites or to friends on social media. Can you identify the motivation? Make a list and compare the different motivation factors.

## Valence and Volume

The positivity or negativity of WOM is neutrally referred to as the 'valence'. Valence of WOM is the positive, neutral, negative or mixed character of any given WOM message, i.e. the sentiment of the message being passed on. Intuitively, valence is often understood as having a substantial influence on consumer choice, i.e. positive valence will lead to increased consumer demand.

However, there is evidence that not all WOM is regarded as equally valid by consumers. It appears that negative reviews are given greater importance than positive reviews by some consumers, especially for experience goods (Park and Lee, 2009), such as travel services.

Much research has been dedicated to exploring the effect of frequently feared negative WOM. However, many of the findings have been highly contradictory and occasionally counterintuitive. While some researchers have noted that negative word of mouth can harm both reputation and sales (Breitsohl et al., 2010), the duration of this effect is uncertain, and might be very short. Other scholars have suggested that mixed reviews actually increase sales (Clemons et al., 2006). Moreover, studies have found that certain customers explicitly seek out negative reviews (Bambauer-Sachse and Mangold, 2011). In fact, in at least one study, researchers claimed that negative reviews actually increase sales (East et al., 2008).

Despite the possible positive effect of negative eWOM, responding, or at least the urge to respond, can be a challenging task. Review sites, such as TripAdvisor, give the possibility to respond directly to reviews, while on Facebook negative reviews can be deleted from Facebook pages and Twitter encourages interactive discussion via @replies. However, as Willemsen and colleagues (2012a) show, only consumers seeking empowerment are likely to desire web care and a resolution of their problems. Others consumers who engage in negative WOM, such as consumers with altruistic motives, are likely to disregard helpful advice and rather engage in further venting. Thus, deciding whether or not to respond to a negative post where possible requires identifying the initial motivation of the eWOM sender.

Trying to move beyond the focus on valence, some researchers have suggested that particularly eWOM evaluation is more based on, and mediated by, other characteristics, such as product characteristics and consumer personalities (Zhu and Zhang, 2010). Moreover, earlier researchers have pointed out the role of volume of WOM as a more potent predictor for actual consumer behaviour. In an example of analysing social media-like conversations, Godes and Mayzlin (2004) show that the volume of online WOM in Usenet groups predicts consumer behaviour – at least for a new television show. Yang and colleagues (2012) confirm the importance of WOM volume, based on box office revenues in relation to consumer-generated reviews collected from a South Korean online portal. Zhu and Zhang (2010) offer a more differentiated view by presenting evidence that WOM volume is a strong predictor for products aimed at the mass market, and that for these types of products valence exhibits little predictive function. However, for niche-market products, such as independent films, and where WOM volume is relatively lower, WOM valence has greater predictive powers according to their findings.

## SUMMARY

This chapter has summarised the key aspects of WOM-related research to date. Although there is a significant body of research, there are still large areas where the evidence is contradictory or even counterintuitive, such as the influence of negative WOM. Similarly, the consumers' evaluation of the credibility of WOM messages appears more complex than often assumed. Further, while traditional WOM and eWOM share certain similarities, there are also subtle differences. Moreover, motivations to engage in WOM appear to be manifold and different depending on the context in which they appear, for example if they are made directly to friends and within established social networks, or towards strangers.

# RESEARCH DIRECTIONS

Because of the multi-faceted dynamics of WOM and eWOM, this area offers ample opportunities for future research. For instance, most research to date is based on books, movies, games and travel, i.e. traditional underpinnings of e-commerce. Much more research is needed on more different types of products and different product categories, especially as there are indications that promotions in traditional, offline environments may counterbalance online reviews (Zhu and Zhang, 2010), and this interaction is not yet well understood. Particular focus should therefore be on how eWOM is connected to events in real life, and products not usually bought over the Internet, but where online communities potentially influence purchase decisions.

# RESEARCH HIGHLIGHT WOM AND LOYALTY

## Walk Your Talk: An Experimental Investigation of the Relationship Between Word of Mouth and Communicators' Loyalty

In two studies in this article, Garnefeld and colleagues (2010) examine the theoretical and practical links between WOM activity and increased loyalty, providing empirical evidence that initiating WOM increases loyalty not only in the receiver of the message, but also increases loyalty of the sender.

The article is based on the theoretical framework of Self-perception Theory (Bem, 1967), which postulates that when engaging a certain behaviour, individuals ask themselves hypothetically what their attitude must be if they are willing to behave in a certain manner. Based on this assumption, the authors postulate that recommending a product or service also has a reverse effect on the sender, increasing affective commitment to the recommended product, which in turn mediates behavioural loyalty.

Moreover, the authors hypothesise that individuals with little experience of the service provider will display stronger affective commitment and loyalty intention than those who are already long-term customers.

In the first study, the authors establish the causal relationship between WOM and loyalty. This is followed by a second study, in which the moderating role of affective commitment was tested on a sample of travellers, based on quantitative analysis of questionnaires.

Based on the results of the two studies, the authors conclude that firstly, WOM activity increases loyalty intentions and affective commitment in the senders. Furthermore, the increase is stronger for those who possess less experience with the service provider, suggesting that organisations should target specifically people who are relatively new customers in order to increase their affective commitment – and potentially turn these customers into loyal customers.

The full article is available on the companion website of this book.

# CASE STUDY #KNOWYOURLEMONS

Breast cancer is the most prevalent type of cancer in women worldwide. Despite years of encouraging talking about breast cancer, it is still a type of cancer many people, especially women, do not want to talk about. The result is that, although its most common appearance in the form of a lump is fairly well known, other warning signs are often missed. For example, changes to the shape and size, the skin tone or the appearance of veins often go unnoticed or are ignored. This ignorance directly contributes to late diagnosis and poorer survival rates. However, as long as women don't feel they can openly talk about breast cancer and all of its symptoms, it is likely that many more signs and symptoms will be missed.

Responding to this challenge, the charity Worldwide Breast Cancer set out to encourage women to talk more freely about changes to their breast, overcome low literacy levels and raise awareness of many different types of changes to the breast that can indicate breast cancer.

The charity's founder, Corrine Ellsworth Beaumont, designed a simple and effective picture, showing twelve lemons in a conventional egg package, with each lemon showing different potential symptoms of breast cancer. The image was originally shared on the charity's webpage and Facebook page. From there it grew in popularity, with the original image being shared around 1,500 times. While the campaign was successful in its own right, the picture gained immense exposure two years later: breast cancer survivor Erin Chieze spotted the image and posted it, together with her story of how she discovered that she had breast cancer. She also asked people to share the image and to raise awareness of the different symptoms. For example, in her case, she found no lump. Instead, she found an indentation similar to one shown on one of the lemons. As a result the picture went viral, becoming one of the most shared pictures on Facebook. Erin's original post was shared over 45,000 times, with many people also sharing the image itself, creating unprecedented exposure for the charity – and raising awareness of the different symptoms.

*(Continued)*

## Questions to Consider

1   Which aspects of the campaign made the campaign successful in terms of generating WOM?
2   Although the original picture gained some attention, which factors explain the campaign going 'viral'?
3   How would you have improved the campaign? Which techniques would you have used to increase WOM from the outset? Justify your answers based on theories!

# FURTHER READING

Carl, W.J. (2006) 'What's all the buzz about? Everyday communication and the relational basis of word-of-mouth and buzz marketing practices', *Management Communication Quarterly*, 19(4): 601–34.

Filieri, R. and McLeay, F. (2013) 'E-WOM and accommodation: An analysis of the factors that influence travelers' adoption of information from online reviews', *Journal of Travel Research*, 53(1): 44–57.

Garnefeld, I., Helm, S. and Eggert, A. (2010) 'Walk your talk: An experimental investigation of the relationship between word of mouth and communicators' loyalty', *Journal of Service Research*, 14(1): 93–107.

Huang, L., Yung, C.-Y. and Yang, E. (2011) 'How do travel agencies obtain a competitive advantage?: Through a travel blog marketing channel', *Journal of Vacation Marketing*, 17(2): 139–49.

## REFERENCES

Accenture (2010) 2010 Global Consumer Survey findings [Online]. Available at: www.accenture.com/us-en/Pages/insight-accenture-customer-satisfaction-survey-2010-summary.aspx (accessed 26 October 2013).

Alexandrov, A., Lilly, B. and Babakus, E. (2013) 'The effects of social- and self-motives on the intentions to share positive and negative word of mouth', *Journal of the Academy of Marketing Science*, 41(5): 531–46.

Arndt, J. (1967) 'Word of mouth advertising and informal communication', in D. Cox (ed.), *Risk Taking and Information Handling in Consumer Behavior*. Boston, MA: Harvard University Press. pp. 188–239.

Awad, N.F. and Ragowsky, A. (2008) 'Establishing trust in electronic commerce through online word of mouth: An examination across genders', *Journal of Management Information Systems*, 24: 101–21.

Bambauer-Sachse, S. and Mangold, S. (2011) 'Brand equity dilution through negative online word-of-mouth communication', *Journal of Retailing and Consumer Services*, 18: 38–45.

Bem, D.J. (1967) 'Self-perception: An alternative interpretation of cognitive dissonance phenomena', *Psychological Review*, 74: 183.

Breitsohl, J., Khammash, M. and Griffiths, G. (2010) 'E-business complaint management: Perceptions and perspectives of online credibility', *Journal of Enterprise Information Management*, 23: 653–60.

Brown, J., Broderick, A.J. and Lee, N. (2007) 'Word of mouth communication within online communities: Conceptualizing the online social network', *Journal of Interactive Marketing*, 21: 2–20.

Chatterjee, P. (2001) 'Online reviews: Do consumers use them?', *Advances in Consumer Research*, 28: 129–33.

Cheung, C.M.-Y., Sia, C.-L. and Kuan, K.K. (2012) 'Is this review believable? A study of factors affecting the credibility of online consumer reviews from an ELM perspective', *Journal of the Association for Information Systems*, 13: 2.

Cheung, M.Y., Luo, C., Sia, C.L. and Chen, H. (2009) 'Credibility of electronic word-of-mouth: Informational and normative determinants of on-line consumer recommendations', *International Journal of Electronic Commerce*, 13: 9–38.

Chevalier, J.A. and Mayzlin, D. (2006) 'The effect of word of mouth online: Online book reviews', *Journal of Marketing Research*, 43: 345–54.

Clemons, E.K., Gao, G.G. and Hitt, L.M. (2006) 'When online reviews meet hyperdifferentiation: A study of the craft beer industry', *Journal of Management Information Systems*, 23: 149–71.

Dahl, S. and Eagle, L. (2012) 'Why not all WOM is created equal', paper presented at the European Marketing Academy (EMAC), Lisbon.

De Matos, C.A. and Rossi, C.A.V. (2008) 'Word-of-mouth communications in marketing: A meta-analytic review of the antecedents and moderators', *Journal of the Academy of Marketing Science*, 36: 578–96.

Dobele, A., Lindgreen, A., Beverland, M., Vanhamme, J. and Van Wijk, R. (2007) 'Why pass on viral messages? Because they connect emotionally', *Business Horizons*, 50: 291–304.

Dye, R. (2000) 'The buzz on buzz', *Harvard Business Review*, 78: 139–46.

East, R., Hammond, K. and Lomax, W. (2008) 'Measuring the impact of positive and negative word of mouth on brand purchase probability', *International Journal of Research in Marketing*, 25: 215–24.

Garnefeld, I., Helm, S. and Eggert, A. (2010) 'Walk your talk: An experimental investigation of the relationship between word of mouth and communicators' loyalty', *Journal of Service Research*, 14(1): 93–107.

Godes, D. and Mayzlin, D. (2004) 'Using online conversations to study word-of-mouth communication', *Marketing Science*, 23(4): 545–60.

Godes, D. and Mayzlin, D. (2009) 'Firm-created word-of-mouth communication: Evidence from a field test', *Marketing Science*, 28: 721–39.

Hennig-Thurau, T., Gwinner, K.P., Walsh, G. and Gremler, D.D. (2004) 'Electronic word-of-mouth via consumer-opinion platforms: What motivates consumers to articulate themselves on the Internet?', *Journal of Interactive Marketing*, 18: 38–52.

Higgins, E.T. (1998) Promotion and prevention: Regulatory focus as a motivational principle', *Advances in Experimental Social Psychology*, 30: 1–46.

Hogan, J.E., Lemon, K.N. and Libai, B. (2004) 'Quantifying the ripple: Word-of-mouth and advertising effectiveness', *Journal of Advertising Research*, 44: 271–80.

Huang, C.-C., Lin, T.-C. and Lin, K.-J. (2009) 'Factors affecting pass-along email intentions (PAEIs): Integrating the social capital and social cognition theories', *Electronic Commerce Research and Applications*, 8: 160–9.

Katz, E. (2006) *Personal Influence: The Part Played by People in the Flow of Mass Communications*, 2nd edn. New Brunswick, NJ: Transaction Publishers.

Kelly, L., Kerr, G. and Drennan, J. (2010) 'Avoidance of advertising in social networking sites: The teenage perspective', *Journal of Interactive Advertising*, 10: 16–27.

Ladhari, R. (2007) 'The effect of consumption emotions on satisfaction and word-of-mouth communications', *Psychology and Marketing*, 24: 1085–108.

Lee, M. and Youn, S. (2009) 'Electronic word of mouth (eWOM): How eWOM platforms influence consumer product judgement', *International Journal of Advertising*, 28(3): 473–99.

Lopez, M. and Sicilia, M. (2013) 'How WOM marketing contributes to new product adoption: Testing competitive communication strategies', *European Journal of Marketing*, 47: 1089–114.

Moldovan, S., Goldenberg, J. and Chattopadhyay, A. (2011) 'The different roles of product originality and usefulness in generating word-of-mouth', *International Journal of Research in Marketing*, 29: 123–33.

Montgomery, K.C. and Chester, J. (2009) 'Interactive food and beverage marketing: Targeting adolescents in the digital age', *Journal of Adolescent Health*, 45: S18–S29.

Munzel, A. and Kunz, W.H. (2014) 'Creators, multipliers, and lurkers: Who contributes and who benefits at online review sites', *Journal of Service Management*, 25: 49–74.

Okazaki, S. (2009) 'The tactical use of mobile marketing: How adolescents' social networking can best shape brand extensions', *Journal of Advertising Research*, 49: 12–26.

Park, C. and Lee, T.M. (2009) 'Information direction, website reputation and eWOM effect: A moderating role of product type', *Journal of Business Research*, 62: 61–7.

Phelps, J.E., Lewis, R., Mobilio, L., Perry, D. and Raman, N. (2004) 'Viral marketing or electronic word-of-mouth advertising: Examining consumer responses and motivations to pass along email', *Journal of Advertising Research*, 44: 333–48.

Porter, L. and Golan, G.J. (2006) 'From subservient chickens to brawny men: A comparison of viral advertising to television advertising', *Journal of Interactive Advertising*, 6: 30–8.

Schivinski, B. and Dabrowski, D. (2016) 'The effect of social media communication on consumer perceptions of brands', *Journal of Marketing Communications*, 22(2): 189–214.

Shin, D., Song, J.H. and Biswas, A. (2013) 'Electronic word-of-mouth (eWOM) generation in new media platforms: The role of regulatory focus and collective dissonance', *Marketing Letters*, 21(2): 1–13.

Shirky, C. (2000) 'The toughest virus of all', *Business 2.0*, 5(14): 87.

Steffes, E.M. and Burgee, L.E. (2009) 'Social ties and online word of mouth', *Internet Research*, 19: 42–59.

Utz, S., Kerkhof, P. and van den Bos, J. (2012) 'Consumers rule: How consumer reviews influence perceived trustworthiness of online stores', *Electronic Commerce Research and Applications*, 11: 49–58.

Van Noort, G., Antheunis, M.L. and van Reijmersdal, E.A. (2012) 'Social connections and the persuasiveness of viral campaigns in social network sites: Persuasive intent as the underlying mechanism', *Journal of Marketing Communications*, 18: 39–53.

Walther, J.B. and Parks, M.R. (2002) 'Cues filtered out, cues filtered in: Computer-mediated communication and relationships', *Handbook of Interpersonal Communication*, 3: 529–63.

Wangenheim, F.V. and Bayon, T. (2004) 'The effect of word of mouth on services switching: Measurement and moderating variables', *European Journal of Marketing*, 38: 1173–85.

Wiertz, C. and de Ruyter, K. (2007) 'Beyond the call of duty: Why customers contribute to firm-hosted commercial online communities', *Organization Studies*, 28: 347–76.

Willemsen, L., Neijens, P.C. and Bronner, F. (2012a) 'Satisfy the unsatisfied? Motives for negative electronic word of mouth and their effect on webcare receptiveness', paper presented at the ICORIA, Stockholm School of Economics.

Willemsen, L.M., Neijens, P.C. and Bronner, F. (2012b) 'The ironic effect of source identification on the perceived credibility of online product reviewers: The ironic effect of source identification', *Journal of Computer-Mediated Communication*, 18: 16–31.

Winer, R.S. (2009) 'New communications approaches in marketing: Issues and research directions', *Journal of Interactive Marketing*, 23: 108–17.

Woisetschläger, D.M., Hartleb, V. and Blut, M. (2008) 'How to make brand communities work: Antecedents and consequences of consumer participation', *Journal of Relationship Marketing*, 7: 237–56.

Yang, J., Kim, W., Amblee, N. and Jaeseung, J. (2012) 'The heterogeneous effect of WOM on product sales: Why the effect of WOM valence is mixed', *European Journal of Marketing*, 46: 1523–38.

Zhu, F. and Zhang, X. (2010) 'Impact of online consumer reviews on sales: The moderating role of product and consumer characteristics', *Journal of Marketing*, 74: 133– 48.

# PART 4

## Understanding Context in Social Media Marketing

The last part of the book examines important factors influencing social media marketing outside of the actual social media environment, i.e. the context in which social media marketing takes place.

The first chapter in this part takes up a core theme from Chapter 7 regarding engagement, and expands on the topic by examining how social media marketing can be measured effectively. Because of the enormous amount of data available for digital, and to a lesser extent, social media marketers, approaching available data with a critical appreciation is important to avoid drawing the wrong conclusions, or over relying on the available data set without realising the data's limitations.

Next Chapter 11 examines cross-cultural aspects of social media. While effectively social media has a potentially nearly global reach, paying attention to cross-cultural aspects is important to avoid pitfalls in the social media marketing strategy. The chapter discusses a number of potential issues, such as the erroneous assumption that popular social media networks are necessarily global, and that all will give global exposure to brand-related messages. In a similar way, it would be erroneous to assume that social media is used in the same way around the world. Rough measurements, such as average number of friends, or average hours spent on social media, indicate that people from different cultural backgrounds approach social media in distinct ways. This in turn clearly has an impact on potential strategies to reach consumers using social media. Finally, reactions towards messages are, just as in the case of messages in traditional media, likely to be perceived very differently in different cultural contexts. It is therefore important to be aware of the potential for different interpretations when using this medium with a frequently cross-country reach.

Finally, Chapter 12 discusses the important concept of privacy together with ethical and legal challenges facing social media marketers. This rapidly evolving area requires particular attention by marketers to avoid being seen as exploiting loopholes or tarnishing the reputation of their brands and their profession through not considering actions carefully.

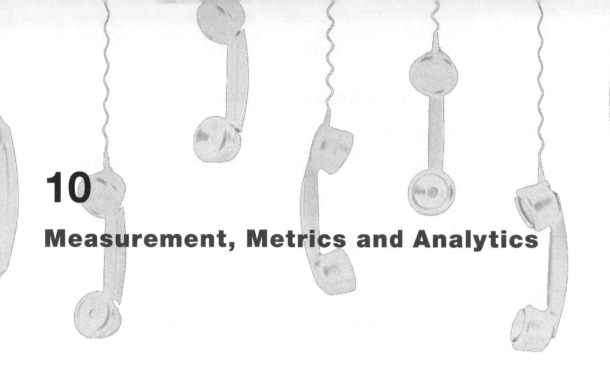

# 10

# Measurement, Metrics and Analytics

## CHAPTER OVERVIEW

Social media offers a multitude of measurements promising to inform marketers about virtually any aspect of their social media campaigns, their brands and their reputation online. Even free services, such as Google Analytics, which measures no less than 127 different aspects of online engagement, are complemented by a significant number of commercial packages all supplementing the data stream for marketers. However, while many of these **metrics** can provide useful insights, it is essential to critically examine what the data actually means, particularly quasi-qualitative metrics which aim to quantify qualitative insights and emotional connections and can give marketers a false sense of certainty. This chapter therefore discusses critically the value of the manifold data available, highlighting the limitations that marketers should be aware of when scrutinising such data reports.

# LEARNING OUTCOMES

On completing this chapter, you should be able to:

- critically discuss digital and social media metrics and their ability to offer relevant marketing insights
- compare and contrast traditional metrics with social media and digital metrics
- understand the likely influence of biases, such as social desirability bias on data derived from social media
- understand how linking value may influence underlying behaviour reported in the data.

## MEASURING SOCIAL MEDIA

Social media measurement is a hotly debated topic as social media, and in fact most Internet activity, gives access to an astounding, and unprecedented, wealth of information. Tracking behaviour on websites is technically easy, and generates much data, for example on which links users click, which tweets they retweet and which posts they like – or even just see. This wealth of information is significantly more than for traditional media, where at best estimates could be given of, for instance, how many people viewed an advertisement. However, the quantity of the measurements available in the digital context does not necessarily translate into quality data and insights. In fact, some of these measurements, in the eyes of many professionals, raise more questions than they answer – with some experts suggesting that social media activity is itself inherently immeasurable (DiStaso et al., 2011).

One argument why social media measurement may prove so difficult could be the sheer variety of different platforms and engagement types. It is hard to compare, for example, the 'value' of a person subscribing to a channel in YouTube with that of a person becoming a fan of a page on Facebook, or the value of someone registering in a non-branded online community discussing fitness activities amongst strangers with someone joining Nike+ to virtually compete with friends using the platform. Even for relatively well-defined and frequent social media actions, the effectiveness is subject to some debate, for example, focusing on assessing a relatively easily quantifiable, common and simple measure, the 'value of a fan' on Facebook, LaPointe (2012) quotes eminent professor of marketing, Tim Ambler, as saying, 'Marketing metrics inspire certainty and confidence. Cannabis has much the same effect' (2012: 287). While such conclusions may be drastic, the arguments for careful examination of any metric are overwhelming. LaPointe, himself a marketing professional rather than an academic, argues that, in relation to fans, the measurement is simply too all encompassing. Thus, 'a fan' combines a wide variety of motives, none of which is reflected in the metric. Such motives can range from the expectancy of a reward for liking a page, to liking the page because of the content rather than the brand, or as a result of social pressure to like a page. As a result any attempt to attribute a uniform value for individual fans becomes meaningless.

Similarly controversial is the influence of 'Twitter followers', a metric as effortlessly established as Facebook fans, but which has been consistently derided as being unreliable;

popularly so after a now famous post of blogger Adi Avnit who coined the term the '**Million Follower Fallacy**' to describe the phenomenon (Avnit, 2009). Avnit bases his conceptual claims on similar arguments to the ones made by LaPointe: many followers don't read the posts of people they follow, as they are not actually interested in the posts, but often follow based on other reasons, for example, some users may follow out of courtesy, as they consider it important to 'follow back'. Consequently, there is little correlation between influence and number of followers. Cha and colleagues (2010) further investigated the fallacy through an analysis of news and gossip items posted on Twitter. In their study they confirm that users who are popular (e.g. have many followers) are not necessarily influential in terms of generating retweets or mentions. They conclude that influence is most likely gained by topic-focused tweets, rather than engaging in a wide variety of topics, however, by doing so, users may limit the amount of followers.

Such critical voices become even more important when there is significant suspicion about many of the fans and followers on popular social networking sites. There is a growing market in Twitter followers, where individuals receive small payments to follow a brand (Stringhini et al., 2012). Such 'fake followers' may be bought or may be machine-generated accounts, trying to gain followers through following back. Either way, these can significantly influence the amount of followers. US President Barack Obama's account, for example, has been reported as having no less than 19.5 million fake followers – over 53% of the total followers (Martosko, 2013). As the number of followers is a key component of many other social media metrics, for instance influencer score, such 'fake' accounts can severely hamper the validity of any metrics relying on these and similar numbers. Unfortunately, such fake followers are by no means limited to Twitter. Service providers offer followers for virtually all social media platforms, from Facebook friends and fans, YouTube views and SoundCloud plays and followers, to Google+1 followers.

Social media measures should, consequently, be interpreted with great care and reflection. However, simply asserting that social media activity is entirely immeasurable would equally be too simplistic, as not all measures are completely meaningless. Rather, it is important to carefully scrutinise the data and avoid being overwhelmed by numbers.

An alternative solution to traditional social media metrics is proposed by Hoffman and Fodor (2010). They argue that **ROI** (Return on Investment) calculations for social media should start 'upside down'. That is to say that rather than taking investment in social media tools as the starting point, social media calculations should be based on the investments consumers make into social media, or in other words the time invested by consumers to engage with the branded content. Consequently, such metrics would rate consumers who read status updates, or share them after reading, much higher than consumers who invest only a split second in becoming a fan – and then no longer engage with the brand.

However, despite the potential of these more imaginative approaches, they are likely to be difficult to implement and achieve reliable measurement tools. Although potentially interesting as an alternative measure, currently there is no attempt at providing such measurements.

Consequently, it is useful to take a brief look at some of the conventional tools, bearing in mind the significant limitations they may have.

**THINKBOX MEASUREMENT BASICS**

Select three different social media accounts of brands on different social networks (for example, a Twitter account, a Facebook brand page and a LinkedIn company page). Take a look at the people following the brands on each of the different social networks by looking at the followers' profiles. How many of these followers are likely to interact with information from the company? What are their likely motives?

## Stages of Social Media Measurement Planning

Taking a very conventional approach to measuring social media, Murdough (2009) advocates that, because of the multiplicity and diversity of different metrics, it is necessary to engage in a three-stage measurement planning process designed to identify which is the optimal measurement tool or tools that should be used depending on the desired outcomes. The three social media measurement planning stages Murdough advocates are:

1.  Align the measurement objectives to the desired business goals.
2.  Establish **key performance indicators (KPIs)** aligned with measurement objectives.
3.  Determine performance benchmarks or targets to gauge success.

The resultant metrics and indicators can then be refined and further aligned as necessary. The result of this activity can be shown in tabular format showing how goals, objectives and appropriate social media metrics align (see Table 10.1).

Keegan and Rowley (2017) propose a slightly more holistic six-stage measurement model, based on interviews with social media marketing managers. Their six stages comprise setting evaluation objectives, identifying KPIs, identifying metrics, data collection and analysis, report generation and management decision making.

## Frequently Used Measuring Tools

Existing social media metrics and measurements can be broadly divided into two types of measures: **volume measures** and **sentiment measures**. While volume measures, such as the number of posts, likes and fans, are always quantitative in nature, sentiment measures are typically said to be qualitative, although they are arguably only pseudo-qualitative or quasi-qualitative. Sentiment measures try to estimate the balance of positive vs. negative engagements, although they often do this by providing numerical data rather than insightful information traditionally associated with qualitative research, such as focus group research. Consequently some of the sentiment measures are actually more quantitative in nature and have significant drawbacks associated with quantitative data; for example, sentiment analysis or sentiment ratio aims to give information about the overall emotions of the social media streams examined, but it will ultimately not be able to explain the reasons for such emotions. The measurement quantifies emotional expressions by relying on computer algorithms to classify brand mentions into positive, neutral or negative mentions. It then calculates an overall ratio, which represents the sentiment ratio for a brand. A particular concern that has been raised is that sentiment analysis, because it is highly automated and reliant on expressions explicitly used, cannot distinguish between ironic and non-ironic mentioning of a brand. Thus interpretability is limited in the cases where ironic expressions are likely, for instance, if someone tweets, 'Well done @someplace_airways for the delay', sentiment analysis is likely to interpret the sentence as positive rather than negative.

**Table 10.1** Three social media measurement planning stages

| Goals | Objectives | Metrics |
| --- | --- | --- |
| Relationship building | Grow social media audience | Number of fans/followers |
| | Create engagement | Number of likes/comments Number of downloads |
| Community-based learning | Obtain feedback | Sentiment analysis |
| Generate purchase intent | Drive online purchases | Web analytics and referrals to purchasing sites |

*Source*: Republished with permission of Taylor and Francis, from *Journal of Interactive Advertising*, 10, Murdough, C., 'Social media measurement: it's not impossible', 2009; permission conveyed through Copyright Clearance Center, Inc.

In a similar way, the popular **Net Promoter Score**, and the social media-specific Social Net Promoter Score, provide a simple tool for assessing the potential loyalty of customers. To calculate the score, the company that developed the score and markets it as the 'one number you need to grow your business', derives the score based on a categorisation of customers as either 'promoters', for example those likely to recommend the company, 'passives' or 'detractors', for example individuals who are engaging in negative word of mouth. The categorisation itself is the result of a simple, direct question, asking customers how likely they are to recommend the company to a friend or colleague (e.g. 'How likely are you to recommend our company/product/service to your friends and colleagues?' which is scored on a scale of 0 to 10). While the score is used by many companies and organisations, research has shown that the promoter score is unlikely to be an effective predictor of future growth of commercial companies (Keiningham et al., 2007) or for charities (Schulman and Sargeant, 2013).

Other measures often used are more apparently quantitative, though nevertheless require careful consideration before being seen as conclusive information. **Share of voice**, for example, calculates the frequency of a particular brand being mentioned in comparison to competitor brands. In this case, knowing the relative frequency of the brand being talked about does not include any measurements about the sentiment or emotions expressed.

Consequently, for example, in the run-up to the Russian Winter Olympics of 2014 many groups called for the boycott of major sponsors such as Coca-Cola, McDonald's and Visa using social networks to exercise pressure on the International Olympic Committee and the Russian government in connection with apparent human- and animal-rights abuses. In these cases, the share of voice of the brands increased; however, the sentiment was evidently negative.

## THINKBOX METRICS

Visit the websites of two social media metrics providers, for example, Jive Engage, Salesforce.com, Social Radar, Klout, etc. Compare the metrics that are provided and critically evaluate their value to an organisation.

## Comparison to Traditional Websites

A key difference between digital marketing, centred on attracting and tracking consumer activity on websites, and social media marketing is the comparative dearth of specific metrics for social media. Proprietary website marketing provides ample data about movements of individuals on a website, with well-established measurements based on site-visitor activity (e.g. page views per visit, bounce rates) or establishing direct links between website cost and sales by calculating ROI ratios such as cost-per-acquisition or cost-per-sale. However, while the data available for traditional websites may be abundant, it is important to consider that such purely quantitative data has no explanatory power to spell out why individuals act in such a manner on a website. Additional data is necessary to understand consumer behaviour; for example, based on traditional website analytics, an organisation can track where people purchasing their products arrive from. However, they cannot explain how these individuals feel about the products, or why they have decided to follow an external link to the organisation's website in order to purchase an item. To obtain such data, further research, for example qualitative studies or visitor surveys, would be needed.

Nevertheless, it is important to acknowledge that such quantitative metrics from proprietary websites are not available on many social marketing platforms, or are made available in different degrees depending on the site policies. For instance, page owners on Facebook can obtain volume metrics about reach, number of likes and engagement actions in addition to basic demographic data about people who like a page. However, such data is not available for Twitter followers, unless it is purchased, and virtually no specific data, such as reach, is available about assessments posted on review websites. In all cases, the data is only an aggregate, and individual users or user groups or segments cannot be identified based on the data provided by social websites. Consequently, many social marketers must rely on relatively futile data when evaluating effectiveness, as the more meaningful data about individual website visitors is only available to website owners, who in turn use the data to target advertising through **behaviourally targeted advertising**.

## Comparisons to Traditional Media

It is equally tempting to make comparisons between the reach of different media, for example by talking about the number of people accessing Facebook on a daily basis, and compare this to the number of people watching television – or indeed a particular television station. Television has long-established audience measures calculating reach over a period of time – or viewers at a particular point of time. However, such comparisons are difficult as social network sites' experiences are by their very nature often personalised and not time-specific – for example, everybody's newsfeed on Facebook is different depending on the friends one has, and therefore personalised and accessible at any time. Television experiences on the other hand are not personalised and, although technology exists to make television less time-specific, such as rewind functions for live TV, by and large the experience of a programme broadcast is simultaneous for the majority of the audience.

This makes it difficult to compare figures, as the figures are potentially misleading. For example, while around 31 million users access Facebook in the UK per month (Kiss, 2013) this number still remains lower than people watching any of the major four television stations per week (BARB, 2013). Conversely though, Facebook has a higher reach than any one of the major television channels, by reaching a far greater number of individuals.

And while the number of fans of Facebook's popular pages rises steadily, the most liked Facebook page in the UK, Skittles sweets, 'only' reaches 2,747,680 (Socialbakers, 2012) – significantly less than popular television programmes such as European football games (16.5 million viewers) or television shows such as *Britain Got Talent* (13.1 million viewers) (*The Guardian*, 2012).

However, more significantly, while a major broadcaster will reach several million people at the same time, a single Facebook user can technically only reach a maximum of 5,000 people, although the average number of Facebook friends per person is far lower, at around 190 friends (Bennett, 2013) – while Twitter users have, on average, only 27 followers (Becker, 2012).

Such numbers, not surprisingly, have resulted in some advertisers criticising new media as hype (Carmichael and Cleave, 2012). While there are undoubtedly examples of extremely popular and effective campaigns that have been shared amongst social media users – positive and negative ones – the majority of social media campaigns reach only a fraction of the potential reach of a single advertisement on television. It is therefore understandable that on the basis of reach metrics alone, social media is unlikely to perform in a similar way to traditional media.

Despite the lower potential reach, social media offers abundant alternative opportunities for 'traditional' online advertising. While there is anecdotal evidence of the effectiveness of advertisements placed on social media sites, there are also significant concerns that advertising on social networks is perceived negatively by users; for instance, Taylor and colleagues (2011) report on one survey which identified that only 22% of consumers hold positive attitudes towards advertisements appearing on social media, and that 8% even abandoned a social networking site because of perceived over-advertising. As an example Taylor and colleagues use the abandonment of MySpace users in favour of Facebook – although mostly driven by seeking the 'next big thing', the feeling of users of excessive unwanted and unsolicited advertising on MySpace in the last phase of the peak popularity of the site was a contributing factor increasing the migration to competing social media platforms. Taylor and colleagues' findings show that the entertainment value of the advert is the most important factor in reducing annoyance. They link their findings to Uses and Gratifications Theory (see Chapter 4), by explaining that users are primarily seeking entertainment when using social networks, and subsequently become annoyed when adverts are failing to be entertaining, or where adverts do not have some explicit value to social media users.

Specifically behaviourally targeted advertising (or **BTA**) has been suggested as a possible solution to overcome the reach issue and the potential problem arising out of targeting users who are not interested in specific products. Behaviourally targeted advertising is advertising that is displayed based on previously captured behavioural data of the user, for example by displaying advertising related to recent searches on websites or items looked at in an online shop – or within social networks specifically, based on demographic and psychographic information of the user based on profile information or friend activity. At least hypothetically, BTA has the potential to offset the more limited but targeted reach of social media in relation to traditional media, by minimising exposure to advertising that is irrelevant to the viewer. A notable point of Taylor et al.'s study is the relative small effect of perceived privacy concerns and interestingly this was highest amongst the youngest participants in the study (15–18 years old) and less so for participants aged over 18. However, as the study did not specifically address BTA, privacy concerns may be more prominent since the widespread use of behaviourally targeted advertising. For more discussion on privacy and ethical aspects of online and behaviourally targeted advertising, please see the Chapter 12.

## Media Usage: Public vs. Private

However, simple comparisons between traditional media and social media show a further fundamental misunderstanding as to what the function of social media is, how it is used – and by extension what role brands play in the 'social media marketing dance' (Kaplan and Haenlein, 2011: 253). The main difference that often gets overlooked is the potential public vs. private nature of traditional and social media. Traditional media, and advertising using these channels, is largely passively consumed. The evaluation of advertising-related information, and engagement takes place often in private, just as consumption takes place frequently alone (or with relatively few friends in the same room) rather than collectively.

In the social media context, participants' actions are actively producing the medium's content, and therefore social media engagement and related consumption activities are a public shared activity amongst often much larger networks than could possibly fit into a small room. Notwithstanding privacy concerns, there is evidence that consumers pursue socially desirable behaviours in a social media context – while other activities, which are perceived as potentially less socially desirable, are less emphasised as a result of the public nature of the medium.

Drenten, for instance, describes how adolescent girls share pictures trying on new clothes in a dressing room with their friends online, who in turn give fashion advice (Drenten, 2012). Thus, a previously almost always very private activity, limited to only those in the dressing room, has become a virtual, socially interactive endeavour. Moreover, there is evidence that some individuals post pictures of themselves wearing branded items, although these individuals only tried the items on in a shop – and had no intention of purchasing the item. However, in the public facing stream, these individuals post pictures of themselves wearing these items in the hope of achieving peer-recognition based on friend feedback.

This function of social media as bridging the gap between private and social consumption is not only limited to actual or potential purchasing, but extends to a wide variety of experiences. Examples include 'food porn' picture sharing, which enables online friends to virtually share meals, virtual debates about football amongst groups of friends not in the same room – or even giving relationship advice in a public forum (e.g. through withluv.com, a self-described 'social community for getting relationship advice or sharing your own').

### Social Desirability Bias

Social desirability bias (**SDB**) is relatively well established in psychological and health research, though it often goes unacknowledged in marketing research and has received virtually no attention in relation to measuring social media engagement.

SDB was first described in the 1950s, and is defined as 'the need of subjects to obtain approval by responding in a culturally appropriate and acceptable manner' (Crowne and Marlowe, 1960: 353). In traditional market research, SDB arises when, for instance, a respondent in a marketing survey tries to impress the market researcher. In such instances, the respondent is likely to answer the questions in a way concurrent with what he or she believes the researcher wants to hear or is likely to increase the chances of approval or admiration from the researcher. For example, when asked about charitable donations, a generally socially desirable activity, most people overestimate the amount they donate (Lee and Sargeant, 2011).

While many practitioners have hailed social media as a natural environment in which to collect data and measure consumer behaviour, social media may nevertheless be subject to extensive social desirability bias and, particularly in social networks where the emphasis is on maintaining links with personally known others, such as Facebook, SDB is a likely influence factor shaping consumer engagement. For instance, as described in the Drenten (2012) study above, the desirability of the brand is likely to influence if a person will engage in 'public' trying on of clothes – with socially desirable brands more likely to be shown than socially undesirable brands. Similarly, activity on Foursquare or other location-based social networks may be heavily skewed in line with SDB. Consequently, relying on social media as an information source may significantly overestimate consumer action and involvement in socially desirable campaigns or linked to socially desirable or largely admired brands. Conversely, it may significantly underestimate the engagement in brands which are less socially desirable or activities which are not seen as socially desirable or culturally acceptable.

**THINKBOX SOCIAL DESIRABILITY BIAS**

Look at your (or a friend's) Foursquare, Facebook or other social network stream. Make a list of places and brands the person has checked in to or posted about (N.B. Foursquare is particularly useful for this as you can see top place categories in the account profile).

What do these places or brands say about the person posting? Which places do not appear – and why?

## MESSAGE CONTENT: INFORMATION VS. LINKING VALUE

In addition to the SDB in social media actions, the impact of brands as 'linking value' is also likely to influence talking about brands. In a social context interactions with brands can be the result of anthropomorphised brands, i.e. seeing brands as virtual, entertaining friends, a concept that is discussed in more detail in Chapter 3, or brands are used as a way to represent oneself online, and act as a symbolic link between members of a particular tribe. The notion of 'linking value' is often associated with post-modern consumption. It assumes that consumers primarily derive value not from a product or the usage of the product, but rather by the social links deriving from such consumption. This phenomenon has been applied long before the emergence of social media as, for example, Godbout and Caillé (1992) studied the concept in relation to gift giving, while Cova (1997) discussed the phenomenon in more general terms (see also Chapter 2 for a more extensive discussion of linking value). One could argue that brands, where used to create linking value, are similar to badges or other symbols worn to display membership of a particular group: they are posted about in order to communicate to the social network something about the poster, for example, when @ClayBrizendine tweets about his new clothes:

> New duds from @ctshirts arrived today. Almost loving the tie more than the shirt! Thanks guys!' http://instagram.com/p/Ys_mvyB0Wh/ (https://twitter.com/ClayBrizendine/status/328978056637210624).

Engaging in such a communication with the brand online communicates information about his fashion sense and style, in a similar way as he would be if actually wearing a shirt or tie from the brand. In this instance, the poster describes himself in his profile as a 'Corporate Trainer'. Talking about a brand that focuses on business-casual and business wear, in this case Charles Tyrwhitt shirts, aligns his desired online persona with his own personal brand as a professional person. Consequently, the point he raises may be less about the shirts themselves, but rather the symbolic value that the explicit mentioning of the brand gives, which in turn shows other consumers of the brand that the poster is 'one of them' – and the poster aligns himself with the brand image.

Therefore, in the example above, the brand is mentioned not primarily because of the product or product attributes, but rather because of the 'linking value' the brand provides.

## SUMMARY

This chapter has highlighted several concerns with the abundance of social media and other digital marketing metrics. For digital content there is a wealth of information and data available to measure the behaviour of users. However, such measures are, ultimately, based on abstract calculations and therefore lack interpretative insight. While some practitioners and academics have argued that digital marketing and social media metrics are inherently useless and deceptive, such a view is probably one step too far. Rather, it is necessary to understand thoroughly the metrics that are being used. This implies extensive planning for how any social media or digital campaigns can be measured before campaigns start, and guarding against pitfalls, such as relying on simplistic measurements which sound comprehensive, but have little empirical support.

As a result of these concerns, any quantitative data (or quasi-qualitative) data derived from social media and digital media metrics should be triangulated through other, independent measures to confirm validity. A simple reliance on online data presented may severely influence the potential for valid conclusions to be drawn.

## RESEARCH DIRECTIONS

With many behaviours being easily measurable and quantifiable, much of the research has focused on analysing the available data. However, as implied by the chapter, the metrics often used are only a visible part of consumer behaviour, and do not clearly show emotional connections or other motivators that have resulted in the observed, and measured, behaviour. Thus, research focusing more on qualitative and insightful reflections of online behaviour is likely to generate future research interest beyond the provision of simple metrics. For example, the influence of social desirability bias on the selection of postings is virtually unstudied. Similarly, while the concept of linking value has been extensively discussed in the literature, the effects on metrics and resulting 'skew' has not been researched.

# RESEARCH HIGHLIGHT
## MEASUREMENTS

Neiger and colleagues (2012) developed a theoretical model of measuring social media engagement in a health promotion context. They propose an evaluation hierarchy and apply the developed hierarchy to a hypothetical promotion campaign using Twitter as the main campaign vehicle.

Before giving examples of appropriate metrics, Neiger and colleagues argue that engagement types can be broadly classified into three stages:

1   low engagement, which includes Facebook likes or following a brand or organisation on Twitter
2   medium engagement, which involves positing of narrative comments or sharing or retweeting of organisation-produced content
3   high engagement, which encompasses behaviours such as individuals creating original content to support an organisation or campaign.

Neiger and colleagues imply that the normal journey of engagement is upwards from low engagement to high engagement, and that each level of engagement represents a stage. During the first stage – the low engagement stage – Neiger et al. argue that the information flow is largely unidirectional towards the follower, for example by providing information. Twitter metrics associated with this stage are simple numerical metrics, such as number of tweets, number of followers and the potential reach, calculated as the number of followers each follower has.

In the second stage, the relationship with the followers becomes dialogic with the emphasis shifting from providing information to the followers to maintaining and eliciting responses. Through mentioning the organisation in tweets, followers can raise the organisational visibility amongst their followers, and typically followers will start to respond directly to questions posted by the organisation. Consequently, metrics include retweet frequencies, @mentions and also a somewhat unusual metric that looks at the quantity of followers who follow other followers. The authors argue that if this latter metric is high, this may indicate that a quasi community is forming, which may be an important milestone towards achieving peer-to-peer support and co-creation for the organisation. Finally, during the high engagement stage, followers start to engage explicitly with the organisation in a fully dialogic relationship, for example, followers take part in research projects conducted by the organisation, participate in programmes or support the delivery of, in this case, health promotion programmes.

While the article explicitly focuses on health promotion programmes, the points raised are equally likely to apply, though possibly with some adjustments, in other contexts. Depending on the context, for a low-involvement good, measures such as purchasing may actually show a low level of involvement and clearer brand advocacy may show higher levels of engagement, for example, by creating a spoof advert and posting it on YouTube for a product such as Marmite.

A more fundamental limitation of the article is, however, the implicit assumption of a progression of followers from low engagement to high engagement, with relatively little guidance on how the progression can be encouraged, a problem that is a well-acknowledged limitation of all stage-based behavioural models, such as Stages of Change or the Transtheoretical Model of Behaviour Change. Thus it is important to be aware that although a follower may start as a low engaged follower, progression to become a medium or highly engaged follower is by no means automatic – nor necessarily sequential. Although the proposed metrics are likely to be able to show how many followers are in each segment, and which segments are growing over time, additional research, for example in the form of qualitative research establishing the motives for moving from low to medium engagement, may be needed to effectively manage such campaigns.

# CASE STUDY GOOGLE 'THE VOICE' TAIWAN

In the 2016 presidential elections in Taiwan, Google aimed to provide more meaningful election coverage for its many users in the country. Targeting specifically young users, Google set up 'The Voice', an online platform for Google users to engage directly with the election debate, candidates and news relating to the election. According to analysis by Google, in previous elections, especially younger voters felt that candidates weren't listening to them. Therefore, Google set out to design a way to connect more easily with the democratic process.

The stated aim was to simplify the way voters connected to their candidates and to allow voters a direct voice in the elections. Google created a one-stop election hub, where users could read the latest stories and news items about the candidates, view the most recent polls and other statistics and even watch live debates broadcast via YouTube.

A key feature of the election hub was the 'Ask a Question' gadget, which allowed voters to ask questions directly to their candidates. More than 6,500 questions were submitted, and voted upon by other users. The most voted questions were then put to the candidates in an exclusive televised debate, and the presidential candidates also answered some of the questions on the platform itself.

The election site itself contained customised and personalised content for users, and the aggregated data was used by Google to display adverts related to the interests of individual voters.

Overall roughly one third of young Taiwanese voters participated in the site. Moreover, while the general turnout fell from 74% in the previous presidential election to 66% in the 2016 presidential election, the youth voting rate increased by 7%.

*(Continued)*

## Questions to Consider

1 What additional data would you like to know in order to measure the effectiveness of Google 'The Voice' of Taiwan?
2 Overall, the winning candidate, Tsai Ing-wen, was ahead in the polls since the beginning of the campaign. Do you think Google had any influence at all?
3 How do you feel about the site customising newsfeeds and adverts according to the users' profiles? What ethical issues does this raise?

# FURTHER READING

Groshek, J. and Al-Rawi, A. (2013) 'Public sentiment and critical framing in social media content during the 2012 US presidential campaign', *Social Science Computer Review*, 31(5): 563–76.

Kwok, L. and Yu, B. (2012) 'Spreading social media messages on Facebook: An analysis of restaurant business-to-consumer communications', *Cornell Hospitality Quarterly*, 54(1): 84–94.

Neiger, B.L., Thackeray, R., Van Wagenen, S.A., Hanson, C.L., West, J.H., Barnes, M.D. and Fagen, M.C. (2012) 'Use of social media in health promotion: Purposes, key performance indicators, and evaluation metrics', *Health Promotion Practice*, 13(2): 159–64.

## REFERENCES

Avnit, A. (2009) The million followers fallacy [Online], Pravda Media Group. Available at: http://blog.pravdam.com/the-million-followers-fallacy-guest-post-by-adi-avnit/ (accessed 24 February 2014).

BARB (2013) Total viewing summary [Online], Broadcasters Audience Research Board. Available at: www.barb.co.uk/viewing/weekly-total-viewing-summary?period_year%5B%5D= 2013&period_month%5B%5D=2&period_week%5B%5D=17&button_submit=View+fig ures&period%5B%5D=201302060117 (accessed 16 March 2013).

Becker, P. (2012) Twitter the latest facts and figures (Infographic) [Online]. Available at: http://wallblog.co.uk/2012/11/13/twitter-the-latest-facts-and-figures-infographic/ (accessed 16 March 2013).

Bennett, D. (2013) 'The Dunbar number, from the guru of social networks', *Bloomberg Business Week*, 10 January.

Carmichael, D. and Cleave, D. (2012) 'How effective is social media advertising? A study of Facebook social advertisements', in *Proceedings of the 7th International Conference for Internet Technology and Secured Transactions (ICITST 2012)*, 10–12 December. pp. 226–9.

Cha, M., Haddadi, H., Benevenuto, F. and Gummadi, K.P. (2010) 'Measuring user influence in Twitter: The million follower fallacy', in *Proceedings of the 4th International AAAI Conference on Weblogs and Social Media*. Menlo Park, CA: AAAI Press. pp. 10–17.

Cova, B. (1997) 'Community and consumption: Towards a definition of the "linking value" of product or services', *European Journal of Marketing*, 31: 297–316.

Crowne, D.P. and Marlowe, D. (1960) 'A new scale of social desirability independent of psychopathology', *Journal of Consulting Psychology*, 24: 349.

DiStaso, M.W., McCorkindale, T. and Wright, D.K. (2011) 'How public relations executives perceive and measure the impact of social media in their organizations', *Public Relations Review*, 37: 325–8.

Drenten, J. (2012) 'Snapshots of the self: Exploring the role of online mobile photo sharing in identity development among adolescent girls', in A. Close (ed.), *Online Consumer Behavior: Theory and Research in Social Media, Advertising, and E-Tail*. New York: Routledge. pp. 3–34.

Godbout, J.T. and Caillé, A. (1992) *L'Esprit du Don*. Paris: La Découverte.

*The Guardian* (2012) 'Most viewed TV programmes in 2012' [Online]. Available at: www.theguardian.com/media/2012/dec/12/most-viewed-tv-programmes-in-2012 (accessed 11 November 2017).

Hoffman, D.L. and Fodor, M. (2010) 'Can you measure the ROI of your social media marketing', *MIT Sloan Management Review*, 52: 41–9.

Kaplan, A.M. and Haenlein, M. (2011) 'Two hearts in three-quarter time: How to waltz the social media/viral marketing dance', *Business Horizons*, 54: 253–63.

Keegan, B.J. and Rowley, J. (2017) 'Evaluation and decision making in social media marketing', *Management Decision*, 55(1): 15–31.

Keiningham, T.L., Cooil, B., Andreassen, T.W. and Aksoy, L. (2007) 'A longitudinal examination of net promoter and firm revenue growth', *Journal of Marketing*, 71: 39–51.

Kiss, J. (2013) 'Facebook UK loses 600,000 users in December' [Online], *The Guardian*. Available at: www.guardian.co.uk/technology/2013/jan/14/facebook-loses-uk-users-december (accessed 16 March 2013).

LaPointe, P. (2012) 'Measuring Facebook's impact on marketing: The proverbial hits the fan', *Journal of Advertising Research*, 52: 286.

Lee, Z. and Sargeant, A. (2011) 'Dealing with social desirability bias: An application to charitable giving', *European Journal of Marketing*, 45: 703–19.

Martosko, D. (2013) 'Barack Obama has 19.5m fake Twitter followers' [Online], *Mail Online*. Available at: www.dailymail.co.uk/news/article-2430875/Barack-Obama-19-5m-fake-Twitter-followers.html (accessed 25 February 2014).

Murdough, C. (2009) 'Social media measurement: It's not impossible', *Journal of Interactive Advertising*, 10.

Neiger, B.L., Thackeray, R., Van Wagenen, S.A., Hanson, C.L., West, J.H., Barnes, M.D. and Fagen, M.C. (2012) 'Use of social media in health promotion: Purposes, key performance indicators, and evaluation metrics', *Health Promotion Practice*, 13(2): 159–64.

Schulman, K. and Sargeant, A. (2013) 'Measuring donor loyalty: Key reasons why Net Promoter Score (NPS) is not the way', *International Journal of Nonprofit and Voluntary Sector Marketing*, 18: 1–6.

Socialbakers (2012) December 2012 Social Media Report: Facebook pages in the United Kingdom [Online]. Available at: www.socialbakers.com/blog/1214-december-2012-social-media-report-facebook-pages-in-the-united-kingdom (accessed 16 March 2013).

Stringhini, G., Egele, M., Kruegel, C. and Vigna, G. (2012) 'Poultry markets: On the underground economy of Twitter followers', *WOSN '12: Proceedings of the 2012 ACM Workshop on Online Social Networks*. New York: ACM Press. pp. 1–6.

Taylor, D.G., Lewin, J.E. and Strutton, D. (2011) 'Friends, fans, and followers: Do ads work on social networks? How gender and age shape receptivity', *Journal of Advertising Research*, 51: 258.

# 11

# Cross-cultural Aspects and Implications

## CHAPTER OVERVIEW

This chapter looks at cross-cultural and social influences when using social media across cultural boundaries. In the first section, the chapter focuses on differences in social media use and adoption, then it moves on to discuss differences in terms of reactions towards social media content, specifically WOM and reviews, before finishing with a discussion about the reflection of cultural values in content posted online.

## LEARNING OUTCOMES

On completing this chapter, you should be able to:

* critically discuss the notion that social media is truly global
* understand differences in adoption and usage of social media
* be able to explain differences in reaction towards reviews and brand-related content in cultural terms
* have a broad idea of cultural and social factors influencing social media content.

## CROSS-CULTURAL ASPECTS OF SOCIAL MEDIA

A multitude of studies have linked various aspects of social media explicitly to existing cross-cultural frameworks, with Hofstede's five cultural dimensions (Hofstede, 1991, 2001) frequently used to explain observed differences (see Table 11.1 for a brief review of these dimensions). Hofstede's dimensions have been linked to technology adoption (cf. Steers et al., 2008), impact of eWOM (Christodoulides, 2012), intentions to become brand page fans (Muk et al., 2013) to name but a few examples.

While the literature shows that such links can be made, at least in certain cases, it is nevertheless important to remember that Hofstede's framework (or other, similar frameworks) has significant limitations that are important to acknowledge. Specifically, Hofstede's framework, while being a popular and frequently used general guide to cross-cultural differences, cannot explain differences at an individual level. In particular in relation to marketing communication, and by extension communication in social media, occasional cultural paradoxes can be observed (see de Mooij and de Mooij, 2009 for an extensive discussion of the effects of culture on advertising). Moreover, while culture can explain certain behaviours and perceptions at a societal level, other factors, only partially or not at all covered by Hofstede's framework, may have a significant impact on observed behaviour or perceptions. For instance, while cross-cultural frameworks like Hofstede's dimensions can explain a propensity for superstition, or Hall's high-context and low-context framework (Hall and Hall, 1987) can explain a tendency to read more into a communication than what is being said semantically, i.e. paying attention to colours or searching for hidden meanings behind the overt meaning of the words being used, no framework can account for red being seen as a lucky colour in parts of the world, for example. It is therefore important to not simply rely on cross-cultural frameworks alone, but to always seek clarification from people highly familiar with a target culture to ensure that any message, especially when it has the potential to reach a global audience, is culturally acceptable.

The remainder of the chapter focuses on different aspects of cultural influence on social media. The first part reviews cultural and social influences in terms of social media adoption and usage. The second part of the chapter then moves on and focuses on the potential differences in perceptions that may arise if people from different cultures are exposed to messages originating in another culture in a social media context. The last part of the chapter explores the reflection of cross-cultural values in social media content, specifically, how brands, organisations and companies display cultural values through the messages they send and other design elements.

**Table 11.1** Five cultural dimensions

---

**Power Distance**

Power distance is the extent to which members of the society with less power accept that power is distributed unequally. High power distance countries, such as Japan, are characterised by comparative respect for authority and acceptance of hierarchical structures. In lower power distance countries, such as the UK, displays of hierarchical power or authority can have a negative connotation and hierarchical power structures are often regarded with suspicion.

**Individualism/Collectivism**

Individuals in individualistic societies tend to put greater emphasis on looking out for themselves and their immediate families, rather than the wider community. Conversely, in collectivist countries the needs of the wider group rather than the individual as a constituent of the group are emphasised. This includes strong differentiation between in- and out-group.

Individualist countries are often characterised by small family units, such as frequently found in many Western countries like the UK or the US, while countries scoring higher on this dimension, such as many Latin American and Asian countries, tend to have larger family units and extended family ties and groups.

**Masculinity/Femininity**

Quality of life and caring for others are more emphasised in feminine societies, while achievement and success are relatively more valued in masculine societies. Gender roles are often strongly differentiated in masculine societies, whereas in feminine societies gender roles tend to be less differentiated. Because of the highly competitive nature of masculine societies, envy of success and rewards are also common. For example, programmes like the 'Employee of the Month' work well in masculine societies. Typical examples of strongly masculine societies include the US and Japan, while examples of feminine societies include the Netherlands, Norway and Sweden.

**Uncertainty Avoidance**

Uncertainty is perceived as potentially threatening in countries with high uncertainty avoidance and therefore preferably avoided – or at least regulated. For example, in countries with high uncertainty avoidance strict rules and formality are frequently apparent. Countries such as Germany, seen as relatively high on uncertainty avoidance, have explicit rules, laws and regulations for many areas of life.

**Long-term Orientation**

Long-term orientation is the extent to which a society collectively holds conventional, historic continuum-oriented views, or emphasises short-term, future orientation. This dimension is derived from the work of Michael Bond related to Chinese values, and is therefore the most 'Asian' of the five Hofstede dimensions. Countries that score highly on long-term orientation tend to have strong order systems, highly value perseverance and often place a greater importance on concepts such as shame and face. For short-term oriented societies, the emphasis is more on immediate, often individual pursuit of happiness.

---

*Source*: Dahl, S. (2014) 'Communication appeal effectiveness', in A.J. Broderick and C. Demangeot (eds), *Contemporary Consumer Psychology*. London: Sage Publications.

## Differences in SM Usage

As social media is largely dependent on social ties, it is easy to forget that, although some players attract a large and nearly global user base, such a user base is by no means universal or equally distributed. Nor is the way in which social media is used universally similar – in fact, there are often surprising differences when comparing social media usage across different countries, for example, the amount of friends, and therefore how many potential interaction partners a user has, differs significantly from country to country. In 2010, as an example, the average Japanese Facebook user was connected to only 29 others, while the average Malaysian user was connected to 233 (BBC News, 2010). Such dramatic differences suggest that Japanese users access social media to share information with relatively few, and most likely quite intimate, friends, possibly friends with whom they are in contact with on an equally regular basis away from the social media site. Thus, in terms of WOM terminology (see Chapter 9) Japanese users, at least on Facebook, are connected to a network with strong ties. Conversely, ties between friends of Malaysian users are likely to be much weaker, and are unlikely to replicate mostly regular, offline social relationships. Similarly, Japanese and French users spend far less time (2.3 hours/day) on social media sites than Indonesians and Saudi users, who use social networking sites on average 5.1 hours a day (MarketingCharts, 2013).

Moreover, some social networks are not as popular, or not available, in some countries than in others – most prominently, Facebook, Twitter and YouTube are banned in most parts of Mainland China, though they are available in Hong Kong and Macau, and there are conflicting reports about potential availability in parts of Shanghai (*The Guardian*, 2013). Consequently local competitors are more popular – and are also rapidly expanding into neighbouring territories. Similarly, Facebook attracts only around 5% of the population in Russia, Belarus or Ukraine (with the local VK network being considerably more popular), while in Iceland over 70% of the population use Facebook (Internet World Stats, 2012).

While some of these differences in usage may be cultural, others are likely to be the result of different factors. As Berthon and colleagues (2012) suggest, social media usage can be said to rely largely on three factors: technology enabling the use of social media, socio-cultural factors, and governmental rules and regulations. While technological advancement means that social media has the ability to reach virtually every part of the world, with only rural areas of developing countries having difficulties in accessing the Internet, governmental regulation and socio-cultural factors are frequently intertwined and more complex, for example, Russian censors have repeatedly threatened to ban Facebook (Galperina, 2013). However, the user base of Facebook itself is, as pointed out before, very small in Russia when compared to other social networks. The small user base can make it relatively simple to block access to the website, at least without provoking the same angry reaction from the majority of Russian social media users, who are relying on social networking sites such as VK. As the VK user base is largely Russian, the network is culturally and socially more relevant to a much larger part of Russian society. Consequently, governmental and technological interference with VK in Russia is subject to extensive Internet debate. For instance, when VK was briefly and supposedly erroneously blocked in 2013, the censorship created an outrage amongst Russian bloggers and other Internet users (BBC News, 2013). No such outrage has ever followed the suggestion of blocking

Facebook completely – or even the required 'hiding' of certain posts on Facebook, Twitter and YouTube in Russia because of restrictive laws (Kramer, 2013).

Moreover, while it is easy to claim nearly global reach of social media, it is important to acknowledge that certain global media are significantly more popular in some areas than in others, even outside of areas where Internet censorship is currently enforced, with stark differences occurring even in the same country or region. In Hong Kong, a special administrative region of China with different laws regarding freedom of speech and no Internet censorship, Facebook is by far the most popular social media platform with 2.6 million people of the around 7 million inhabitants using Facebook daily. As Facebook is blocked in Mainland China, users there rely on local websites, which are clearly more relevant for them. Consequently, websites such as Sina Weibo, largely a hybrid of Twitter and Facebook, attracts around 300 million users daily, or Renren, which is fundamentally similar to Facebook in terms of functionality. These websites are also starting to grow outside of the original, Mainland China territory. However, while many Hong Kongers are proud users of Facebook, other social networks popular in other countries, including in Asia, are not doing nearly as well in Hong Kong. Twitter, for example, while very popular in South Korea and Japan, and fully accessible in Hong Kong, is struggling to gain users. While it is hard to gain accurate figures, Twitter has been reported as having only approximately 3,500 estimated users (Zhai, 2013) in Hong Kong. However, social ties to Mainland China may offer a partial explanation as to why services such as Sina Weibo are more popular and in fact, Sina Weibo is the second most popular social networking platform in Hong Kong, with around 600,000 users (Global Web Index, 2011). Consequently, many brands in Hong Kong do not market themselves on Twitter – rather it is very common to see Facebook pages and Sina Weibo addresses in adverts, encouraging consumers to connect with businesses and organisations on these two platforms. Sina Weibo, on the other hand, is currently only available in Chinese, thus, the user base outside of China is typically limited to overseas Chinese, although other international versions have been announced.

## THINKBOX SOCIAL MEDIA USAGE

Make a list of social media sites you use. Now compare this list with other people from your class. Are there differences? Compare the reasons for using the same and different social media sites.

## Cultural Factors in Social Media Adoption

In general terms, there is an extensive literature linking information and communication technology adoption to underlying cultural values. Erumban and de Jong (2006), for example, examined computer ownership across 42 countries and showed that both uncertainty avoidance and **power distance** affect private computer possession. Cognate with cultural dimension descriptions, they showed that in countries with high uncertainty avoidance scores, uptake of ICT (information and communication technology) equipment was slower. According to the authors, this is a reflection that in countries where uncertainty avoidance is high, individuals are more likely to wait and evaluate ICT purchases before making a decision. However, they also pointed out that once the uncertainty regarding the worth of the ICT adoption has been lifted, people in countries with high uncertainty avoidance scores would be swifter to adopt the new technology than in countries where scores are lower, i.e. there is a delayed effect, followed by a strong increase in adoption. This link between uncertainty avoidance and uptake of ICT has also been reported by Srite and Karahanna (2006), who showed that, in relation to the Technology Acceptance Model, the relative importance of perceived social norms are linked to uncertainty avoidance. Consequently, through the relative importance, social norms influence behavioural intentions and ultimately actual behaviour.

Further, Erumban and de Jong found that in countries with high power distance, ICT adoption was lower. They relate this finding to previous findings that organisations and countries with hierarchical structures tend to show lower innovation and adoption of new technologies, and, furthermore, are less open to new ideas as these may entail decision making for which no historical pre-requisites are available and consequently require the decision to be made at a higher level.

Potentially, one could argue that ICT adoption is similar to the adoption of new technology in the form of using different social media sites, as the Technology Adoption Model has been used previously to study adoption not only of technological equipment, but also in terms of engaging in behaviours involving technology – such as using social media. However, contrary to the uncertainty avoidance propagated as underlying technology adoption, Okazaki (2013) points out that, more intuitively, social networks are likely to be closely linked to societies which are individualistic, as people in these societies are linked to often numerous others with relatively weak ties between individuals. He argues that in societies that are more collectivistic in nature, individuals are most likely to form fewer but stronger ties, and thus are less likely to engage in self-promotion activities frequently encountered in social media contexts, and therefore are less likely to adopt social media as a means to communicate amongst intimate friends. However, while the average number of Facebook friends may only be a very rough indicator of such cultural influence factors, such claims are hard to empirically verify, suggesting a much more complex relationship. Malaysia, for example, is a highly collectivistic country – just like Japan – yet both countries are, as previously mentioned in this chapter, at opposite extremes when it comes to the average number of friends each user connects with.

Trying to examine the motivators for online engagement with social networks more closely, a comparative study between social media users in the US and South Korea (Kim et al., 2011) also found that motivators are similar across both culturally highly distinct countries. Looking for friends, obtaining social support, entertainment, information and convenience motivated users in both countries. However, on a more subtle basis, the study found that the weighting of these motivators differed as American students emphasised the entertainment acquired through social media more than their South Korean counterparts. Thus, activities such as following updates from friends perceived as funny or entertaining were particularly important motivators for US social media users, while

South Korean students, on the other hand, emphasised accessing social support using social media more than their American counterparts. They also based their friendship circles largely on existing social relationships, i.e. South Korean students used social media predominantly to communicate more with already existing social networks – and with people they already knew outside of the social media context. Conversely, American students tended to accept friend requests more freely and corresponded with both people they had strong ties with as well as relative strangers.

### Agency-communication Theory

**Agency-communication Theory** gives a hypothetical, theoretical explanation for this difference (Okazaki, 2013). Agency-communication theory was originally introduced by Zarbatany et al. (2004), suggesting that friendship is not a consistent and single construct, but rather encompasses two different types of friendship. These two types are 'communal' and 'agentic' friendships.

Within an agentic friendship type, friends provide self-worth through validation and support for the individual, however, normally in a non-committal and sporadic way. Agentic friends tend to be looser friendships where both friends mutually support each other when needed and convenient for both. Typical examples of such friendships might be friends that occasionally 'like' status updates, but generally have little other interaction, such as chats or emails, or rarely see each other outside of a virtual environment.

Communal friendship types on the other hand are based on a wider variety of factors, including companionship, mutual affection and shared experiences. Thus, such friendships tend to be deeper and more profound, and expressions of friendship are not dependent solely on mutual convenience. Rather, in terms of tie strengths, communal friendships tend to be significantly tighter and more stable over time.

Consequently, communal type friends are likely to be friends whom individuals connect with online and offline, i.e. with regular social contact via social media as well as other means.

While both agentic as well as communal friendship types can be found in all countries, a preference for the one over the other has been linked to both culture and gender. Some researchers have suggested a link based on Hofstede's individualism and **collectivism** (Hupfer and Detlor, 2007). Hupfer and Detlor found that people with high individualism scores placed greater emphasis on establishing and maintaining agentic friendships, while individuals with higher collectivist scores emphasised more communal friendships. Further, and in line with the characterisations of agentic and communal friendships, Hupfer and Detlor found that people with a preference for communal relationships engaged more with relationship-enhancing networking practices, such as messaging, sending eCards and meeting new people.

Thus, Okazaki speculates, within cultures where more emphasis is placed on agentic relationships, strategies targeting individuals would require enabling them to 'show off' more – although to date no empirical evidence has endorsed such a proposition.

While the research into the role of both social and cultural factors in the adoption and usage of social media is still nascent, the observed usage differences and emerging research findings suggest that both factors may have some influence; as a concrete example, Amaro and Duarte (2017) showed that Portuguese travellers relied more heavily on social media when planning their vacations than UK travellers. They explained this difference by an underlying difference in uncertainty avoidance, which is higher in Portugal than in the UK. Consequently, when engaging in social media marketing activities, it is therefore important for the marketer to understand how people are using social media, for example, brand-related eWOM in a culture where strong ties dominate social media usage may be significantly more 'valuable' (or indeed damaging, if negative) than in a culture where loose ties are dominant (see for instance the discussion in Chapter 9 regarding the importance of tie strength in word-of-mouth recommendations).

However, the influence of cultural and social factors is not only limited to the adoption or ways of using social media. These factors are also likely to influence reaction to messages received when using social media, including messages both from friends and organisations that users like or follow.

## THINKBOX AGENTIC VS. COMMUNAL FRIENDSHIP

Think of ten friends you connect with on a given social media site. Can you classify these friends into agentic or communal friends? What differences would it make to you if one of these friends recommends you to sign up to a deal that sounds too good to be true, for instance, an online casino where you are nearly always winning?

## Reaction to Social Media

Going beyond the notion of tie strength discussed in the previous section, Christodoulides (2012) shows that there are differences in how Chinese and UK consumers react to negative or positive eWOM. Studying evaluations based on online reviews, i.e. in cases where pre-existing ties were unlikely, Christodoulides found that individuals with different cultural backgrounds reacted differently when forming opinions based on reading reviews. Chinese respondents were found to adjust their evaluations dynamically, anchoring on the most recent evaluation available. Conversely, UK users were most likely to anchor their evaluation on the most negative reviews. This suggests that some of the observed differences can be explained through Anchoring Theory, and different anchoring biases dependent on cultural factors.

### Anchoring Theory

Anchoring and adjusting, or **Anchoring Theory**, was first introduced in the 1970s by Tversky and Kahneman (1974). The theory postulates that, when forming evaluations, individuals anchor these on certain attributes, for instance, the amount of stars given on a review website, a test result score – or indeed particular features in a written review. Once an anchor is established, any subsequent information leads to an adjustment of the original 'anchored' evaluation. However, importantly, any adjustments are made relative to the original anchor. For instance, if a review website has many positive reviews and ranks a hotel as the best in town, and an individual anchors his/her evaluation on this information, then, based on Anchoring Theory, the individual is likely to adjust their evaluation skewed towards a positive evaluation, i.e. a very good hotel overall or even the best hotel in the world. That is to say, individuals are less likely to think of the hotel as being completely hideous, even if they would have made such an evaluation in the absence of a previously set anchor (or indeed if they would anchor on the most negative review).

Anchoring Theory, while well established and often used in marketing as a way to explain decision making (cf. Wansink et al., 1998), has interestingly not been evaluated extensively across different cultures. Particularly in the context of the anchoring effects of WOM, apart from the previously referred to study by Christodoulides (2012), there has been little work in the area. In this case, the permanence of eWOM is an interesting example making a previously hard to research area more easily researchable, although further research is needed to establish the different reactions specifically towards brand-related communications in a social media context. Nevertheless, cultural differences in anchoring may be a suitable explanatory basis for observed differences in response to reviews, which in turn are an important part of social media and brand engagement for consumers. Consequently, while more research is needed to establish the exact nature of anchoring influences, social media marketing managers should carefully consider which anchors they may be able to use and 'set' in the mind of users – and what the likely effect would be. For instance, displaying warranties and awards may set anchors, which, particularly if current, are likely to lead to more positive evaluations in some cultures. On the other hand, negative reviews may have a much longer effect for readers from other cultural backgrounds, and may be less counterbalanced by more positive and more recent reviews. Thus, social media marketers should think of creative strategies as to how to deal with negative eWOM.

Apart from the reactions towards messages, the values displayed in messages and other content is equally likely to be influenced by cultural and other factors differing across different countries and regions. Thus, the remainder of the chapter now focuses on the messages sent, rather than the way messages are received.

## THINKBOX ANCHORING

Go to TripAdvisor, booking.com or a similar site that carries reviews. Based on the reviews, make a choice for a hotel in a foreign city you have never visited. Pay attention to how you get to the overall evaluation of the hotel. Discuss which features or reviews you are anchoring on.

## Reflection of Cultural Values

It is important to remember that social media marketing is often not taking place in a vacuum, but is part of wider branding and marketing communication campaigns of the company or organisation. Okazaki (2013) argues that, consequently, social media marketing can be assumed to be a component of globally integrated marketing communications – although a potential global reach, or indeed national targeting if required, would greatly depend on the technical abilities of the platform used. Facebook, for example, allows pages to be visible only in certain countries, i.e. certain pages can be specifically targeted at certain geographic regions. Twitter does not offer this functionality, and has no technical functionality to hide a Twitter feed in one country. Consequently, for platforms with no geo-targeting possibility, if an organisation wants to have country or territory-specific feeds, it would have to create those feeds and hope that consumers would choose the feed or channel that is relevant to their country. For example, users have the choice to follow and interact with both the global Coca-Cola account (https://twitter.com/CocaCola) and the British Coca-Cola account (https://twitter.com/CocaCola_GB) on Twitter. The challenge for a brand with presence in several markets, like Coca-Cola, would be to direct consumers to the right account.

A potential issue with globally accessible marketing communication campaigns is that traditionally marketing communications tended to reflect, by and large, the underlying cultural values of the target country. Reflecting underlying cultural values has been an important cornerstone for many national as well as global marketing campaigns and brands, resulting in significant cultural differences in appeals being used in different countries (Cheong et al., 2010). Hofstede's dimensions of culture (2001), despite the previously mentioned important methodological limitations and theoretical concerns, have, by and large, been useful in explaining these differences, especially in culturally very distant countries, such as Asian countries and Western countries, with mixed results in 'culturally close' countries (Czarnecka et al., 2013). Another popular framework has been Halls' (Hall and Hall, 1987) classic high-context and low-context communication preferences, which has been used to explain advertising content from a cross-cultural perspective. For instance, using Halls' theory, information content has been shown to be higher in cultures with a low-context culture and communication style, while in countries with a high-context communication style, advertisements contained fewer information cues.

In a traditional marketing communication context, appeals (sometimes referred to as values) are frequently used to examine the reflection of cultural differences in company-originated communication, such as advertising (Dahl, 2014). The rational for focusing purposely on appeals is the existence of a large body of previous research, which has resulted in a well-established and frequently used methodology focusing on appeals identified originally by Pollay (1986). Pollay's list of 42 advertising appeals has been widely adopted to show that the much hyped globalisation of marketing communication including cultural convergence of target audiences, as controversially advocated by Levitt in the 1980s (Levitt, 1983), remains elusive. A significant body of research has since established that, at least for print and television advertising, the appeals in culturally different parts of the world remain distinct, despite the undeniable globalisation of financial markets, brands and to some extent products.

Despite the large body of research examining traditional advertising, within the social media context, only a few studies have compared social media appeals, or values, across countries. In a study comparing the Chinese Renren pages of companies with American Facebook pages, Tsai and Men (2012) show that pages of organisations on the Chinese social media site are more likely to promote values in line with collectivism and high power distance, characteristic of Chinese society. Moreover, companies posting on Renren use a more high-context communication style than their American counterparts. American Facebook pages, in contrast, promoted more individualistic values. However, while this study may indicate that cultural values are reflected on social media sites, it is important to point out that the findings were not completely as hypothesised: no significant differences were found for appeals related to low power distance, which is more prevalent in US society, nor were US sites employing lower context strategies, such as comparative claims or highlighting product features. The latter finding may, at least theoretically, be explained by the circumstance that lower context strategies may be counterproductive in social media environments (see, for example, the discussion in Chapter 3 on anthropomorphism), as social media pages usually focus on brand building rather than on low-context sales arguments.

Apart from value or appeals differences, which would become apparent in the content of messages and texts posted, culture is also likely to affect other types of visual displays, for instance in pictures posted on social media websites, or other design features of social media campaigns. There is a well-established body of literature within the context of web design suggesting cultural adaptation for traditional online content. Social media sites, however, offer less flexibility in terms of design, as practically many features, such as page design or font type, are standardised depending on the website used. Nevertheless, there are significant visual and content styles of social media that can be adopted to reflect cultural differences. For instance, Marcus (2004) describes how website elements should be adopted based on Hofstede's cultural dimensions. As previously noted, not all of his suggestions are applicable or achievable in the context of social media. Marcus suggests, for example, that in high power distance cultures, access restrictions and password requirements make websites more attractive. Such access restrictions are more problematic to implement on, for example, Facebook pages and most other social media websites where the content is visible to all who follow. However, other elements are clearly comparable, and can be implemented both in a social media and traditional web environment. Marcus, for example, suggests displaying more status-implying buildings in a high power distance culture, while relying on displaying more informal buildings or places in low power distance cultures. Similarly, he suggests focusing on products, individuals and dynamic imagery in individualistic cultures, while in collectivistic cultures images displaying groups are suggested to be preferable.

Specifically to a social media environment, Lin et al. (2017) suggest emphasising more individual posts in individualistic cultures and communal messages in collectivist cultures; focusing on consumers' identity in short-term oriented cultures and conversely emphasising functional information in more long-term oriented cultures; engaging in one-way communication in higher power distance countries while emphasising two-way communication in lower power distance countries; and avoiding direct messages in higher-context cultures while addressing more directly in lower-context cultures.

Most of the suggestions for web design are similar to suggestions made for traditional marketing communication, such as advertising design. However, while it is tempting to argue that social media is in many ways similar to traditional marketing communication, the early evidence suggests that in some cases subtle differences exist, potentially due to the more egalitarian nature of social media. Thus, further research in this area would be valuable to show how these subtle differences manifest themselves.

## THINKBOX CULTURAL DIFFERENCES

Go to three websites of companies from different countries – these could be the same companies operating in three different markets (e.g. McDonald's in Hong Kong, Australia and Italy) or three local companies which serve a similar market (e.g. Café de Coral from Hong Kong, FEBO from the Netherlands and H3 Burgers from Portugal). Based on the look and feel of each of the companies, discuss how you could achieve a similar brand message using social networks.

## SUMMARY

This chapter described the socio-cultural influences on social media. While social media is assumed to be relatively global, and many social media websites are indeed globally accessible, there are, nevertheless, many differences in terms of usage and motives for using social media websites.

Similarly, the way messages sent via social media websites are likely to be interpreted from a culturally distinct perspective, depending on the receiver – and may be conveying culturally different values dependent on the sender.

## RESEARCH DIRECTIONS

The area of socio-cultural differences in social media remains largely under-researched and is one of the promising areas of future research (Okazaki, 2013). Consequently, there are multitudes of differences – and similarities – that have not been extensively researched. For instance, research into image transfer across cultures is largely nonexistent, especially in such areas as advergaming (Okazaki, 2013), where image transfer is less cognisant, but may have strong cultural implications. Similarly, motivators to engage in eWOM, facilitated by and as a result of social network activity, remain largely under-researched. This is even more crucial in areas where there is at least conjectural convergence of cultures, forming a universal 'global teen' segment in which children around the world are proposed to share more similarities than differences (Taylor, 2005).

Similarly, early studies suggest that linking culture and appeals used on social networking sites offers room for further research, but more evidence of such links is needed. Future research can explore if this link is mostly because of social networking sites reflecting traditional advertising, or if the social media environment is an even more distorted mirror of cultural values than traditional advertising. Similarly, if organisations' communications reflect cultural values, future research needs to focus on the effect that culturally non-congruent communications might have, particularly if they are globally accessible.

# RESEARCH HIGHLIGHT CULTURE

In their article 'Cultural differences and switching of in-group sharing behavior between an American (Facebook) and a Chinese (Renren) social networking site', Qiu and colleagues (2012) examine how users perceive and act differently depending on the cultural context of the social networking website that they are using. They examine these differences by conducting two studies based on a sample of students from Mainland China currently studying in Singapore, who use both the 'American' platform Facebook and the Chinese social networking site Renren. As both sites offer near identical functionality, comparisons could be made by examining if the same users use or perceive each site differently.

In the first study, the authors asked students to rate the activity they were exposed to on both Facebook and Renren, based on a scale measuring perceived cultural characteristics, including cultural characteristics linked to collectivist culture (such as 'hierarchical' and 'sharing-orientated'), individualistic attributes (such as 'egalitarian', 'assertive' and 'competitive') and social networking attributes ('self-expressive' and 'supportive'). Based on the answers of 37 students, they conclude that Renren and Facebook, despite similar technical capabilities, are perceived differently on some, but not all of the attributes tested. Specifically, Renren was rated significantly higher on collectivist attributes than Facebook; however, Facebook was not rated significantly more individualistic than Renren – and both networks did not differ in terms of the perceived social networking attributes.

The authors then followed up the perception study by coding how participants used both networks, based on coding of the 20 most recent events on participants' profile pages and newsfeeds. Events for 100 students were coded as either 'in-group sharing'-oriented, or as non-sharing. Examples of 'in-group sharing' activities included all events that involved clicking the 'share' button: such as sharing of links to other websites or videos, pictures created by others or sharing of posts made by others. All other events, such as for example posting a status update about oneself, were coded as non-sharing activity.

The results showed that on Renren, participants engaged in significantly more sharing activity than on Facebook: this implies that participants 'switched' their behaviour when acting on Renren and acted in a more culturally consistent manner by engaging in greater sharing activity than when using Facebook. A further, unexpected, result was that users on Renren tagged people less frequently in pictures than on Facebook. While Qui and colleagues are cautious about interpreting this result, they suggest that a possible explanation might be that tagging increases the chance of being identifiable to out-group members, something that is not preferred in an Asian cultural context (Cho, 2010).

The authors conclude that users access different social networking sites with culturally congruent content, noting that collective knowledge sharing, although common on both platforms, is more frequently used as an in-group sharing tool on Renren. Specifically, they note that, from a cross-cultural perspective, motives for sharing differed. As previously researched, Americans tend to share information as a way to establish a sense of individuality while Chinese are motivated to share information to enhance in-group harmony (Jiacheng et al., 2010).

The full article can be found on the companion website of this book.

# CASE STUDY LIFE OF FARAH

Domestic violence is a problem in all parts of the world, including in Dubai. In Islam, domestic violence is sometimes argued to be justified based on religious verses that imply a 'light tap' is acceptable. However, even a 'light tap' can be domestic violence and this was the message the Dubai Foundation for Women & Children (DFWAC) wanted to share with a wider audience.

To convey the key message, they used Instagram's Story 'tap to see the next image' feature. Using the handle lifeof_farah, they posted a series of pictures of a woman's face, with more bruises appearing following each tap. Thus, someone who viewed the lifeof_farah story and tapped forward to the next picture would gradually wound the protagonist. DFWAC then tagged influential social and traditional media personalities in the pictures to nudge them to share and talk about the campaign. Around 124,000 men shared the campaign

Following the innovative campaign, the message was picked up by many influencers globally and reported widely in the media. The public debate surrounding the issue also started to significantly sway public opinion: pre-campaign, 64% of men surveyed in Dubai found that a 'light tap' was not acceptable. This increased to 82% of men surveyed after the campaign. Importantly, the charity registered a 39% drop of domestic violence cases in the year after the campaign.

## Questions to Consider

1  How do you explain the success of the campaign?
2  Do you think this campaign can be 'translated' into other cultures?
3  Which ethical and cultural challenges do you foresee with this campaign? And when using this campaign in other parts of the world?

# FURTHER READING

Magnini, V.P., Kara, D., Crotts, J.C. and Zehrer, A. (2012) 'Culture and service-related positive disconfirmations: An application of travel blog analysis', *Journal of Vacation Marketing*, 18(3): 251–7.

Mesch, G.S., Talmud, I. and Quan-Haase, A. (2012) 'Instant messaging social networks: Individual, relational, and cultural characteristics', *Journal of Social and Personal Relationships*, 29(6): 736–59.

Qiu, L., Lin, H. and Leung, A.K.-Y. (2012) 'Cultural differences and switching of in-group sharing behavior between an American (Facebook) and a Chinese (Renren) social networking site', *Journal of Cross-Cultural Psychology*, 44(1): 106–21.

## REFERENCES

Amaro, S. and Duarte, P. (2017) 'Social media use for travel purposes: A cross cultural comparison between Portugal and the UK', *Information Technology & Tourism*, 17(2): 161–81.

BBC News (2010) Japan has fewest digital friends on social networks [Online]. Available at: www.bbc.co.uk/news/technology-11501625 (accessed 14 November 2017).

BBC News (2013) Error blacklists Russia's top social network VKontakte [Online]. Available at: www.bbc.co.uk/news/world-europe-22651973 (accessed 19 February 2014).

Berthon, P.R., Pitt, L.F., Plangger, K. and Shapiro, D. (2012) 'Marketing meets Web 2.0, social media, and creative consumers: Implications for international marketing strategy', *Business Horizons*, 55: 261–71.

Cheong, Y., Kim, K. and Zheng, L. (2010) 'Advertising appeals as a reflection of culture: A cross-cultural analysis of food advertising appeals in China and the US', *Asian Journal of Communication*, 20: 1–16.

Cho, S.E. (2010) *A Cross-cultural Comparison of Korean and American Social Networking Sites: Exploring Cultural Differences in Social Relationships and Self-presentation*. New Brunswick, NJ: Rutgers University.

Christodoulides, G. (2012) 'Cross-national differences in e-WOM influence', *European Journal of Marketing*, 46: 1689–707.

Czarnecka, B., Dahl, S. and Eagle, L. (2013) 'Is food advertising culture-bound? Contradictory results from three European countries', *Journal of Customer Behaviour*, 12: 2–3.

Dahl, S. (2014) 'Communication appeal effectiveness', in A.J. Broderick and C. Demangeot (eds), *Contemporary Consumer Psychology*. London: Sage Publications.

De Mooij, M.K. and de Mooij, M. (2009) *Global Marketing and Advertising: Understanding Cultural Paradoxes*. London: Sage Publications.

Erumban, A.A. and De Jong, S.B. (2006) 'Cross-country differences in ICT adoption: A consequence of culture?', *Journal of World Business*, 41: 302–14.

Galperina, M. (2013) Why Russia's Internet watchdog threatened to censor Facebook, again [Online], ANIMAL. Available at: http://animalnewyork.com/2013/why-russias-internet-watchdog-threatened-to-censor-facebook-again/ (accessed 4 November 2013).

Global Web Index (2011) Usage Statistics Reports, London/Singapore: Global Web Index [Online]. Available at: www.globalwebindex.net/products/data_pack/social-platform-usage-frequency – sina-weibo (accessed 31 July 2014).

*The Guardian* (2013) 'China opens Shanghai free-trade zone' [Online]. Available at: www.theguardian.com/world/2013/sep/29/china-shanghai-free-trade-zone (accessed 26 February 2014).

Hall, E.T. and Hall, M.R. (1987) *Hidden Differences: Doing Business with the Japanese*. New York: Doubleday.

Hofstede, G. (1991) *Cultures and Organizations: Software of the Mind: Intercultural Cooperation and its Importance for Survival*. New York: HarperCollins.

Hofstede, G. (2001) *Culture's Consequences: Comparing Values, Behaviors, Institutions, and Organizations Across Nations*. London: Sage Publications.

Hupfer, M.E. and Detlor, B. (2007) 'Beyond gender differences: Self-concept orientation and relationship-building applications on the Internet', *Journal of Business Research*, 60: 613–19.

Internet World Stats (2012) Internet and Facebook usage in Europe [Online]. Available at: www.internetworldstats.com/stats4.htm (accessed 4 November 2013).

Jiacheng, W., Lu, L. and Francesco, C.A. (2010) 'A cognitive model of intra-organizational knowledge-sharing motivations in the view of cross-culture', *International Journal of Information Management*, 30: 220–30.

Kim, Y., Sohn, D. and Choi, S.M. (2011) 'Cultural difference in motivations for using social network sites: A comparative study of American and Korean college students', *Computers in Human Behavior*, 27: 365–72.

Kramer, A. (2013) 'Russia begins selectively blocking internet content' [Online], *New York Times*. Available at: www.nytimes.com/2013/04/01/technology/russia-begins-selectively-blocking-internet-content.html?_r=0&adxnnl=1&adxnnlx=1393444473-1SDF8rJLdBp7Jt kqaXrtjg (accessed 26 February 2014).

Levitt, T. (1983) 'The globalization of markets', *Harvard Business Review*, 61: 92–102.

Lin, H.-C., Swarna, H. and Bruning, P.F. (2017) 'Taking a global view on brand post popularity: Six social media brand post practices for global markets', *Business Horizons*, 60(5): 621–33.

Marcus, A. (2004) 'User interface design and culture', in N. Aykin (ed.), *Usability and Internationalization of Information Technology*. London: Taylor and Francis. pp. 51–78.

MarketingCharts (2013) Social networking eats up 3+ hours per day for the average American user [Online]. Available at: www.marketingcharts.com/wp/interactive/social-networking-eats-up-3-hours-per-day-for-the-average-american-user-26049/ (accessed 4 November 2013).

Muk, A., Chung, C. and Kim, J. (2013) 'Cultural influence on young consumers' intention to become brand-page fans: Individualism versus collectivism', in Kevin J. Shanahan (ed.), *Marketing Identity: Annals of the Society for Marketing Advances*, 2013 SMA Conference, South Carolina. pp. 123–4.

Okazaki, S. (2013) 'Social media and international advertising: Theoretical challenges and future directions', *International Marketing Review*, 30: 56–71.

Pollay, R.W. (1986) 'The distorted mirror: Reflections on the unintended consequences of advertising', *Journal of Marketing*, 50: 18–36.

Qiu, L., Lin, H. and Leung, A.K.-Y. (2012) 'Cultural differences and switching of in-group sharing behavior between an American (Facebook) and a Chinese (Renren) social networking site', *Journal of Cross-Cultural Psychology*, 44(1): 106–21.

Srite, M. and Karahanna, E. (2006) 'The role of espoused national cultural values in technology acceptance', *MIS Quarterly*, 30(3): 679–704.

Steers, R.M., Meyer, A.D. and Sanchez-Runde, C.J. (2008) 'National culture and the adoption of new technologies', *Journal of World Business*, 43: 255–60.

Taylor, C.R. (2005) 'Moving international advertising research forward: A new research agenda', *Journal of Advertising*, 34: 7–16.

Tsai, W.-H.S. and Men, L.R. (2012) 'Cultural values reflected in corporate pages on popular social network sites in China and the United States', *Journal of Research in Interactive Marketing*, 6: 42–58.

Tversky, A. and Kahneman, D. (1974) 'Judgment under uncertainty: Heuristics and biases', *Science*, 185: 1124–31.

Wansink, B., Kent, R.J. and Hoch, S.J. (1998) 'An anchoring and adjustment model of purchase quantity decisions', *Journal of Marketing Research (JMR)*, 35: 71–81.

Zarbatany, L., Conley, R. and Pepper, S. (2004) 'Personality and gender differences in friendship needs and experiences in preadolescence and young adulthood', *International Journal of Behavioral Development*, 28: 299–310.

Zhai, I. (2013) 'China may only have 18,000 active Twitter users: Infographic' [Online], *South China Morning Post*. Available at: www.scmp.com/comment/blogs/article/1119055/china-may-only-have-18000-active-twitter-users-infographic (accessed 19 February 2014).

# 12

# Privacy, Ethical and Legal Issues

## CHAPTER OVERVIEW

This chapter takes a look at the impact of social media on privacy, ethical considerations and self-regulation and statutory regulation of social media marketing, critically evaluating how far current codes of practice and regulations are applicable or indeed transferable to social media. Using examples from the alcohol industry and advertising to children, the chapter highlights areas of ethical concern and potential regulatory consequences of ethically questionable behaviour.

# LEARNING OUTCOMES

On completing this chapter, you should be able to:

- critically discuss the difference between ethical and legal marketing
- reflect on privacy and the data protection implications of social media marketing
- elaborate on the implications of using social media, especially in relation to marketing of potentially harmful products or to vulnerable groups.

## PRIVACY, ETHICAL AND LEGAL ISSUES

The rise of digital media, and particularly social media, has resulted in a variety of ethical, legal and privacy problems, for example, much of the current marketing communication regulation has no effective means of dealing with social media-based marketing campaigns, and until very recently digital and social media were outside the remit of advertising regulators. Similarly, the vast amount of sharing of personal data, often with the intention of sharing content amongst trusted friends, gives rise to the potential for manifold privacy concerns. This is especially true in cases where such data is accessible, particularly unintentionally, by third parties, such as employers or organisations using the data to target marketing communication campaigns. This chapter focuses on these novel aspects of widespread social media use, firstly by exploring privacy concerns before moving on and discussing the concerns and challenges about new media marketing in relation to existing regulatory frameworks.

## Privacy

**Privacy** has been a major issue for social media websites, particularly because of the complexity of managing privacy settings (Lee, 2014). Although many users express concerns for privacy, they actually fail to adjust settings to protect their privacy (Gross and Acquisti, 2005). Social Capital Theory has been used to explain privacy concerns, and privacy enhancing actions, in relation to social media behaviour, and has been highlighted in the research literature (Chakraborty et al., 2013). It is therefore useful to briefly review Social Capital Theory before examining the applicability to social media.

### Social Capital Theory

There are many theoretical discussions surrounding the notion of social capital. The main argument of **Social Capital Theory** is the concept that access to social networks and social credibility within these networks have an appreciable value, and that this value can be measured similar to the value of goods or services. Consequently, investment in social relationships, for example, in the form of building and maintaining relationships both online and offline, has an expected return, in the form of enhanced outcomes of actions (Lin, 1999). The explanations for the more favourable outcomes of actions within an established social network can be said to be fourfold:

- Established social relationships enable the flow of information.
- Established social relationships open up the possibility to exert influence.
- Social relationships bring with them social credentials, in the form of trust and access to parts of the social network not readily accessible by others.
- The social capital and an extensive or effective social network reinforces an individual's identity and recognition, which in turn is essential for maintenance of mental health and a feeling of entitlement to resources (Lin, 1999).

Consequently, social capital adds to the 'value' of individuals beyond the traditional notion of human capital, for example the knowledge and skills a person has.

In a similar way to traditional relationships, social capital can be gained, or indeed lost, through the use of social media interactions. Many individuals mix different networks of people on social media, for instance, colleagues and friends, and actions may be shared across different networks unintentionally, and have the potential to destroy social capital in those networks. For instance, there have been several cases where sharing of spare time activities intended to be accessible only to friends has led to the termination of employment for some individuals. However, even adjusting privacy settings may not in all cases suffice to protect the individual's privacy. In a case in New Zealand, a woman was asked by her employer and subsequently ordered by an employment tribunal to hand over Facebook data to prove she was actually sick on the days she claimed sick leave.

Similar to the unintentional sharing of private information amongst different networks is the unintended sharing, or making available, of data to third parties, specifically advertisers. Behaviourally targeted advertising (see also Chapter 11), i.e. advertising that relies on a longitudinal profiling of users, has been the subject of intense debate. The debate has led to a largely negative rhetoric in the popular media, and regulators as well as academics expressing concerns about the privacy aspects of this technology. In response, the advertising industry has emphasised consumer relevance, rather than focusing on privacy issues, for example the UK-based Internet Advertising Bureau defines this form of advertising as 'a growing way of making the advertising you see on websites more relevant to your interests and preferences. It is based upon previous unidentifiable web-browsing activity, such as pages viewed, searches made and ads clicked on' (Internet Advertising Bureau, n.d.). The World Privacy Forum (World Privacy Forum, n.d.) is more explicit about the technical aspects of behavioural targeting, and highlights the incumbent privacy issues. It emphasises that a user is tracked over time to gain a profile of the consumer's online activities, their interests and preferences, and/or communications, which is then used as a basis to serve advertising or market goods.

The main concerns regarding this type of advertising are conflicting claims about how aware consumers are of this tactic, what levels of understanding consumers have, and the perceived difficulty of opting out. Pressure groups, such as American Consumer Affairs, claim that consumers are largely unaware of the practice (Bosworth, 2006), while academic research asserts that consumers are more aware than popular media assumes (Alreck and Settle, 2007). However, although consumers are aware of the tactic, consumers are also reported to be highly critical. Alreck and Settle, for instance, report that over half of the consumers think behavioural tracking and targeting should be illegal.

Regulators have responded to these concerns by requiring identification of behaviourally targeted advertising (for example, by a stylised i being displayed on behaviourally targeted advertisements in the European Union). However, despite awareness campaigns, there are concerns that a sizable part of the population does not realise, or at least fully appreciate, the meaning of the symbol.

Behaviourally targeted advertising does raise an interesting issue at the crossroads of this chapter. Because of the potential for data collection, social media and new technology present both privacy and ethical concerns, even for an activity that is clearly legal. However, as many individuals object to being tracked online, but either lack the skills, knowledge or motivation to opt out of the tracking, such practices raise concerns as to what effect such actions may have in the long run. For instance, if people object to companies using such technology, will they eventually refuse to purchase products from such companies?

Similar issues in relation to privacy and details becoming available to marketers have been raised in relation to other social network activity, though largely depending on the network used and the type of campaigns being run. Facebook applications, for example, often make much of the profile information of users available to the developers – a feature frequently overlooked by users. Consequently, by installing an application, a user may make contact lists, emails and relationship status and other personal details available without fully realising that these details are being passed on. Moreover, the majority of applications request the ability to post to user profiles, i.e. for example, sharing high scores for online games on a user's Facebook wall. This in turn may alienate consumers, particularly in cases where the users have not realised, or are overwhelmed, by the privacy settings and their control. Thus, such tactics may result in the users removing the application rather than adjusting the security and privacy settings. Considering carefully the extent to which individuals would like to engage publicly with apps is therefore important, particularly considering if there are potential implications for the social capital of users.

Other social media tools, for example Facebook pages, following on Twitter or subscribing on YouTube are less likely to generate privacy concerns to the same extent as apps and other functions which allow posting on behalf of users. Nevertheless, most interactions in social networks are public, and thus can have a direct influence (both positive and negative) on the individual's social capital. For instance, liking a brand page or following a brand on Twitter is publicly visible. Consequently, iconic brands or brands with strong symbolic character for certain tribes will benefit based on Social Capital Theory, with users following or liking the brands not only because they may (or may not) be actual customers, but as a form of self-expression. Brands that are likely to erode social capital for their users, for example because they are either not iconic or unfashionable, may struggle.

## THINKBOX SOCIAL CAPITAL

Think of the brands you follow on social networks. Make a list of them, and compare how they enhance (or erode) your social capital.

Think of brands or organisations you would not follow. Are there organisations or brands that you may engage with (i.e. buy products from or visit), but you do not wish to follow them on social networks? Compare the list with others.

Privacy, the right to privacy, the voluntary disclosure of usually private information and the changing nature of privacy has been the subject of intense debate – and considerable concern by some, often citing confusion about data being shared amongst other users or with organisations. Yet others have responded to these concerns by pointing towards personal and individual responsibility about which data is being shared, and pointing to benefits, such as better targeted information, as a result of shared information. Frost and Massagli (2008), for example, examining the online community PatientsLikeMe.com, show that sharing of personal health information can, on the one side, lead to valuable benefits such as better disease management. And while such benefits are clearly valuable, the public availability of health related data, as an extreme example, or even added automatic matching of patients in an online community based on conditions and treatments, has led to some serious concerns regarding privacy of such information.

While many users may arguably think more carefully before disclosing highly sensitive data, such as health information, and may choose to take protective measures such as choosing a user name that is not easily identifiable, more conventional social media activity has given rise to equal concern regarding privacy. For instance by examining conventional 'liking' of movies and pages on Facebook, an activity relatively few people restrict or are aware is being shared, Kosinski and colleagues (2013) showed that the researchers could predict sexual orientation, ethnic background and political affiliations of Facebook users. Similarly, Quercia and colleagues (2011) showed that Twitter profiles could be used to predict with high accuracy personality scores of users based on a five-factor model of personality.

These problematic situations regarding privacy are the often naïve assumptions of users that the data they share is being used exclusively by people they are consenting to, or users not being aware of the potential issues arising from data collected. For instance, Kosinski's study was based on relatively few movies and pages. Similarly, others have demonstrated that personally sensitive data is available to advertisers for targeting purposes, for example, in a seminal blog post, Gawker columnist Chen (Chen, 2012) showed how behaviourally targeted advertising settings on Facebook could be used to find out sexual preferences of employees in different companies.

## Data Protection

In addition to privacy issues, more legal **data protection** issues can also arise as a consequence of using social media marketing methods for organisations, although most of the data protection issues, from a legal perspective, are likely to arise outside of the social media sphere and primarily within the context of an organisation's website, as most social media websites themselves will have appropriate safeguards for data protection. Consequently, as a user of, for example, Twitter, an organisation is less likely to encounter significant data protection issues. Nevertheless, it is useful to consider the potential for data protection issues, as these can arise, for instance, when an organisation links social media activity with content on their own website, for example, in the case of asking people to complete an online form to enter a contest.

In cases where personal data is collected, such as in the case of apps on Facebook, or where data is made available, it is important to review the data based on the current legislation of the country the organisation is located in and/or the data is collected in, especially as simple errors can create a significant legal issue. For instance, exporting data from the EU or by an EU domiciled company to a jurisdiction outside of the European Economic Area can pose a legal problem, for example, if the data is transferred to a website or host in the US which is not part of the Safe Harbour Scheme.

A potential grey area in relation to social media is the applicability of anti-spam legislation. It is technically possible, for example, to message directly any user following an organisation on Twitter. Such mass messaging could potentially be a violation of anti-spam legislation, if users feel that direct messages are different and more personal than following updates of a brand, which is what the users have opted-in for when they followed a brand.

Consequently, while social media activity is likely to pose less purely legal data protection issues than conventional digital marketing, where the ability to collect and store data is larger, it is prudent for organisations to remain cautious and consider potential issues that may arise prior to communicating directly with social media users or encouraging users to disclose personal information.

## Legal and Ethical

The question of ethical and legal marketing activity is by no means restricted to marketing communication, digital marketing or even more specifically to social media marketing. With full or partial bans on marketing communication activities in place in many industries, such as gambling, tobacco, drugs and alcohol – or towards certain target groups, for instance, children – many marketing communications are highly regulated. However, legal restrictions are not necessarily ethical, and unrestricted marketing communications are not always ethically appropriate (see Table 12.1).

**Table 12.1**  Ethical and legal

|          | Ethical           | Unethical             |
|----------|-------------------|-----------------------|
| **Legal**   | legal and ethical   | legal but unethical     |
| **Illegal** | illegal but ethical | illegal and unethical   |

We now briefly review legal and ethical issues in relation to digital and social media marketing.

## Legal Frameworks/Self-regulation

At first glance it would be understandable to assume that legal issues in relation to marketing communication (online or offline) would be relatively straightforward, and simply require the knowledge of the applicable laws or regulations. However, unfortunately, this is often not the case, and the regulations can be confusing, lacking specifics – or can have unintended consequences. For instance, the UK introduced a ban on advertising food high in fat, sugar and salt ('junk food') to children in 2007. However, despite this ban, children are actually exposed to more junk food advertising on television than before the ban (BBC News, 2012), not accounting for any marketing activity through advergames or other digital and social media, which is not currently regulated in the same way as television advertising.

Moreover, even where clear regulations exist for traditional media, such regulation may not be applicable, or may be applicable in other ways in social or digital media – and there again it may depend on which types of websites' product or brand information appears. In the US, for example, the Food and Drug Administration regulates advertising of pharmaceuticals in traditional media. However, no such regulation exists in relation to Internet-based information (Bartel-Shehann, 2012). Similarly, the British Advertising Standards Authority rules governing traditional media started to apply to websites only from 2011; however, many digital media formats, such as advergames, were not mentioned in the current regulation. The ASA later ruled that advergames may be regarded as paid for advertising, but to date has extended rulings in only a handful of cases. However, even while the ASA has now an extended remit, other organisations maintain a more focused approach on broadcasting. For instance, Clearcast, an organisation providing pre-broadcasting clearance of advertisements for organisations wishing to broadcast these ads on television in the UK, does not screen other forms of media, including social media.

Further than simply applying current rules, such as the ASA codes or similar regulation, the fundamental basis of conventional advertising regulation contributes to the ethical and legal dilemmas created by emerging media forms. For traditional media, the regulations are based on two important principles: firstly, that advertising should be clearly recognisable as such, for instance by identifying a sponsored tweet; and secondly, the regulation of advertising content, i.e. regulations concerning what can and what cannot be said.

In new and social media, much of the communication is, however, blurring the lines between social and commercial communication – and commercial communication is frequently indistinguishable from social-like communication (see also Chapter 3 on branding and anthropomorphic marketing).

Concerning the identification of commercial communication, there are contradictory regulations of disclosure depending on which country is concerned; for example, the US guidelines suggest adding 'Ad:' at the beginning of a space-constrained communication, for example, in the case of a sponsored or commercial Twitter update. However, adding 'Ad:' is only recommended in cases where the update might be confused with a personal communication, so in cases where a celebrity posts a sponsored update, adding 'Ad:' is recommended. There are, however, no guidelines as to communication which is originating from the brand, based on the argument that a follower of the brand will recognise that this is a commercial message. Moreover, the US guidelines make it clear that consumers might not understand alternative forms of identification, such as the **hashtag** #spon, suggesting that the message was sponsored by an advertiser. Consequently, the US guidelines suggest that if a significant proportion of 'reasonable' viewers of such communication would not understand the commercial nature of the communication, then such communication would be deemed to be deceptive under the US guidelines. Likewise, simply putting an abbreviated link, as in the form of 'bit.ly/disclosure', which contains the disclosure of the commercial nature of the message, would be regarded as deceptive (see Federal Trade Commission, 2013 for further examples).

Yet, these rules are by no means universal. In contradiction to the US guidelines, the UK Advertising Standards Authority considers #spon a suitable identifier – and cleared a controversial campaign by Snickers as not being in breach of the advertising code based on the fact that the tweets contained #spon and @snickersUK. In New Zealand, the Advertising Standards Authority recommends using the #ad (Advertising Standards Authority, 2012), while in Australia the sponsored update or tweet should include the wording 'sponsored', 'client' or 'paid' (Interactive Advertising Bureau Australia, 2013).

Many other countries, for example India (Krishnamurthy, 2012), have no specific regulations regarding social media, although some generally agree that the same principles that govern traditional media advertising should be applied. However, in the absence of any specific regulation, how such regulation would work in practice is not clear.

With regards to the content, the applicability of the regulations is even more problematic as current regulations are based on controlling what is being said, for example, the Advertising Standards Authority regulates that claims in advertising must universally be truthful. Further, particular product groups have more specific regulations restricting what can and what cannot be said. For example, current regulations do not permit for products that are considered high in fat, such as cheese, to make health claims, such as claims relating to the high content of calcium. Similarly, alcohol products are not allowed to claim that they enhance social success or sexual attractiveness.

While such rules are relatively easy to monitor in traditional advertising, where often comparatively overt product claims are being made, in a context where the majority of the communication is subtle and human-like, monitoring potential content breaches of content guidelines is significantly harder. For instance, Dahl and Desrochers (2013) show that many alcohol brands regularly post pictures of parties. These pictures show the product in use, but usually do not contain any direct marketing claims. A potential interpretation of such pictures would be that alcohol contributes to social success, which would be a breach of the current guidelines. However, as the message is implied and reliant on interpretative rather than explicit decoding of the messages, enforcing such content restrictions would be difficult if not impossible.

Moreover, **content restrictions** are not enforceable for user-generated content, as this content is not originating from brands. However, such content is often indistinguishable from brand-originating communication, for example, there are many 'spoof' commercials on YouTube or other video-sharing websites. One of the most prominent examples, and with several thousand spoof commercials on YouTube, are commercials for MasterCard based on their well-known slogan 'for everything else there is MasterCard'. 'Indecent Proposal', one of the most infamous spoof commercials, with millions of views and shared widely across social media networks, contains for example references to sexual intercourse, references to alcohol as a means to obtain courage and lacks any disclosure information normally required to be included when advertising financial products.

## THINKBOX REGULATION

Download the product-specific regulations for advertising from one of the regulators (e.g. the ASA in the UK). Make a list of ten brands in the product category. Look up the companies' social media presence, such as Facebook pages, Twitter feeds or Instagram profiles. See if the companies obey the regulations. How easy is it to assess if the companies are in compliance or breaching the regulations?

## Ethical Frameworks

In addition to legal and regulatory issues, social media marketing also faces a number of ethical dilemmas, which can often be substantially more complex than regulatory problems. Many issues encountered by companies using social media can be complex or even questionable from an ethical perspective, yet may not be subject to existing regulation. This situation is further exacerbated because of the novel technical possibilities, which are often complex and have not been explored enough in terms of their impact in existing regulation. For instance, marketing to children, or other vulnerable groups, is subject to stringent regulation in traditional media in many countries. However, even in countries where regulation of online and social media exists, the regulations often get enforced less stringently. Moreover, while companies may target specific social media activities, such as Facebook pages, at a country or region, and in compliance with local regulations, there is frequently the technical possibility of accessing information from other countries or areas freely. For instance, Goldfarb and Tucker (2011) show that in US states where there is a ban on traditional advertising of alcohol products, online advertising substitutes for traditional advertising. Similarly, while prescription drug advertising is only allowed in the US and New Zealand, and banned in the rest of the world, websites related to prescription drugs are freely available in other countries; for example, the website of Nexium (www.purplepill.com/), a top prescription-only drug to treat heartburn and acid reflux, is freely available to Internet users outside of the US. The site includes a small warning that the information is intended for US customers only. Limiting the site to users from the US only would be technically extremely easy, yet customers beyond the US can freely access all the information.

As with all ethical decisions, having a clear answer is often difficult, and decisions therefore depend on a variety of different factors that need to be balanced. Ethical decisions can be made using one of four ethical frameworks as decision criteria. These four are **Teleology**, **Deontology**, **Relativism** and **Social Contract Theory**. Depending on which framework is chosen, there are likely to be different ethical outcomes.

- *Teleology/Consequentialism* is a framework that evaluates actions based on the outcomes or effects of actions. Usually teleological decision making is further divided into either: a) utilitarianism, where actions are striving for the greatest good for the greatest number; or b) egoism, where individual benefit is stressed, thus de-emphasising the communal benefit.

- *Deontology* focuses on the intentions behind an action rather than outcomes. Deontology is often associated with the work of eighteenth-century philosopher Immanuel Kant, contending that ethical 'absolutes' are identifiable and universally valid.
- *Relativism* contests such moral and ethical absolutes. Relativists stress that there is no universal set of ethical principles; and that individual cultures, societies or social groups may have their own ethical structures. Consequently, no set of ethical principles is superior to others and each group should refrain from judging other groups' ethical standards.
- *Social Contract Theory* builds on the assumption that a usually implicit contract exists between the state and/or organisations and individuals or groups concerning rights and responsibilities towards each other and regulating a symbiotic co-existence.

Given the multitude of potential ethical problems, the chapter now focuses on two areas where there is both extensive regulation, but also widespread new and social media usage, as examples of potential ethical and regulatory problems: advertising to children and alcohol promotion.

## Children and Games

Advertising to children, particularly advertising of junk food (i.e. food that is high in sugar, salt or fat), is amongst the most vigorously regulated marketing activities in many countries, not least because food marketers have often been criticised for their potential contribution to rising obesity rates amongst children (Boyland and Halford, 2013) and encouraging the use of pester power in children causing domestic conflict (Marshall et al., 2007).

The industry has responded to widespread concerns about their products by imposing voluntary and relatively strict self-regulatory programmes. In the US, for example, the Children's Food and Beverage Advertising Initiative (CFBAI) includes some of the largest food advertisers, amongst them Mars, PepsiCo, Kraft, Kellogg's and Nestlé. Similar, though less stringent, programmes exist in Australia, in the form of the Responsible Children's Marketing Initiative, and in the UK the Food and Drink Federation (FDF). Despite the laudable rhetoric, however, there have been concerns regarding the reality of the promotions by companies signing up to these schemes. Quilliam and colleagues (2011), for example, found that companies who signed up to the CFBAI initiative were more likely to include unhealthy food items in their Internet-based advertising than those companies not part of the scheme. Yet, the explicit CFBAI programme aim is to reduce the exposure to unhealthy food items. Similarly, while many food companies publically defended strong regulatory measures and responsible marketing, Dahl and colleagues (2009) found that advergame content mostly ignored these guidelines.

Particularly the rise of advergames and other immersive advertising techniques has resulted in substantial concerns, yet little regulatory activity. Extended brand exposure, through repeatedly playing a game, is one of the appeals for advertisers using advergames. In some cases, children have been reported playing advergames more than a 100 times, resulting in more extended brand exposure than would be possible through traditional advertising, for example, on TV.

Moreover, while advergames were originally largely placed only on food manufacturers' websites, or websites specifically dedicated to advergaming, social media has added a wider network capability to these games. In other words, games are designed to be promoted across social media websites, to be placed on social media websites and to encourage players to use social media websites to spread the word about the games. In addition, advergames have further matured from being essentially web-based activities to mobile activities, especially popular on platforms such as the iPhone, iPad and other tablet computers. The connectivity between these mobile devices and social media further allows that the games become a ubiquitous activity in a similar way to mobile social media itself – they can be played at home, on the bus, at school.

In a review of mobile advergames, Dahl and colleagues (2013) show that, similar to the traditional advergames, there are serious concerns about how food marketers put into practice their alleged ethical advertising practices, and are breaching the spirit and substance of advertising codes. For instance, some games required purchase of food items for full access. Other games had contradictory age settings – with a low setting they would not be blocked by parental controls being activated on the iPad or Android tablets, yet, these games required a one-time activation by clicking or entering a much higher age when launched for the first time.

Although marketing practices as observed in the games are for the most part not illegal, largely because the regulations do not extend to advergames, such inconsistent behaviours by some, and in the case of advergames large, players, the industry is particularly problematic, as it fosters a perception that the industry is actively circumventing advertising codes and actively engaging in unethical marketing practices.

## Alcohol Promotion

Similar to unhealthy food items, alcohol is a controversial product with highly regulated marketing communications. For traditional advertising, alcohol messages in the UK and other countries are restricted in what they can say or imply, for example, alcohol advertising is not allowed to suggest that alcohol consumption raises the chances of social success, for example, by saying that a party can only be successful if alcohol is present. Alcohol cannot be linked to increased sexual attractiveness; advertising is not allowed to show people appearing to be under 25 and so forth. In the UK the regulation of marketing communications is overseen by the self-regulatory Advertising Standards Authority, and the industry body The Portman Group, which develops voluntary standards for marketing from the alcohol industry.

Again, similar to unhealthy food items, many alcohol companies engage in social media marketing: most of the top advertisers have a large social media presence, especially on social networks such as Facebook, Twitter and increasingly on Instagram.

Investigating how alcohol brands use Facebook pages, Dahl and Desrochers (2013) find that a majority of alcohol brands engage in continuous behaviour that can be characterised as subtle brand reminders; for example, when updating their status, less than half of the brands name their brand name in the status update. Of these, nearly 80% of updates are unrelated to the product, rather, alcohol brands engage their followers through discussion based on other topics, from sports to current affairs, arts, parties and nature. Consequently, the majority of updates are wholly unrelated to the product and make no reference to the product they are allegedly advertising.

While there are isolated instances of updates which may be against the regulations (e.g. pictures of very young consumers, or pictures which may condone irresponsible drinking), most updates do not contravene regulations. Talking about something unrelated, posting daily pictures of parties where people are drinking the advertised brand or liking of comments and sharing of pictures taken by followers is clearly not against the regulation. However, it represents a ubiquitous contact between brand and consumer, where the brand is increasingly seeking to be anthropomorphic and displays much human-like behaviour (for instance, talking about being relieved that a strike on the London underground is called off, and a football game can go ahead).

Concerns about such behaviour focus on the possibility that, because of the subtlety of the communication, persuasion knowledge (see Chapter 7) may not be activated, similar to non-activation during advergames. Consequently, recipients cannot activate coping behaviours. Similarly, in the long term, ubiquitous, peripherally processed communication, while less effective in the short term than centrally processed communication, can have a powerful effect on emotions linked to a brand and brand purchasing intentions (see also Chapter 3 for an explanation of the Elaboration Likelihood Model).

In a similar way to the food industry, there is widespread suspicion of the alcohol industry as exploiting marketing communication, especially to younger adults. For instance, Mart and colleagues allege that the alcohol industry is 'exploiting youth and young adults' (Mart et al., 2009) in social networks. Likewise, Bond and colleagues (2010) draw similarities between the alcohol industry and the tobacco industry, and accuse the alcohol industry of circumventing traditional advertising regulations, including, for example, the placement of products and brand names in the text of pop music (Primack et al., 2008), while Huhmann and Limbu (2016) show that prescription drug companies are active users of social media, while advertising of their products is forbidden outside of the US and New Zealand.

These examples show the potential ethical and regulatory issues that can arise when engaging in social media marketing. On the one side, regulation may be slow to catch up with new technology, and in many cases, even prior to social media, regulation has been accused of being slow in terms of providing a coherent framework for new promotion vehicles (Hoek, 2004). Equally, the fundamental notion of regulation based largely on defining which product attributes can be explicitly referred to and which ones not, is largely superfluous in an environment of ubiquitous brand connectivity, where promotional emphasis is on the creation of emotional connections rather than sales arguments. Nevertheless, while there are often possible avenues for circumventing regulation, doing so can have significant negative consequences in the long run. For instance, having been found to be circumventing the regulations for advertising content to children, foods high in sugar, fat and salt have been banned from advertising during programmes aimed primarily at children. However, even after such a radical step, the industry has continued to exploit regulatory loopholes, through greater emphasis on online and advergame based marketing communications and by focusing advertising on programmes with large underage audiences, such as soaps, which are nevertheless not primarily directed at children and teens – and therefore not covered by current regulation. The result of these activities is that increasingly there are calls to ban all promotions for these types of food, largely based on the assumption that the industry is inherently unethical and cannot be trusted.

## THINKBOX ETHICAL VS. LEGAL

Go back to the sites you have investigated in the previous ThinkBox exercise. Discuss the ethical implications of what you see. Do you think the advertisers are behaving ethically? How can you evaluate if they are? What do you think could be causes for concern? What might be the long-term consequences of unethical behaviour?

## SUMMARY

This chapter has briefly reviewed the ethical and regulatory/legal implications of social media marketing. By using the examples of online alcohol marketing and marketing towards children, the chapter has highlighted that the regulatory frameworks are ineffective, as present regulation is based on product-centric marketing, i.e. what can and cannot be said about a product, while social media marketing is about establishing an emotional connection beyond product attributes through ubiquitous brand presence. Consequently, regulatory frameworks have been criticised as unfit for purpose in relation to social and new media activities.

Many legal and regulatory frameworks are struggling to cope with social media activity, making ethical principles an important aspect when engaging in social media marketing. Moreover, unethical activities, including raising the suspicion that companies may be avoiding regulation, can have long-term significant impact on future marketing activities, and marketers should very carefully consider how their actions may be perceived if they are to avoid tougher regulation.

## RESEARCH DIRECTIONS

Future research can tackle a wide array of different topics in relation to regulation and ethical principles in a social media context. Past research has highlighted that many companies appear to be breaking regulatory codes designed for broadcast advertisements when advertising online. However, the effect of breaking these rules has not been extensively studied. Similarly, what effect does ubiquitous brand presence have? What is the long-term effect of daily brand exposures, and how can these subtle brand reminders be regulated? Other interesting future avenues of research include cross-cultural comparisons of ethical issues, reactions towards ethical and unethical behaviour – and actual behaviour of companies when targeting different markets, that is, how do social media messages differ when targeted towards a global audience? Or towards a local audience?

# RESEARCH HIGHLIGHT
## ADVERGAMES

In 'Analyzing advergames: Active diversions or actually deception. An exploratory study of online advergames content' Dahl and colleagues (2009) evaluate advergames aimed at children and promoting snack foods by using existing regulatory codes for broadcast advertising. In the article, the authors give a brief overview of the advergames, including who uses them and the theories that explain advergame effectiveness (see also Chapter 5 of this book for some of the theories discussed in this article).

Based on visits to websites of 15 well-known international food companies, the authors present data on the amount of advergames and the content of these. They further analyse each website and game to see how far these games are obeying the spirit of the regulation. For instance, the regulations require that advertising is clearly distinguished from entertainment content; however, only a handful of the websites actually reminded visitors that the content they were engaging with was commercial in nature. Similarly, the regulations ask for nutrition information to be made available, yet, most of the websites made no such information available. Similarly, regulations require advertisers not to require or condone purchasing of unhealthy products. Yet, some games were found to require entering of codes to continue playing. Similarly, the regulations state that peer pressure and pester power should not be encouraged. Despite this, most websites allowed invitations to be sent to friends in the form of eCards or emails.

Although the sample for the study is relatively small (only 15 companies), the evidence from the visits is concerning. Many advertisers appear to engage in practices that would be in breach of the regulations if advergames were regular advertisements. It is particularly concerning that such behaviours, legal as they may be, occur at a time when there are increased calls for much tougher regulation on these advertisers.

The full article is available on the companion website of the book.

# CASE STUDY  WHO IS LOUISE DELAGE?

Her Instagram bio reads simply: 'Louise Delage, 25 yo, Paris. Whatever you are, be a good one'. And she is an Instagram star: within two months Louise gained 16,000 followers and hundreds of likes for the pictures she posted every day. Louise is attractive and she leads an extraordinary life of sun, beach, travelling and parties, sharing it with her followers.

*(Continued)*

Chic, cheerful and fashionable, Louise appeared to be the friend everyone enjoys following on Instagram, living life to the full. However, there was another side to Louise. A little over six weeks, and 50,000 likes after Louise appeared on Instagram, a video was posted on her account, revealing the truth about the charming French Instagram star, by pointing out something that was staring every follower in the face from day one, but most didn't realise: In nearly every picture she posted, she was holding a drink. And she was always alone. In fact, Louise has an alcohol addiction. And her followers literally liked her addiction.

Louise didn't really exist at all. Louise was a social media campaign, designed to highlight the problem of frequently overlooked addictions in close friends and relatives. The campaign was created on behalf of the charity Addict Aide, an organisation that highlights and helps identify addicts. The campaign specifically focused on making people aware of how easy it is to overlook addiction, rather than notice the problem and acting on it: no follower of her many pictures ever pointed out that Louise appeared to be constantly accompanied only by an alcoholic drink, instead, followers liked the pictures and engaged in friendly and sometimes flirty banter with Louise.

After the revelation, the story made national headlines in France and many news outlets picked up on the issue. Thus, while the campaign might have been fake, the campaign definitely managed to raise awareness in real life.

## Questions to Consider

1   How do you feel about the social media agency setting out to create a deliberately fake social media profile?
2   Which ethical questions do you think the case raises?
3   Which legal questions does the case raise?
4   Imagine you would have followed Louise. How would you react when she revealed her 'secret'?
5   How would your answers change if Louise was promoting a commercial cause (for example, an alcohol brand)?

# FURTHER READING

Huang, E. and Dunbar, C.L. (2013) 'Connecting to patients via social media: A hype or a reality?', *Journal of Medical Marketing: Device, Diagnostic and Pharmaceutical Marketing*, 13: 14–23.

Jacobson, W.S. and Tufts, S.H. (2013) 'To post or not to post: Employee rights and social media', *Review of Public Personnel Administration*, 33: 84–107.

Khan, G.F., Swar, B. and Lee, S.K. (2014) 'Social media risks and benefits: A public sector perspective', *Social Science Computer Review*, 28: 24–44.

# REFERENCES

Advertising Standards Authority (2012) *ASA Guidance Note on Social Media*. Available at: www.asa.co.nz/pdfs/ASA%20Guidance%20Note%20on%20Social%20Media%20October%20 2012.pdf (accessed 3 March 2014).

Alreck, P.L. and Settle, R.B. (2007) 'Consumer reactions to online behavioural tracking and targeting', *Journal of Database Marketing & Customer Strategy Management*, 15: 11–23.

Bartel-Shehann, K. (2012) 'Direct-to-consumer advertising of prescription drugs: Consumers, physicians, messages, and complexity', in S. Rodgers and E. Thorson (eds), *Advertising Theory*, Routledge Communication Series. New York: Routledge. pp. 269–81.

BBC News (2012) Call for pre-watershed ban on junk food advertising [Online]. Available at: www.bbc.co.uk/news/uk-scotland-17414707 (accessed 3 March 2014).

Bond, L., Daube, M. and Chikritzhs, T. (2010) 'Selling addictions: Similarities in approaches between Big Tobacco and Big Booze', *Australasian Medical Journal*, 3(6): 325–32.

Bosworth, M. (2006) Consumerists want FTC probe of online advertising [Online]. Available at: www.consumeraffairs.com/news04/2006/11/ftc_online.html (accessed 28 February 2014).

Boyland, E.J. and Halford, J.C. (2013) 'Television advertising and branding. Effects on eating behaviour and food preferences in children', *Appetite*, 62: 236–41.

Chakraborty, R., Vishik, C. and Rao, H.R. (2013) 'Privacy preserving actions of older adults on social media: Exploring the behavior of opting out of information sharing', *Decision Support Systems*, 55: 948–56.

Chen, A. (2012) Use Facebook's targeted ads to find out how many people are into kinky sex in any workplace [Online], 13 January. Available at: http://gawker.com/5875937/ heres-how-many-facebook-employees-are-into-kinky-sex-according-to-facebook (accessed 14 November 2017).

Dahl, S. and Desrochers, D.M. (2013) 'My friend Bud: Alcohol promotions using social media', in S. Sezgin, E. Karaosmanoglu and A. Elmadag Bas (eds), *Proceedings of the 42nd Annual EMAC Conference, Lost in Translation: Marketing in an Interconnected World*. Istanbul: Istanbul Technical University, 4–7 June.

Dahl, S., Eagle, L. and Baez, C. (2009) 'Analyzing advergames: Active diversions or actually deception. An exploratory study of online advergames content', *Young Consumers*, 10: 46–59.

Dahl, S., Eagle, L. and Low, D. (2013) 'Mobile phone-based advergames: Simply fun or slightly deceptive?', presented at the 16th Biennial World Marketing Congress: Looking Forward, Looking Back: Drawing on the Past to Shape the Future of Marketing, 17–20 July, Melbourne, VIC, Australia.

Federal Trade Commission (2013) .com Disclosures: How to make effective disclosures in digital advertising [Online], BCP Business Center. Available at: www.business.ftc.gov/ documents/bus41-dot-com-disclosures-information-about-online-advertising (accessed 25 November 2013).

Frost, J.H. and Massagli, M.P. (2008) 'Social uses of personal health information within PatientsLikeMe, an online patient community: What can happen when patients have access to one another's data', *Journal of Medical Internet Research*, 10(3). Available at: www.jmir.org/2008/3/e15/ (accessed 27 November 2017).

Goldfarb, A. and Tucker, C. (2011) 'Advertising bans and the substitutability of online and offline advertising', *Journal of Marketing Research*, 48: 207–27.

Gross, R. and Acquisti, A. (2005) 'Information revelation and privacy in online social networks', in *WPES '05: Proceedings of the 2005 ACM Workshop on Privacy in the Electronic Society*. New York: ACM Press. pp. 71–80.

Hoek, J. (2004) 'Tobacco promotion restrictions: Ironies and unintended consequences', *Journal of Business Research*, 57: 1250–7.

Huhmann, B.A. and Limbu, Y.B. (2016) 'Content and compliance of pharmaceutical social media marketing', *Marketing Intelligence & Planning*, 34(7): 977–99.

Interactive Advertising Bureau Australia (2013) Social advertising best practice guidelines. Available at: www.iabaustralia.com.au/uploads/uploads/2013-09/1380474000_4e7b1ea67 b2b9243ff4fb8a96b367455.pdf (accessed 14 November 2017).

Internet Advertising Bureau (n.d.) IAB Guide to Behavioural Targeting [Online]. Available at: www.iabuk.net/disciplines/behavioural-targeting/guide (accessed 28 February 2014).

Kosinski, M., Stillwell, D. and Graepel, T. (2013) 'Private traits and attributes are predictable from digital records of human behavior', in *PNAS: Proceedings of the National Academy of Sciences*, 110(5): 5802–5.

Krishnamurthy, J. (2012) 'Live issue: Can advertising on social media be regulated?' [Online], *Campaign India*. Available at: www.campaignindia.in/Article/311948,live-issue-can-advertising-on-social-media-be-regulated.aspx (accessed 25 November 2013).

Lee, M. (2014) Is privacy too complex for social media to handle alone? [Online]. Available at: www.zdnet.com/is-privacy-too-complex-for-social-media-to-handle-alone-7000025067/ (accessed 28 February 2014).

Lin, N. (1999) 'Building a network theory of social capital', *Connections*, 22: 28–51.

Marshall, D., O'Donohoe, S. and Kline, S. (2007) 'Families, food, and pester power: Beyond the blame game?', *Journal of Consumer Behaviour*, 6: 164–81.

Mart, S., Mergendoller, J. and Simon, M. (2009) 'Alcohol promotion on Facebook', *Journal of Global Drug Policy and Practice*, 3: 1–8.

Primack, B.A., Dalton, M.A., Carroll, M.V., Agarwal, A.A. and Fine, M.J. (2008) 'Content analysis of tobacco, alcohol, and other drugs in popular music', *Archives of Pediatrics and Adolescent Medicine*, 162(2): 169–75.

Quercia, D., Kosinski, M., Stillwell, D. and Crowcroft, J. (2011) 'Our Twitter Profiles, our selves: Predicting personality with Twitter', *Proceedings of the 2011 IEEE International*

*Conference on Privacy, Security, Risk, and Trust, and IEEE International Conference on Social Computing*. Los Alamitos, CA: IEEE Computer Society. pp. 180–5.

Quilliam, E.T., Lee, M., Cole, R.T. and Kim, M. (2011) 'The impetus for (and limited power of) business self-regulation: The example of advergames', *Journal of Consumer Affairs*, 45: 224–47.

World Privacy Forum (n.d.) WPF resource page: Behavioral advertising and privacy [Online]. Available at: www.worldprivacyforum.org/2011/03/resource-page-behavioral-advertising-and-privacy/ (accessed 28 February 2014).

# 13

# Afterword

# Where Next for Social Media Marketing?

This book set out to examine to what extent social media really is a game-changing technology, in fact, as some would argue, so fundamentally game-changing that traditional models and theories of communication no longer apply.

While social media has, unquestionably, created new forms of communication, and has had a profound impact on the choice of channels through which, and the manner in which, communication is conducted, it is also true that many fundamentals of communication and communication theories have not been replaced or annihilated by the rise of social media. Rather, for some theoretical frameworks, such as those related to word of mouth, the rise of social media has made it easier to verify existing theories because something as elusive as word of mouth can now be more easily captured and tracked.

In a similar way, other theories, such as Uses and Gratifications Theory, Elaboration Likelihood Model or Persuasion Knowledge Models have been enriched by the additional data available thanks to new technology. With increasing speed and ease of communication, new technology has, rather than replacing established theories, shown that marketers need to engage with theory to make decisions based on aggregate experience accumulated in existing theoretical frameworks. In today's fast-paced communication environment it is more essential than ever to understand the why rather than focusing wholly on the how. It is thus equally important to understand why brand communities form online, what motivates participation and how, for example, brand communities are different from Facebook pages and Twitter followers, which uses and gratifications participants seek and so forth – rather than focusing only on knowing the technical aspects of operating social media. Only by understanding the why can marketers successfully brace for the future.

While it is infamously difficult to predict the future, there are several innovations which are slowly emerging as technologies of the future. Berners-Lee and Fischetti (1999), for example, envisage the development of the current World Wide Web (and Web 2.0) into a truly semantic web, a web where machines become 'intelligent agents' able to interpret available information, and can take over mundane tasks for humans. One step in the direction of a semantic web is the 'Internet of Things'. The ideology and philosophical foundations of this stretch back to the 1990s, but through wearable technology and high-speed mobile data networks, this Internet of constantly connected, intelligent devices will potentially become a reality in the next few years.

Similarly, predictive technology, i.e. intelligent agentry, is starting to emerge. While its current inception as behaviourally targeted advertising still suffers from significant limitations, more advanced technology is emerging on the technological horizon; for example, Amazon is currently testing technology predicting future orders from customers (Bensinger, 2014). Relying on data analysis of comparable customers and their purchases, this 'predictive shipping' distributes goods as closely as possible to customers' homes, so that they can be delivered within minutes of the customer realising they wish to purchase the item.

Consequently, although the exact path of future technological developments remains uncertain, one thing is definite: a thorough understanding of the fundamental theories explaining human behaviour, persuasion and motivation is invaluable to succeed. And a sound theoretical basis can guide marketers through future technological developments.

## REFERENCES

Bensinger, G. (2014) 'Amazon wants to ship your package before you buy it' [Online], *Wall Street Journal.* Available at: http://blogs.wsj.com/digits/2014/01/17/amazon-wants-to-ship-your-package-before-you-buy-it/ (accessed 1 May 2014).

Berners-Lee, T. and Fischetti, M. (1999) *Weaving the Web: The Original Design and Ultimate Destiny of the World Wide Web by its Inventor*, 1st edn. San Francisco: HarperSanFrancisco.

# Appendix

## EXAMPLE OF A SOCIAL MEDIA MARKETING PLAN

When planning a social media marketing campaign, the broad stages of the planning process are similar to those for traditional marketing campaigns. The main difference is that in the context of a social media campaign the media choice is likely to be driven by social media choices, rather than traditional media choices – although, if the budget allows, combining both has obvious advantages because of synergistic effects, for instance, the synergistic effect of advertising and eWOM discussed in Chapter 9.

Table A.1 shows a comparison of traditional marketing planning frameworks.

**Table A.1** Comparison of marketing planning frameworks

|  | APIC | SOSTTMMMM | SOSTAC |
|---|---|---|---|
| Analysis stage | Analysis | Situation analysis | Situation analysis |
| Objective setting stage | Planning | Objectives | Objectives |
| Strategy decision stage |  | Strategy Targets | Strategy |
| Details stage | Implementation | Tactics | Tactics |
|  |  | Men Money Minutes | Actions |
| Evaluation stage | Control | Measurement | Control |

## ANALYSIS STAGE

During the analysis stage it is important to get as much detail about the organisation, the customers, competitors and the general environment as possible. It is important to get this fundamental research right, as this stage influences all the remaining parts of the planning process.

Another important point is to approach the wider organisation without trying to force any behavioural or marketing objectives into the research agenda at this point – the general analysis is really about a 360° view of the organisation. Appropriate objectives are part of the next step.

Traditional marketing planning frameworks can, of course, help at this stage. Generic planning tools, such as PEEST (Political, Economic, Environmental, Socio-Cultural, Technological factors) and SWOT (Strength, Weaknesses, Opportunities, Threats) can be useful to establish a context in which the organisation operates, and the background for the segmentation process which is at the heart of the analysis stage.

Particular attention should be paid to the segmentation process.

## Segmentation

Primary and secondary research of this stage should be enough to gain insights about the customer segments. While there is no right and wrong way to segment, within social media, segmentation tends to be less on geographic or other demographic criteria, but more based around communities. As discussed in Chapter 1, these communities can, of course, have a geographic or demographic focus, but more often they tend not to. As the ultimate aim of social media marketing is leveraging the brand as a linking value brand for a community, or at least encouraging eWOM in these communities, it is important to locate the various communities and study their interactions. Remember that at this point, the research is just about finding out about these communities and what interactions are likely to encourage establishing the brand or organisation as a helpful and trusted ally for the communities. Thus, it is important to observe and not act at this stage!

## OBJECTIVE SETTING STAGE

With the information from the analysis stage, it is then possible to set the objectives of the campaign. To define the objectives, it is often useful to start by setting out broad goals for the campaign, for example, divining WOM recommendations, encouraging online discussions about a new product, or increasing the number of Facebook likes. These broader goals can then be distilled down to measurable objectives, remembering that objectives should be SMART, i.e. specific, measurable, achievable, realistic and time-specific. It is important to consider how the objectives will be measured at this stage, as the measurements need to be spelled out and will form the basis of the latter evaluation stage as well as any interim measurements and evaluations which should be part of the details stage.

## STRATEGY DECISION STAGE

Once the objectives for the campaign have been set, suitable strategies can be identified to achieve these. The strategy development must commence by identifying suitable targeting and positioning strategies. This includes identifying suitable target audiences based on the research carried out during the segmentation phase in the analysis stage and the identification of suitable tools to engage the targeted segments, and the positioning or 'core message' that is being conveyed.

## DETAILS STAGE

At the details stage, individual tactics and actions should be identified, including a timeline of such actions to help ensure knowing when which actions need to take place, and how they interlink with other actions. It may be useful to use flow charts or other ways of planning the individual actions and deadlines when designing this stage. Note that it is useful for most campaigns to have interim evaluations, so that campaigns can be adjusted if necessary.

## EVALUATION STAGE

During the final stage, the final evaluation needs to take place. During this stage, and once the campaign has finished, interim results and any end-of-campaign measures should be collated and recoded.

# SAMPLE OF AN ANNOTATED SOCIAL MEDIA MARKETING PLAN

## Company Background

Susie's Deli is a small takeaway food outlet close to a university in a town in northern England. It specialises in mostly vegetarian Mediterranean food, serving a largely student population together with some local residents, passing trade and employees of the university, which is situated nearby. A large proportion of the customers are students who have discovered that Susie's is good value, relatively healthy food at prices similar to the prices of food served on campus. However, buying the food requires walking approximately 10 minutes from the campus to the shop and back, while food on the campus can be purchased often much quicker.

As Susie's offers daily specials, making the trip is often rewarding. However, getting the news out about the daily specials has been difficult, and keeping students informed of daily specials via flyers has been too costly and ineffective.

Attention: This gives you some insights, but it would be helpful to know more about the students (and other segments) whom Susie is trying to target. For example, what other reasons do they have not to purchase food from Susie's? What barriers are there for switching from university food outlets to Susie's? How price sensitive are the various segments (students, staff, etc.)? Which means of communications do they use? While it is often difficult to relate small businesses to analytic frameworks such as PEEST, it is often useful to consider the potential impact of the various aspects. Similarly, a SWOT and Competitor Analysis would be useful to show where additional information is required and to have a systematic overview of the potential competitors and issues facing the business.

## Goals and Objective

- To increase knowledge about daily specials as a means to drive loyalty and increase awareness of Susie's amongst students who have yet to discover the deli.

Attention: this isn't a SMART objective. It would be better to have clear and measurable objectives here after the goal, for example: 'To increase awareness of the daily specials from currently 20% to 30% of the student population over the course of 6 months' or 'To increase the number of new customers to the shop from currently X per day to Y per day during the next 12 months'.

## Strategy Decision Stage

- To create a social media-based campaign to inform current and potential customers of the daily specials.

## Details Stage

- Create a Facebook page for the business.
- Update the page daily with the special of the day, including a description and picture.
- Offer a free coffee for people who like the page during the first three weeks as an incentive for current customers to engage with the page.
- Plan and create weekly posts that have 'engagable' content, such as sharable pictures or competitions.
- Conduct more market research to find out which other social networks current and potential customers are using, and how they can be encouraged to share page content amongst their networks.

## Evaluation Stage

Output measures:

1. Successfully post each day's special around 10am.
2. Post an 'engagable' item each week by Friday.
3. Number of surveys completed regarding other networks/content etc.

Other measures:

1. Like counts for the page each week.
2. Numbers of coffees served.
3. Number of engagements with content, engagable items and daily updates.

Overall this is a simple but potentially effective marketing plan for a small business. A potential issue is that once established, it will be important to maintain the social media activities. In some cases, such as the example case of the Taiwan election in Chapter 10, there will be a finite end date. However, in the majority of cases engaging in social media marketing has no finite end date, and is likely to require commitment over and above the duration of the initial plan.

# Glossary

**3G**   Third Generation mobile data and voice network

**4G**   Fourth Generation mobile data and voice technology, an upgrade of previous standards such as 3G

**7S Framework**   Framework for persuasiveness of mobile applications, using 7 factors: Simplification, Sign-posting, Self-relevance, Self-supervision, Support, Suggestion and Supervision

**Advergames**   Games embedded on websites or social media sites which contain commercial messages

**AESAR**   Adopted model of the DAGMAR purchasing behaviour model for social media engagement

**Agency-communication Theory**   Theory delineating two types of friendships: a non-committal and sporadic agentic friendship, and communal friendship based on companionship, mutual affection and shared experiences

**AIDA**   Model explaining purchasing behaviour as a series of stages: Attention, Interest, Desire and lastly Action

**Anchoring Theory**   Theory asserting that when forming evaluations, individuals anchor evaluations on certain attributes, for instance, the amount of stars given on a review website, a test result score – or indeed particular features in a written review

**AOL**   America Online – an early 'walled garden' online provider, later offering Internet access

**ARF**   Advertising Research Foundation

**Attitude–behaviour gap**   The discrepancy between an attitude and actual behaviour, for instance, many people have a positive attitude towards environmentally friendly products, but few people actually purchase these products

**Augmented reality**   Applications which synthesise location-specific information and supplementary information

**BBS**   see Bulletin Board System

**BCG** Boston Computer Group

**Behavioural engagement** A form of brand-contact that involves some form of behaviour on behalf of the consumer, such as making contact with a brand via email, liking a page, etc.

**Behaviourally targeted advertising** Advertising that is displayed based on previously captured behavioural data of the user, for example, by displaying advertising related to recent searches

**Brand communities** A subculture-like group, dedicated to the consumption of a particular brand

**Brand personality** A way of describing and categorising brands on five core dimensions

**Brand recall** A measure of promotional effectiveness where the brand name recall, either aided or unaided, is measured

**Brand recognition** A measure of promotional effectiveness, where the recognition of a brand's key attributes is measured

**Brand relationship** Description of the relationship type between consumer and brand

**BTA** Behaviourally targeted advertising

**Bulletin Board System** An early form of online community often not immediately linked to the Internet

**Buzz marketing** Planned marketing activity with the specific aim of increasing WOM activity (i.e. creating 'buzz' around a product or brand)

**CCCS** Centre for Contemporary Cultural Studies

**CCT** Consumer Culture Theory

**Collectivism** A measure of cultural similarity or difference, based on the extent to which societies tend to put lesser emphasis on looking out for themselves and their immediate families and rather more emphasis on group cohesion (see also Individualism)

**CompuServe** Early online provider offering chatrooms and forums, and later Internet access; similar to AOL

**Consequentialism** see Teleology

**Consumer Culture Theory**   A variety of theoretical perspectives focusing on the contextual aspects of consumption, such as the symbolic nature of consumed products and services, and experiential aspects of consumption activity

**Content restrictions**   Restrictions on what can be said about products, for example, health claims, usually for traditional media and increasingly also for online media

**Credibility**   The presumed, reputed, surface or experienced trustworthiness of a message or sender

**Cultivation Theory**   Theory explaining why people hold views of reality based on what is portrayed in the media, rather than what is happening in the 'real world' around them

**Culture jamming**   Form of social activism distorting commercial or official messages in an ironic or subversive way, for example, by hijacking a Twitter hashtag

**DAGMAR**   Defining Advertising Goals for Measured Advertising Results – model to explain purchasing behaviour in four stages: Awareness, followed by Comprehension, followed by Conviction and finally Action

**Data protection**   The protection of personal data collected by third parties

**Deontology**   Evaluation of actions based on intentions (rather than effects – see Teleology)

**Elaboration Likelihood Model**   Model of persuasion relying on two distinct routes of persuasion: a peripheral and a central route. The peripheral route relies on understated cues to subtly shift or associate attitudes towards a product or brand. Conversely, the central route relies on 'elaboration' (or cognitive engagement) on behalf of the consumer to aid consumers forming or changing attitudes towards a product/service or brand

**ELM**   Elaboration Likelihood Model

**Emotional engagement**   A form of emotional or cognitive engagement, or contact, with a brand

**Engagement**   A widely used term to describe some form of interaction with a message, usually referring to behavioural interaction, e.g. liking or retweeting, but is also sometimes used to refer to mere exposure to a message

**eWOM**   Word of mouth communication using electronic means, from social media networks to sharing of information by other electronic means (e.g. SMS)

**Experience Economy**   In an Experience Economy, the value of a product is measured not by the value of the actual product, but rather by the consumer's experiences surrounding it

**FAQ**  Frequently Asked Questions – an early form of user-generated document in the form of common questions and answers on a topic

**Flow**  Mental state of full immersion in and complete control of a task resulting in intense enjoyment of the experience (usually in a game)

**Functional Triad**  Theoretical framework categorising technology into one of three roles: technology can serve as a tool, increasing a user's ability; a social actor, creating relationships; or a medium, providing an experience

**Gamification**  Application of games-like principles to achieve desired outcomes in non-games contexts

**GeoCities**  Early web-based online community, where people could establish a virtual home in the form of personal web pages, organised around themed neighbourhoods

**Gopher**  Early hypertext linked document retrieval system on the Internet, often said to be a predecessor to the World Wide Web

**GPS**  Global positioning system – a satellite-based system that provides location and time information for electronic devices such as navigation systems or mobile phones

**GSM**  Global System for Mobile Communications – effectively the 2G standard for mobile voice and data communication (see also 3G and 4G)

**Hashtag**  A common keyword identifier on some social media websites, e.g. Twitter and Facebook: #

**Heuristics**  Simple decision rules for consumers

**Heuristic–Systematic Model**  A theoretical concept complementary to the Elaboration Likelihood Model, relying on two different routes to persuasion, that is, a systematic route, where the receiver engages in a systematic way with an argument presented, and a heuristic route, where a recipient evaluates claims made on simple heuristics

**HSM**  Heuristic–Systematic Model

**HTML**  Hypertext Markup Language – the computer language in which websites are programmed

**HTTP**  Hypertext Transfer Protocol – the technical standard for transfer of information between web-servers and web-browsers

**iBeacon**  GPS enhancement technology

**IGA**  In-game advertising

**Individualism**  A measure of cultural similarity or difference, based on the extent to which societies tend to put greater emphasis on looking out for themselves and their immediate families (see also Collectivism)

**In-game advertising**  Advertising messages or placements of advertisements inside of games

**Integrated Model of Persuasion**  A three route model of persuasion, consisting of systematic/central routes, peripheral/heuristic routes and experiential processing routes, followed by an evaluative stage

**Internet Relay Chat**  An online, text-based, real-time chat programme based on rooms

**KPI**  Key performance indicator

**L4MP**  Limited-capacity Model of Motivated Mediated Message Processing

**Limited-capacity Model of Motivated Message Processing**  A theoretical framework which asserts that users have only limited cognitive ability to elaborate on messages

**Linking value**  The value of a brand as a 'link' between tribe members

**Location-based social networking**  A convergence of social networking and location-based features

**Locative media**  see location-based social networking

**Mere virtual presence**  A series of mini-engagements of emotional connections with a brand

**Metrics**  Common term to describe social media and other marketing-related effectiveness measurements

**Million Follower Fallacy**  Term used to describe over-reliance on useless metrics, e.g. number of followers many of whom may not see updates

**Mobile devices**  Phones, tablets and other devices which are easily carried on the person

**Mobile marketing**  Activity conducted through mobile devices

**Mobile social media**  Social media applications used on mobile devices

**Mosaic**  Early web-browser software released in 1993 by the National Center for Supercomputing Applications

**MUDs**  Multi-User Dungeons

**Net Promoter Score**  Popular customer loyalty metric

**Open Diary**  The first public diary system, and effectively the first blogging website, launched in 1998

**Opt-in**  Communication where the user has to subscribe to receiving the message (e.g. a newsletter, or following someone or a brand on Twitter)

**OS**  Open source

**Parasocial Interaction Theory**  Interactions perceived as immediate, personal and reciprocal by the receiver but not by the sender of a message

**Parasocial relationships**  A relationship where the recipient has in-depth knowledge of the sender, while the sender has almost no knowledge of the recipient (e.g. follower of a celebrity tweeter and the celebrity)

**PDA**  Personal digital assistant

**Persuasion knowledge**  Level of awareness of a persuasion attempt taking place (see Persuasion Knowledge Model)

**Persuasion Knowledge Model**  A theoretical model explaining the coping mechanisms used by individuals in response to recognised persuasion attempts

**Phablets**  A mix of phones and tablet computers, e.g. large smart phones

**Placements**  Insertion of identifiable branded products into a game, movie or other context

**Power distance**  A measure of cultural similarity or difference, based on the extent to which members of the society with less power accept that power is distributed unequally

**Privacy**  The ability to selectively communicate information about oneself, e.g. deciding which information is shared and with whom

**Prosumer**  A producing consumer in the co-creation process

**Push service**  Data service where data is 'pushed' to mobile devices

**QR code**  Quick Response code – a machine readable matrix code which can contain product specific further information, e.g. links to websites

**Qualitative data**  Based on word-based, narrative and in-depth analysis

**Quantitative data**   Based on statistical, mathematical or numerical data

**Reach**   Measure of the total number of people exposed to a message at least once

**Reactance Theory**   Theory explaining 'boomerang' effects of marketing or other campaigns directed at behaviour change

**Referral marketing**   Marketing technique encouraging individuals to directly suggest a product to friends

**Relativism**   Assertion of no moral superiority of one framework or evaluation over another

**ROI**   Return on Investment

**SDB**   Social Desirability Bias

**S-D Logic**   Service Dominant Logic

**Sentiment measures**   Metrics aiming to quantify qualitative data, such as feelings or likeability, e.g. the balance of positive vs. negative eWOM generated

**Share of voice**   Measurement of the frequency of a particular brand being mentioned in comparison to competitor brands

**Smart phone**   Mobile phone with more advanced features than a standard mobile phone

**SMS**   Short Message Service – text-based messaging service on mobile devices

**SNT**   Social Network Theory

**Social Capital Theory**   Theory asserting that access to social networks and social credibility within these networks have an appreciable and measurable value

**Social Cognitive Theory**   Theory showing that knowledge can be acquired through observation rather than experience alone

**Social Contagion**   Theoretical model explaining the social influence on decision making

**Social Contract Theory**   Assumption of a usually implicit contract between the state and/or organisations and individuals or groups concerning rights and responsibilities towards each other

**Social Information Processing Theory**   Theoretical framework explaining the potential for deep online relationships amongst users in a virtual environment

**Social messiness**   Marketers are forced to share brand ownership with consumers, replacing conventional hierarchy and control in contemporary consumer society

**Social Network Theory**   Theory explaining how individuals and organisations are linked through interconnected ties and how information passes amongst these networks

**Subcultures of consumption**   Subculture-like groups, largely comprising of self-selected members, defining themselves based on a shared commitment to a particular brand, product or other consumption activity

**Tablet**   Mobile computer, generally in the form of a large, touch sensitive screen

**TAM**   Technology Acceptance Model

**Technology Acceptance Model**   Technology-focused adaptation of the Theory of Reasoned Action, a model for predicting technology uptake as a result of attitudes and behavioural intentions

**Teleology**   Evaluation of actions based on outcomes or effects (rather than intentions – see deontology)

**Theory of Planned Behaviour**   Explains behaviour based on attitudes, social norms and self-efficacy resultant in an intention to perform the behaviour

**Theory of Reasoned Action**   Precursor of the Theory of Planned Behaviour, and the basis of the Technology Acceptance Model, explaining the often weak correlation between attitude measures and actual performance of behaviour

**Tie strength**   Relative strength of the relationship amongst individuals and other individuals or organisations, e.g. close friends have strong ties, acquaintances have weak ties

**Tribe**   A subculture-like group, different from the traditional view of a market segment, in that they are fluid and self-selected

**TSFT**   Two-step Flow Theory

**tWOM**   Traditional form of word-of-mouth communication, i.e. face-to-face communication

**Two-step Flow Theory**   Theoretical framework explaining the passage of messages, initiated via mass-media or social media, first amongst opinion leaders followed by their followers

**UBB**   Ultimate Bulletin Board

**UGT**   Uses and Gratification Theory

**Usefulness**  A key concept, along with ease of use, in the Technology Acceptance Model

**Usenet**  A networked platform for the exchange of messages and online discussions in hierarchically ordered groups

**Uses and Gratifications Theory**  Theory explaining media choices made by audiences

**UTAUT**  Unified Theory of Acceptance and Use of Technology

**Valence (of WOM)**  The positive, neutral, negative or mixed character of any given WOM message

**Value–action gap**  see attitude–behaviour gap

**Viral marketing**  Passing along of commercial messages, for example amongst friends

**Virtual worlds**  Online versions of fantasy worlds

**Volume measures**  Metrics related to the volume, number or frequency of social media interactions or followers, for example, number of followers, number of likes, etc.

**WAP**  Wireless Application Protocol, an early technical standard of accessing data on a mobile device

**Warranting Theory**  Theory which explains that messages with a 'warrant', i.e. whose information content cannot be easily manipulated by the subject of the information, is attributed higher credibility than information that is more readily manipulated

**Web 2.0**  Controversial name describing World Wide Web sites using technology going beyond the static pages of earlier websites

**WOM**  see Word of mouth

**Word of mouth**  Traditionally person-to-person communication related to a brand or a product (see also eWOM and tWOM)

**World Wide Web**  Abbreviated 'web' or 'www', a system of hyperlinked Internet-based documents, later becoming often used synonymously as a term referring to the Internet

# Index